THIS CITY OF CORK
1700 – 1900

THIS CITY OF CORK
1700 - 1900

By

DR. S. F. PETTIT

STUDIO PUBLICATIONS,

CORK

First Published 1977

by Studio Publications,
Winthrop Avenue, Cork.

©   Sean F. Pettit 1977

Printed in the Republic of Ireland

FOR ARUBA

TABLE OF CONTENTS

INTRODUCTION

This book has grown out of a series of twelve radio talks delivered in 1975 under the title "Cork in the Nineteenth Century." For the kind invitation to give the series I express warmest appreciation to Mr. Diarmuid Ó Súilleabháin, then producer of the Radio Telefis Éireann programme, "Corkabout." I thank Miss Donna O'Sullivan for introducing each presentation. A request from the Adult Education Department of University College, Cork, to give a series of six lectures on the city's history gave final shape to the book. In thanking the Director of the Department, Mr. Seán Ó Murchú, for the honour of being his guest I wish to pay grateful tribute to the one hundred and forty participants who followed the course with deep attention and unfailing courtesy.

The following pages were written in the hope that the general reader might find interest and pleasure in considering certain aspects of the story of this old and charming city. The main emphasis is on the people who made it, on how they lived and worked in their everyday lives, and on some of the outstanding personalities whose memory lingers on. The passions of politics are touched on only incidentally, for if this book has any message it is that the citizens of Cork put aside the divisions of creed and party when it came to promoting the welfare of the place they called home. How well they succeeded can be appreciated not simply by reading any book but by walking about in the city that is encircled by the hills and watered by the river Lee. For thirteen hundred years the routine of everyday life has been lived here by rich and poor, by young and old, by natives and settlers. To know their story is not only to know about the past but also about the present, if only because the very streets we walk on and the bridges we cross and the churches we pray in were given to us by our forefathers. This book is a celebration of their achievements.

But it aims to see the development of Cork against the broader background of events in Ireland and Europe. In a unique way every city is a microcosm of the world, influenced by political, religious, economic and social trends that ebb and flow across time and space. In addition to its own distinctive personality it will exhibit certain chraracteristics common to city life throughout the ages and across the world. For this reason care has been taken to see local happenings against a larger backcloth. This is especially so in the rather long first chapter which attempts to compress the story of Cork from the seventh to the eighteenth century.

The remaining chapters each deal with some one aspect of life from 1700 to 1900; each is self-contained and the reader must forgive a certain amount of overlap. The book is not designed as a formal history; readers who wish to pursue matters more fully will find source material mentioned in the text and in the bibliography. I regret that the present state of my own knowledge did not allow me to devote separate chapters to those highly significant developments of the nineteenth century, the steamships and the railways.

Because of the very nature of his task a historian must depend largely on help from others. I wish to acknowledge my debt to all who have written in the Journal of the Cork Historical and Archaeological Society, the most valuable source in studying the history of the city. To its current editor, Professor John A. Murphy, I owe a special thanks. The citizens have reason to be grateful to the County Librarian, Mr. P. Ó Maidin, for his lengthy series of articles in the "Cork Examiner," this book owes much to them and to his fund of knowledge so generously shared. His staff and the staff in the City Library have been most helpful at all times. Mr. Walter McGrath, editor of the "Hollybough," has kindly published three articles on material incorporated in this book as well as giving the benefit of his knowledge in convivial conversations. Special thanks are due to the editor of the "Cork Examiner" for serialising the chapter "Out and About in Old Cork." The Curator of the City Museum, Mr. Ó Coigligh, and Mr. Ó Tuama gave every help when I was working on the Minutes of the Butter Market. To the Keeper of the State Paper Office, the Deputy Keeper of the Public Record Office, and the Librarians and staff of University College, Cork, Trinity College, Dublin, the National Library, the British Museum and the Royal Academy of Art, London, many thanks are due. Mr. J. Byrne has generously supplied photographic equipment. I thank the various organisations who have done me the honour of asking me to talk to them or lead them on historical walks: the Cork Historical and Archaeological Society, An Taisce, Tuairim, the History Teachers' Association, the Cork Literary and Scientific Society, the Teacher Centre, the Junior Chamber, the Federation of University Women, the Donna Club and the Gurranabraher Parish Festival Committee. I thank one of my students, Miss Mena O'Brien, for her helpful comments on reading the typescript.

Finally, I express deepest appreciation to my wife for her encouragement and patience while this book was being written.

A THOUSAND YEARS OF LIVING BY THE LEE

Chapter I

A city is there to be appreciated and to be experienced. The best way to do so is to go out and about on the streets to see with one's own eyes the shape, the colour and the texture of its houses, churches, public buildings, bridges, shops, railway stations, quays and places of industry. It is from these creations fashioned by the hands of succeeding generations that the city gives its immediate impression of the way of life and the sense of values of the citizens. The streets are the hallmark of the city. To these handprints of man must be added the shape given by Nature, the rise of a hill, the course of a river, the colour of local stone. For in the long process of change and expansion the citizens will have been profoundly influenced by their geographical location, as much in the goods they have made and sold to earn a living as in the appearance of their city and the influence of climate. A city, therefore, is a living thing fashioned by men against the background of Nature. But if the streets display the physical panorama of stone and wood and metal, of hills and water, they also introduce the citizens themselves as they move about in their daily round of business and leisure, displaying their characteristic gestures, their accent, their public personality. The citizen blossoms on the street, enlivened by a hurried greeting, a handshake or a passing smile. Men, women and children feel at home against the familiar silhouettes of houses and shops just as the countryman feels contented as he chews a blade of grass and follows his cows down a boreen. City streets are a rendez-vous with humanity. Be they long or short, dignified or shabby, they recall the human drama of life and labour which has been enacted over the passing centuries. These reflections find an echo in that most interesting book, "Victorian Cities," when author Asa Briggs states that, "there is no substitute for knowing a city, reading about it is second-best." If the city happens to be an old one there is the extra bonus of having something of the quaintness, of the long memories of a shared past, to add to the interest of the present. To walk about in any of the old cities of Ireland, Britain or Europe can, therefore, be a most interesting experience. That interest gains an added dimension from an awareness of how it was that the present grew out of the past. Such is the purpose of this book on Cork.

A Thousand Years of Living by the Lee

To walk about in Cork can be especially enjoyable for it has an atmosphere evoked by visual beauty and a history of thirteen hundred years. Like ancient Gaul it is all divided into three parts; a limestone ridge on the south, a steep sandstone ridge that climbs to the sky on the north, and a flat city centre that nestles in the valley below. This in turn is watered by two channels of the river Lee as it flows in from the austere beauty of Gougane Barra and leaves the city behind to meet the sea in the magnificence of Cork Harbour. The hills and the river create picturesque patches at almost every turn, while the views are enhanced by the vivid colours of the natural local stone, white limestone and red sandstone. Red and white are splashed about profusely in churches, public buildings, banks and warehouses, creating that richness of visual appeal so peculiar to old stone. The city has a harmony that has been fashioned by its natural setting and the creations of its citizens.

This evocation of things gracious and ancient well becomes a city that has its roots away back in the first half of the seventh century when St. Finbarr founded his monastic settlement on the southern hill. It befits a city that received its first municipal charter in 1174 and that was a recognised European port by 1300. But it would be entirely out of character to see Cork only as something of an atmospheric relic from the past, or as a genteel place with nothing more to offer than fine views and eddies of water and bits of old stone. It has been full of sharp-nosed businessmen since its significant commercial expansion as a centre of the butter and cattle trade in the middle of the eighteenth century, and today it is regarded as one of the leading commercial cities of Ireland. Indeed, with the sniff of natural gas off Kinsale there are winks and nudges of big business ahead. Its long lines of quays, stretching up into the heart of the city, see ships from across the world at berth; its airport links with Europe; its annual international Choral and Film Festivals bring the cultures of many lands to open wider horizons in song, dance and film. As an episcopal and university city it shares in the greater world of the church and scholarship. Nor have the political and military upheavals of the past left it untouched; in the seventeenth century it was embroiled in the tangle of Irish, English and French affairs when Oliver Cromwell stalked its Main Street and James II heard Mass at the riverside abbey on the North

Mall, and the Duke of Marlborough battered the old city walls on what is now the Grand Parade. The great political movements of the nineteenth century, that most political of centuries, brought their passion and drama to Cork. It was in the Imeprial Hotel on the South Mall that the Liberator, Daniel O'Connell, was given his last public dinner; Charles Stewart Parnell, the "uncrowned king of Ireland," was its Member of Parliament and addressed dense crowds from the first floor of the Victoria Hotel in Patrick Street. Father Theobald Mathew founded his mass Temperance Movement in a back lane near the quayside in 1836, and when the shadow of the Famine lay across the country in 1846 the city workhouse sent its daily cartloads of victims to be buried in the pauper graveyard at Carr's Hill. The Fenians were strong in the city, and in 1914 many thousands of Corkmen joined the regiments of the British Army to fight for the freedom of small nations. Again the city was actively caught up in the military and political activities that led to the establishment of the modern Irish State; the names of its chief magistrates, Terence MacSweeney and Tomas Mac Curtáin, are in the history books, while Michael Collins, William Cosgrave and Eamon de Valera each won a large allegiance in times of crisis and decision.

Such is the broad scenario of the shape of the city and the life of the citizens. The greater portion of this book deals with selected aspects of the social, commercial and cultural life of the eighteenth and nineteenth centuries. But it seems desirable to devote this first chapter to a bird's eye review of the origins of Cork and to a general survey of its development down to the close of the last century when the broad patterns of the present city had been laid down. In its origins Cork owes something to Ireland and something to Europe; to Ireland it owes its original monastic foundation, to Europe it owes its initial trading tradition and its formal incorporation as a city. What is a city and how did cities emerge? It might be worth while to spend a little time considering these issues in the general European context before relating them to any particular place. In the Europe of today most people live in cities, so much so that city life is taken as the norm in discussing general affairs and in planning for patterns of living and work. This is the age of the global village with more and more of the countryside being transformed into suburbs. The important thing to remember is that this is a relatively recent phenomenon that began to manifest itself only after 1800. It was the Industrial Revolution in Britain, gathering momentum in the middle decades of the last century, that brought into being the early urban sprawls. It was the new age of the machine, of factories, of blazing furnaces, of men of enterprise fashioning a whole new way of life. Instead of the immemorial power of horse and sheer human strength there was now the new power of the steam machine making for greater and quicker production of a vast range of goods from pins to iron ships. It was the beginning of the age of mass production in which we now live. It was also to see profound and enduring social change as more and more country people left the land and crowded into the industrial cities and towns in search of work. They exchanged the fresh air and the community life of the countryside for the long hours and the repetitive labour of the factory, and these operatives, to use the terminology of the age, helped to swell the population of the growing cities, mostly living in slum courts and alleys within earshot of the factory hooter. This bizarre combination of new commercial wealth and a new horde of rootless poor either fascinated or appalled contemporary observers. There were those who saw the age of the machine as the herald of the New Jerusalem of prosperity; for others it was nothing more than a sordid manifestation of commercial greed and human exploitation.

But whether the age of the industrial city was to be blessed or cursed, it certainly could not be ignored. It had come to stay. Apart from the phenomenon of the growth of the cities there was the parallel phenomenon of a population explosion, and sociologists are not yet agreed on an accepted explanation for that happening. Was it a fall in the death rate due to improving medical knowledge or a rise in the birth rate? Whatever the explanation there was considerable incredulity when the 1801 Census revealed England, Wales and Scotland as having a total population of 10.6 million people, with Ireland having 5.2 million. Previous to that there had been the notional idea that Britain had four million people and Ireland two million. Just forty years later the 1841 Census revealed an even more dramatic figure with the four countries having a combined population of 26.7 million. Statistics also showed a radical change in the way of life of the people of Britain: whereas in 1831 only

25% of the people of Britain lived in towns with a population exceeding 20,000, the 1851 Census showed that for the first time in history a majority of people lived in towns. The quoted figure from the 1801 Census giving the population of Britain as over 10 million and that of Ireland as 5 million underlines a point rarely noted in general histories, namely the relative importance of Ireland in terms of population. The Irish figure was to climb to over 8 million in the 1841 Census; however the disaster of the Famine with a dramatic death rate at home and the haemorrhage of emigration abroad set Ireland on a scale of decline. In addition, the lack of industrial expansion meant that this country was progressively left behind in the new trend of urban growth. Yet in relation to Cork city another set of figures is of interest in highlighting its industrial importance just before the industrial boom so radically changed the British scene. In 1760 when its provision trade was capturing markets in Hamburg, Rotterdam and Amsterdam, as well as in Jamaica, Barbadoes, Newfoundland, Carolina and Georgia, the population of the city was given in a contemporary history of commerce as being 60,000 while that of Liverpool was estimated at 35,000 and Birmingham at 30,000. Despite the fluctuations of politics, trade and Famine, the city was to maintain that level all through the nineteenth century.

This consideration of the phenomenon of the growth of the big city is intended to paint the contrast between the nineteenth and all previous centuries. In that long vista of European living the man in the city was very much the odd man out. The greater proportion of people lived in the countryside and earned their living from the land, whether as the mass of the peasants or as landed gentry. Indeed, there was a widespread latent suspicion of town life as expressed in the old adage, "God made the country, man made the town." It was somehow regarded as natural and wholesome that men and women should spend their lives following the immemorial rhythm of the seasons as designed by a benevolent Providence; tending the soil and caring for the animals and using their hands to make their clothes and simple utensils, constituted the simple way of life of the vast majority of the people of Ireland, Britain and Europe until the coming of the nineteenth century. It was an agricultural economy, a largely static society, a way of life based on clearly defined orders of social importance ranging from the church, the lord, the lesser gentry down to the great mass of the hewers of wood and the drawers of water. To state that it was so is not to imply any judgment as to whether it was more or less happy or virtuous or wise than the industrial society which overtook it. It is the historian's task to try to show how and why things happened, not to pontificate on their relative merits. It was in the twelfth century that there was a new stirring of city life after the desolation of the barbaric invasions of the Roman Empire, which had had a highly sophisticated tradition of city life including such refinements as central heating, the theatre and splendid public buildings laid out in elegant squares. The classical cities of Greece and Rome have given us much of the heritage of European civilisation with their sophisticated philosophy, their political thought and their traditions of theatre, dance, sculpture, architecture, oratory and the codification of law. It is hardly an exaggeration to claim that the city states of Greece and Rome, despite their slaves, were the cradle of our civilisation. But in the fifth and sixth centuries most of this creation was swept away in the struggles between the Roman Empire and the hordes of the Ostrogoths, the Visigoths and the Vandals. Such is the resilience of human nature that city life stirred anew from the twelfth century onwards, small but significant, bringing the craftsman and the merchant as a contrast to the rural life of lord, abbot and husbandman. This rebirth of urban living first showed itself in Italy, then in the Low Countries, northern Germany and France. It was caused by the same reasons that make every modern city function, the manufacture, the buying and the selling of goods. A city is all about trade. Venice became the pioneer of this exciting new dimension in living; shipping wine and grain to Constantinople, she sold the returning silks and spices to her inland customers. Gradually small centres for weaving cloth and selling the finished article emerged into commercial towns. Cloth, and all associated with it as regards raw material, formed, with wine, the chief article of trade for Europe as for Ireland until a century and a half ago. The Crusades greatly accelerated the growth of commerce in supplying the Christian armies with provisions and in selling the new exotic products brought back from the East, the spices, the carpets, the silks. Venice was the port of departure and entry for most of that whole enterprise of God and Mammon. But

Genoa and Pisa were rising up to compete. So there grew up a vast trade route stretching from Baghdad, then the world's great emporium, through Damascus and across to Venice, Genoa and Pisa, and then out to the ports of Marseilles in France and Barcelona in Spain. Meanwhile, the small towns of Flanders were beginning to sell their cloth to Scandinavian merchants in return for furs, and by the end of the twelfth century Bruges, Ypres and Arras were hives of spinners and weavers. The source of most of the raw wool was England, and when the Cistercian monks organised sheep-farming England became the chief wool-producer of Europe. It was this quickening of commercial activity combined with the emergence of a money economy instead of barter, that gave birth to city life in Europe in the twelfth and thirteenth centuries. The story of any one of those cities is full of colour and human enterprise. As will be indicated later, the city of Cork showed much of that European pattern.

What pattern did the early cities have? If one were to dissect what might be called the anatomy of the growth of a city it would be seen to have three parts. First, there is a community making, selling and buying goods, possibly situated near an earlier monastic foundation, probably placed where horse or mule trails meet, or better still on a river with access both to the hinterland and the sea. Few things are more important to a trading city than a river. Growing wealthy from commerce the citizens move to the second stage, which is to seek the power to order their own affairs through magistrates chosen from among themselves. This involved winning from the pope or king or local lord or abbot the right to self-government and immunity from tax and outside interference. Such a statute of rights and obligations was called a Charter, and it was the securing of this that gave the city its municipal status. In reading the history of such new towns as Leeds and Bradford in the last century it becomes clear what enormous importance was placed on securing a municipal Charter. Cork was granted its first such document in 1174. With the merchants and craftsmen growing prosperous through trade, with their liberties secured by Charter, the third phase was reached when they set about embellishing their city with the outward trappings of civic dignity. It is to this thrust of corporate municipal pride that Europe today owes the glory of its great Gothic cathedrals and its ornate Guild Halls, where the merchants and craft guilds met to deliberate and to celebrate with feasts of venison and partridge and hogsheads of wine, while musicians played in their special gallery and jugglers tumbled on the floor. Later there came the patronage of sculptors and painters and the civic glory of Renaissance Florence and Rome, when popes and merchant princes bestowed their favours on a Michelangelo and a Leonardo da Vinci.

It would be impossible to appreciate the early growth of Cork without some understanding of the European pattern which it repeated from 1200 onwards. But though the city was to be in many ways typical of other small cities in Britain and Europe, its origin came not from trade but from the monastic school established on the southern limestone ridge by St. Finbarr some time between 600 and 620. It was the Dark Age in Europe with the spoliation of the babarian invasions, but Ireland was experiencing a remarkable spiritual and cultural flowering. It was the epoch when this country gave to the world the intricate beauty of the Book of Kells and when Irish monks brought the light of Christian faith and scholarship to many parts of Britain, France, Switzerland and Italy. The relics of their work in illuminated manuscripts are scattered in libraries and muniment rooms across Europe. As the "insula sanctorum et doctorum," the island of saints and scholars, Ireland served the cause of European civilisation in a manner out of all proportion to her size or her material power. That era in Ireland's history was memorably recalled by the illustrious eighteenth century writer, Dr. Samuel Johnson, as "those times when Ireland was the school of the West, the quiet habitation of sanctity and literature." The school at Cork took its place in that high effervescence, with Finbarr and those who came after him looking down from what is now Gillabbey Rock on the marshland in the valley below and across to the tree-lined hill on the north. The marsh was known as Corcach Mor na Mumhan, the Great Marsh of Munster. Interesting to recall that the area is still locally referred to as the Marsh, so linking it with those far-off centuries. The monastic settlement was centred on the spot now occupied by St. Finbarre's Cathedral, while the farm lands stretched southwards towards the Lough and westwards to the site now occupied by University College.

Those early citizens of Cork spoke their native Irish but they also brought the languages of the new faith, the Latin and Greek of the church. It was around the monastery that the first native settlement grew up on the southern hill where today are situated Dean Street, Vicar Street, Barrack Street and Gillabbey Street. Despite their everyday ordinariness these streets bring echoes of a long and storied past. Those early Irish monks very definitely had the wanderlust and soon a disciple of Cork, St. Colman, set out to found a new settlement at Cloyne, a little place that even today retains much more of its early glory than does the Cork site; it has a very fine Round Tower, part of its medieval Cathedral, and, of course, the memories of the eighteenth century philosopher and bishop, Dr. George Berkeley, remembered for his book "The Querist." Waterford, too, was served from Cork and so was the island of Barra in Scotland. Whether Finbarr was buried in Cloyne or Cork is a matter of uncertainty among local historians, but his foundation attracted followers from all over Munster and from many other parts of Ireland and Britain. They spent their days in the monastic routine of prayer, study and labour in the fields. The cattle were watered in the low-lying swamps now reclaimed to form the grounds of the University and Jury's Hotel, formerly the old Muskerry Railway station. Until late in the last century old Irish-speaking residents of the area used to refer to Gillabbey Rock as Carraig an Aodhaire, the herdsman's rock, from which he could watch his cattle standing in the swamp below.

But this quiet habitation of prayer, study and pastoral calm was to be rudely disturbed by the wrath of the plunderer. In the ninth century many parts of Europe and Britain received the unwelcome attentions of the Danes, coming in their longboats to plunder and seize slaves. Ireland did not escape, though in fact it is inaccurate to refer to them as the Danes in the Irish context, as the history books normally do. It was from the fjords of Stavenger, Trondheim and Bergen in Norway that the Scandinavian or Viking influence was felt in this country and so it is more correct to speak of those important intruders as Norsemen. The suddenness and savagery of their impact is reflected in the surviving monastic chronicles of the time. Two main reasons can be advanced for their descent on the coastlines of western Europe, one demographic and one technical. A rise in the population and a shortage of land in Norway enticed the more adventurous warrior to risk going overseas in search of wealth in the form of slaves and silver. Then, too, the Norse had an advanced skill in the construction of sea-going longboats; they were probably the best seamen in Europe. From 780 onwards they appeared on the North Sea coasts of Britain, attacking the Irish monastic foundations at Lindisfarne and Iona. In the following century Dublin, Limerick, Waterford, Wexford came into being largely as Norse trading settlements. They came to plunder the monastery on the hill in Cork in 820 and again in 860, their oarsmen splashing the water as they made their way up along what is now the tree-lined tranquillity of the Marina. But as in the other Irish centres some remained as settled traders, congregating around the foot of the present Shandon Street. By 900 they were, apparently, a Christian community. But one intriguing piece of evidence puts a question mark over that received opinion as to where they settled, namely the existence of Keyser's Lane off Frenche's Quay. A street with this name is frequently found in Norse settlements elsewhere, for instance at Wexford, so leading to the assumption that here off the quay the settlers had depots for goods or shops for selling craftwork. Not the least interesting fact about Keyser's Lane is that it would seem to be the most ancient surviving street in Cork. In Norse the name meant "the passage leading to the water-front." If archaeological excavations at Cork has not yet yielded the wealth of Norse artefacts found in Dublin recently there can be no doubt but that these early invaders brought a European tradition of trading to the marshland below the monastery on the hill. With saints and scholars up at Gillabbey Rock and Norsemen at Shandon Street and Frenche's Quay, old Cork was beginning to get rather crowded. It was to become much more so when the next strand was interwoven into the pattern that was part of Ireland, part of Europe.

The coming of the Normans was to have a profound and enduring influence in the development of the city, an influence still visible today with names such as Barry, Roche, Burke, Cogan and Fitzgerald over shop windows. If the Normans were to become more Irish than the Irish themselves their arrival was, nonetheless, strictly without appointment. But who were those Normans? It is necessary to pose this question because the Normans have had a rather bad press in Irish history; simplistic notions have been purveyed to the effect that the small band of mail-clad warriors who appeared on a strand in Wexford in 1169 were simply a later version of the earlier Norse and Dane gentry. Furthermore, that first Norman landing is proclaimed as the root of all the woes of Ireland, and over the centuries tears have been shed and dirges have been intoned lamenting the evil day. The impression has equally been conveyed that somehow Ireland was the unique victim of a malign fate. These assumptions, however flattering they may be to national self-pity, need a hard second look before being accepted as the gospel of history. In his widely accepted standard work, "A History of the Middle Ages," Professor Painter talks about "the political genius of the Norman race" when dealing with their kingdom of Sicily. Both there and in Normandy they displayed a sophisticated flair for organisation, and they established a legal code of justice which won a grudging respect even from those on whom it was imposed with a ruthlessness characteristic of the age. The Normans were professional adventurers; they had the blessing of the Pope on many of their enterprises, always proclaiming their readiness to put down laxity in the church and to impose the authority and the orthodox practice of the See of Rome. Their most spectacular achievement was the conquest of England at the Battle of Hastings in 1066, to be followed by a ruthless eviction of the native Saxon lords from their lands, by the bringing of the English church into line with Roman liturgy and administration, and by the erection of strong castles to keep the natives from rebellion. By a combination of iron rule, strict justice before courts accountable to the king, and a highly organised central administration, Norman rule prevailed in England. There was internal peace, a growth in trade and the introduction of those features of European city life already described, walls, charters, guilds, municipal government. It was only a matter of time before these international adventurers would turn their attention to Ireland inspired by a mixture of motives such as the love of conquest, the need to reform the Irish church and to consolidate the conquest of England. Dermot McMurrough brought down upon himself seven centuries of bad publicity for an event that would most probably have happened had he never been born.

Who then were those Normans? Conquerors they certainly were; equally so they were ruthless; but in their concepts of justice, order and culture they represented a high point in the Christian civilisation of their day. It has to be especially borne in mind that they were international adventurers who saw Normandy, Sicily, England and Ireland as theatres for their exploits. To represent their invasion of Ireland in 1169 as a confrontation between England and Ireland in the sense that we in modern times envisage nation states involves a serious distortion of the facts and a grave misunderstanding of the times. Henry II was something of a cosmopolitan figure, concerned with his dukedom in France as much as with England; concerned, too, with his relations with the Papacy following the notorious murder in the Cathedral of Archbishop Thomas a Becket. His trip to Ireland in 1172, when he received the submissions of most of the Irish chiefs, was not so much to subdue Ireland but to control the Norman barons and prevent the possibility of their setting up an independent Norman Irish dukedom. A plaque in one of the streets in Wexford proclaims that Henry spent some time in the town doing penance! What interpreation is to be put on the submission of the Irish chiefs and petty kings to the Norman monarch? Did they see themselves as betraying Ireland to a foreigner? Firstly it must be appreciated that had they chosen to act in unity they would have in all probability swept the invaders out of the country in a short time, even allowing for the prowess of the mail-clad knights. In giving their allegiance to an overlord they were acting in a tradition which was the accepted pattern throughout Christendom at the time and for centuries afterwards. Many were also being severely realistic; they gambled on retaining a far greater measure of local autonomy under an overseas overlord than under an Irish high king. Being Irish or French or Spanish in the twelfth century did not involve the issues of political territorial unity and national sovereignty as these have come to be understood in modern times. Italy, so rich in its culture and so influential in its ideas, was only a geographical expression until 1870. What must be borne in mind is the clear distinction between the ancient concept of nation, based on a common origin, religion and language, and its modern expression as a politically unified state. A professional medieval historian has ventured the opinion that the real tragedy of the Norman invasion of Ireland was not that it happened but that it failed. Had it succeeded, as it did in England, the country might have achieved an administrative unity while retaining that rich culture which soon absorbed the Normans themselves, making them "more Irish than the Irish themselves." It was this capacity to become assimiliated into a new environment which resulted in the Normans fading out of Europe as a distinct race.

One result of their presence in Ireland was an enormous increase in church building in many parts of the country, bringing the Gothic style side by side with the Romanesque which had been in earlier favour. This architectural expansion was due to an increase not only in the number of Benedictine and Cistercian foundations but to the generosity of the Anglo-Norman lords in giving lands to the Mendicant Orders from the Continent, the Franciscans, the Dominicans, the Carmelites and the Friars and Canons of St. Augustine. The remains of these foundations such as Jerpoint, Ardfert and St. Mary's, Youghal, are highly regarded examples of Ireland's architectural heritage. But perhaps the most immediately appealing remains of the Norman presence are the ivy-covered ruined castles which dot the countryside, conjuring up the mystery and the romance of an historic past. However, it is not because of their military or political significance that the Normans are important in the history of Cork; rather it is due to the fact that they consolidated the growth of towns in places where the Vikings had earlier established small trading centres. Medieval Cork was largely a Norman creation.

When Henry II parcelled out the spoils of conquest in Ireland he gave the kingdom of Cork, stretching from Lismore to Kerry, to Milo de Cogan and Robert Fitzstephen in a charter signed by him at Oxford in 1177. But he reserved the city of Cork and the Cantred of the Vikings to himself as a source of revenue for the royal coffers. In its English translation the command of Henry to Messrs. de Cogan and Fitzstephen reads like a piece of pastoral poetry; they were to rule "well and peaceably, fully and quietly, entirely fully and honourably, in wood and in plain, in meadow and pastures, in waters and mills, in warrens, ponds and fishing, in ways and paths, and in all other places and things belonging thereto." When Milo de Cogan selected his particular piece of meadow and pasture he built his castle at Carrigaline, a few miles outside the city. Its ruins still stand among the gently rolling hills, with the water and the woods stretching out to the sea. Its meadows and pastures, its ways and paths are still peaceful and quiet. The acts of war which often accompanied the invaders did not happen at Cork; the re-constituted monastery at Gill Abbey had nothing to fear from intruders basking in papal approval with Henry empowered by a Bull to impose the full Roman discipline on an allegedly lax Irish church. With the arrival of the Normans a whole new European lifestyle begins to emerge in the physical shape and in the municipal govern-ment of the city of Cork. By 1188, when Prince John issued a new charter, the city had apparently already built its fortified walls as well as its South and North Gate bridges. The citizens had the rights and obligations of the "burgesses of Bristol in England." So Cork came to have the right to elect its own municipal officers, to be free from certain tolls and taxes payable to the king and the lord justiciar in Dublin, to have courts of justice held locally, to have the right to exclude outside traders and to establish merchant and craft guilds for the regulation of standards of workman-ship, hours of work and the fixing of a just price. The Normans brought to the monastery on the hill and the trading settlement in the valley that pattern of urban life which marked their influence in other centres in Ireland as it had done in England. The European civic strand of merchant and craftsman came to be woven into the earlier Gaelic pattern.

In relation to Dublin, London and other ancient cities the phrase "within or without" the walls is often used to describe historic churches. In medieval Cork the church of St. Finbarr was without the city walls which converged at the South Gate Bridge; incidentally, before the building of the present gracious Gothic building which was opened for worship in 1870, none of its predecessors ever had anything of marked architectural merit; there was nothing of the grand style of church building which was one of the glories of the medieval world in other parts of Ireland and in the great ecclesiastical centres of England and Europe. The two main parish churches within the walls were the Church of the Holy Trinity, or Christ Church, in the South Main Street and St. Peter's Church in the North Main Street. Both before and after the Reformation Christ Church was the venue for civic and legal religious ceremonies with the Mayor and circuit judges coming in state for Mass or Divine Service. Many of the Irish chiefs of south Munster specified in their wills that they wished to be buried in St. Finbarr's churchyard, just as many of the merchant citizens of the city desired to be laid to rest at Christ Church. Christ Church Lane also shares these venerable historic associations, having witnessed the daily passage of citizens for almost a thousand years. In whatever developments are being contemplated in the latter area and in the vicinity of St. Peter's Church it is most necessary that loving care be taken to maintain these present links with the long past. So many of the newer cities in Europe and America would consider themselves indeed fortunate to have so venerable a visual heritage. The citizens must see to it that the developer with his bulldozer respects the character of the place he has chosen to make his millions !

Other churches outside the walls were St. John's, St. Nicholas, St. Brigid's and St. Mary Nard. In the wake of the Normans there soon came the new town-based mendicant friars who were already at work in the emerging cities of Europe. Unlike the Benedictines or Cistercians who followed their vocation in the wildernesses of the countryside, the newer religious orders of the Franciscans, Dominicans and Augustinians ministered to the townspeople, earning their keep not by farming but by charity — hence the name mendicant, or begging, friars. The Franciscans were on the North Mall by 1214 while the Dominicans came to St. Marie's of the Isle in 1229. It is a happy development that this quaintly-named piece of old Cork now holds the convent of the Sisters of Mercy. By 1430 the Canons of St. Augustine were at the Red Abbey whose square tower is the oldest pieces of architecture surviving in the city; adjacent to it was a foundation of the Knights Hospitaller of St. John of Jerusaleum, one of the military orders to emerge during the Crusades. The old cemetery off Douglas Street recalls the association. How big was the city at any time between 1200 and 1600? Like all medieval cities it was ridiculously small by modern standards. Dublin was clustered around the Liberties of St. Patrick's and Christ Church; London's first historian, John Stow, in his "Survey of London," published in 1598, informed his readers that a walk around the walls of the city covered a distance of just over two miles.

The eastern wall of medieval Cork began at Dun Mhuire on the Grand Parade looking over the marshland which covered the whole of that broad area and the present South Mall, formerly known as the Rape Marsh because the rape seed plant used for making lamp oil grew on its marshy wasteland. Continuing along the present Cornmarket street, the wall met the north channel of the Lee. What is now Castle street was a city centre inlet of water where small ships from Bristol and Bordeaux bobbed in the tide having brought in their cargo of wine and pottery; their sailors made merry in the taverns before sailing away with a fair wind and a cargo of hides and wool. The western wall began in Hanover street, below Clarke's bridge, and continued past the present Courthouse, down Grattan street and so to the river. Outside this small expanse there was water everywhere, water on the Grand Parade and the South Mall until after 1750, water in Cornmarket street, water in Grattan street, water in Sheares street and, of course, water in Patrick Street. Such was the length of Cork; a walk through Christ Church lane and on to Hanover street was the breadth of Cork.

But how did one get in and out of Cork? Apart from the fortified walls nothing was more important to a medieval city than its gates, guarded by day and locked by night— the present-day ceremony of conferring the freedom of the city on distinguished personages is a throwback to those older times, the freeman is considered to have a key to the city gates. The North and South Gate bridges mark the sites of the medieval entrances. Such was the shape of the little medieval city nestling in the valley beneath its protecting walls, secure within its gates, watered by numerous channels, with the little ships trading in wine and hides, and with the ordered life of priest and friar, of merchant and craftsman. Most likely it had the conscious exclusiveness of medieval cities whose citizens felt little affinity with those outside their walls. Yet undoubtedly the citizens traded with the native Irish who brought in their produce and set up their stalls in the shadow of the walls; in 1443 an act of Edward IV permitted the citizens of Cork, Limerick, Waterford and Youghal to buy and sell "all manner of merchandise" to and from the native Irish. The wills of prominent fifteenth century citizens also witness to business transactions with their Irish neighbours, but to what extent Irish was spoken in the streets of Cork, and how much intermarrying there was between natives and settlers are matters which await further study. The assimilation into the Gaelic tradition of language, dress and custom which made the Normans "more Irish than the Irish themselves" was more normally a feature of the countryside than of the introverted towns and cities.

Just how extensive was the trade of Cork, what exactly was being brought in and sent out? The city's trade received a considerable boost in 1326 when in company with Dublin and Drogheda it was constituted a "staple' town by royal decree, a staple town alone had the privilege of holding the "staple" or market for wool. Furthermore, only in such towns could foreign merchants barter and buy hides, wool and tin; these towns in return were obliged to keep to minute regulations for the safety and welfare of their visitors. An official government document of 1284 lists imports to Cork as wine from Bordeaux and Bayone, cloth and kitchen utensils from Bristol, and spices. It would be hard to exaggerate the importance of spices to the European economy of medieval and later times; they were essential to preserve meat at a time when cattle were slaughtered in the autumn and the meat had to be preserved for many months. The spices from the East became one of the most important imports to Europe following the Crusades. Moving on in time another glimpse into the basic activity of a city, that of making, buying and selling goods, can be had from the description of the cargo of a ship from Cork captured in 1551 by English pirates, but later apprehended by Customs at Bristol; it carried 15,000 yards of wollen cloth, Irish Frieze, 6,000 sheep skins, 4,000 calf skins, 500 deer skins and 20 mantles of woollen cloth. The city merchants living in their tall and mainly wooden houses in the narrow laneways off the main street had obviously been doing brisk business with the Irish dealers who came into the city or sold from stalls without the walls. The Port Book of Customs for England for the period 1519-1560 lists the following exports to Cork; iron, small household brass and iron articles, knives, brass ornaments, combs, girdles, mirrors, buttons, medals, thread, gloves, calico, silk, taffeta, soap, lard, pitch, lead, tin, pewter, hops, tar, glue, starch, paper, cotton, wool and earthenware. Much history is written on the assumption that somehow only men mattered—it is almost forgotten that before they did their struttings on the stage of history they

29

needed a mother, if only for the little matter of being born! A good deal of feminine accessories is included in the thread, taffeta and calico, the silk and the gloves of this list of imports, though, of course, silk stockings were part of the wardrobe of a sixteenth century gentleman just as they were to be of the eighteenth century dandy with his powdered wig lending enchantment to his head. Another ship tells another tale. On November 26th 1518, there arrived in Bristol the "Patrick de Kork," of which "Nicholas Gregory est Magister" as the Latin record states, with Nicholas Gregory as Master. It carried merchandise under the names of the following Cork merchants: David Roche, Willelmus Fynne, Johannes Roche, Robertus Murrowe and Romandus Savage. Apart from the splendidly resounding Latin Christian names, this list simply gives the sixteenth century ancestors of people still prominent in the public life of today. But apart from what he exported or imported in the small ships that berthed in Castle street, Patrick street and along the quays from the present Opera House to the North Gate Bridge, what articles of utility and adornment did the merchant have in his house?

A delightfully realistic glimpse at the domestic effects of one such merchant is given by the nineteenth century local historian, Richard Caulfield, in the introduction to his monumental transcription of the old Corporation Minute Books. On March 13th 1570, the following inventory was made of the goods of David Tyrry, merchant of Cork City:: "A standing cup, double gilt. Seven spoons. Two pots or pans of brass. A service of brasnet. Three spits. Nine platters. A porringer with two saucers. Five pewter cups, a laver and basin of pewter. Six candelsticks of brass. A pewter pot, two quarts, two pints, an ink, a crossbow, a sword, three chests or coffers. A table and a pair of trestles. A new Flanders table cloth, a new Irish table cloth, an old Irish table cloth. Three towels and a towel of damask-work. A feather bed and six flax beds, a pipe, a hogshead of Spanish wine, and a milch cow." From this description and the previous list of imports one obvious deduction can be made, namely the comparative lack of a profusion of luxury items even in the household of a wealthy citizen. This was a feature common to such homes all over Ireland and Britain until well after 1600; indeed, stately country residences and palaces were sparsely furnished with hand-carved wooden tables and chairs, large chests for storage and travel, and a sideboard for holding serving dishes and pewter goblets. The modern refinements found in most working-class homes such as soft armchairs, deep-pile carpets and fancy wallpaper were all still very much in the future. Imports were mainly of small goods for immediate domestic or personal use, with a Flemish tablecloth counting as the very height of high fashion. With such hot beverages as coffee and tea still also very much in the future, pewter cups were the normal everyday means used for drinking beer, porter and whiskey. Interestingly enough, much of the documentary evidence of imports to Cork between 1200 and 1700 is being corroborated by the excavations being carried out over the past two years by the Archaeology Department of the University at sites in Adelaide street, off the North Main street and in Christ Church lane off the South Main street. The artefacts unearthed include pieces of pottery from England, Spain, France, Holland and Germany, and from the early settlements in North America. Included are Saintonge green-glazed ware, Ham Green ware, dishes from La Chapella, Beauvais ware, Dutch cockeral dishes, German stoneware, Devon and Staffordshire combs and ware. The genteel use of tablecloths was only beginning after 1600; thick slices of stale bread, known as trenchers, did service as plates in the best of houses; floors were covered in rushes; and only in the odd great house were tapestries and fine cloth being hung on the bare stone walls.

But while the Cork citizens, the Tyrrys, the Galways, the Roches, the Skiddys and the Coppingers, were laying in their hogsheads of Spanish wine and exporting their bales of Irish frieze, momentous events were giving a new shape to the life and thought of Europe. That century and a half between 1450 and 1600 was itself a rich and varied tapestry of human experience. It was the age of the Geographical Discoveries, of the Renaissance and the Reformation. It gave new horizons to the physical world, a new creativity to the world of art, and a new interpretation to ancient Christian belief. These lines are being written while the citizens of the United States celebrate the bicentenary of their independence, but in 1492 the men of Europe heard with a mixture of wonder and incredulity of the discovery of the New World, a vast continent unknown to civilised man through all the passing centuries, a land of strange people and unaccustomed products, a land beyond the pale of the Christian view of the world. It was at once a disturbing and an exciting opening of horizons. Such was the impact of Columbus, of Magellan, of da Gama and of Drake. They changed the world more dramatically and more permanently than had been done since the days of the Old Testament. But the era saw more than physical expansion; it witnessed also an unprecedented enlargement in men's minds and in the mode of their expression in literature, science and art. It was the age of the Renaissance, of a questioning of old assumptions, of a quest for a more satisfying and rational understanding of the universe and of human life. There was the beginning of scientific observation and experiment with such monumental figures as Copernicus and Galileo; there was the new thinking of Erasmus and Thomas More, there was the rediscovery of classical art and the use of the human form in painting and sculpture. It was the age of Michelangelo and of Leonardo da Vinci and of the breathless beauty of Florence and the Sistine Chapel.

Out of this ferment of thought and questioning there came the Reformation which shattered the immemorial unity of Christian faith and discipline, with Luther, Calvin and Henry VIII giving rise to national churches owing no allegiance to the Pope. This in turn set the stage for the Counter-Reformation, the era of Ignatius Loyola and Philip II of Spain, of the Wars of Religion in Germany, France and Holland and the defeat of the Armada. It is only in the past decade that concerted efforts are being made to heal the wounds of division inflicted by that acrimonious family quarrel among Christians. To what extent did this wide sweep of human experience impinge on the citizens of Cork? When did they hear about America? These must remain matters of conjecture, but as to how they came to know and discuss the news of the world it can be stated that this news was literally brought up the river and into the city in ships, possibly in letters written in Latin from the Continent and from England, and most certainly through the stories and accounts of merchants and sailors. There certainly was much to talk about and much to ponder on. In an age before television, before radio, before newspapers, before printed books had become even remotely common to the man in the street, an age in which the vast majority of ordinary people could not read or write, the circulation of news was slow and uncertain and was largely a matter of word of mouth. Nor was this peculiar to the far-off days of the sixteenth century; it is interesting to recall that almost a year had gone by before the church bells rang in some remote north country villages in Britain to announce the news of the most famous battle of the nineteenth century, the battle of Waterloo. The world was still a terribly big place; it is only in our day that it has become a global village.

Of all the momentous events which were giving new horizons, new shapes and new thoughts to the people of Europe it was the Reformation which had more immediate impact on Ireland and on any city such as Cork. With Henry and Elizabeth there came the State Church, owing allegiance not to Rome but to the person of the English monarch as its head on earth. The most dramatic manifestation of the new religious system was the holding of divine worship in English, in the spoken language of the people of England. This was regarded by the adherents of the old Faith as certainly blasphemous and obviously comic. All through the long Christian centuries the people of Europe had participated in the great mystery and art form of the Mass in Latin; the retention of the Latin liturgy became henceforward the most obvious mark of tradition as between the Catholic Church and the new Christian Churches that grew out of the Reformation. The Book of Common Prayer was in time to become a sensitive expression of Christian spirituality and of literary grace, but for the majority of the people of Ireland and of the citizens of Cork it was the Mass in Latin that mattered. The religious upheavals initiated by Henry, and more especially by Elizabeth, had little lasting impact on the spiritual allegiance of the great mass of the Irish people, but they did have a significant role in developing something of a national resistance to English rule in Ireland. Though Elizabeth's own Protestantism was mild and not unduly cluttered with theological niceties, and though her enforcement of the new religious practices in Ireland was hardly more harsh than similar efforts in Catholic and Protestant countries in Europe, yet the liturgy in English and the style of the Queen as Supreme Governor of the Church marked a clear line of departure between the old Faith and the State Church. Out of this fusion of the ideals of Faith and Fatherland the great Hugh O'Neill attempted to weld together a national movement with the assistance of Philip II of Spain, the champion of the Counter Reformation and England's rival for mastery of the sea. Yet O'Neill failed largely to win the support of the towns, and even though he pitched camp at Inniscarra, the citizens of Cork did not flock to his banner.

Neither did they accept the Queen's religious policy. Matthew Sheyn, or Sheehan, the Queen's bishop from 1572 to 1582, caused general revulsion when he publicly burned a venerated image of St. Dominick at the Town Cross situated in the North Main Street opposite Portney's Lane. His successor, William Lyon, a native of Chester, was appointed in 1583 and in an official letter he complained of his problems in enforcing the new dispensation. The "young merchants of Cork went to Mass with daggers and pistols ready prepared." Nor were their elders any more accommodating: "the Pope's legate, friars, priests and seminaries, of whom this country is full, also the city of Cork; whereas seminary and seducing priests resident within the city, maintained and kept daily by the aldermen and merchants of the city, to say Mass, baptise, minister the sacraments and their other popish and heretical ceremonies in their private houses, and when I am out of the town they walk openly and commonly in the street accompanied with the aldermen and officers of the city . . .and now lately within this quarter of this year I made search myself in schools for books and what books were taught there, whether according to her Majesty's lawes, and searching I found to my great grief her Majesty's stile and title torn out of all the grammars to the number of 74 in one school: the leaf in the grammar quite torn out which containeth in it: 'Elizabeth, by the grace of God, Queen of England, France and Ireland, Defender of the Fayth." In fact, despite spasmodic periods of tension, the full public practice of the Catholic Church was maintained openly in Cork until the harsher days of the Penal Laws which came after the Battle of the Boyne in 1690. Even then the intermission was relatively brief and by 1740 Mass houses were freely open and some religious communities of men were re-establishing themselves. The most tangible and irritating aspect of the Penal Code was not the lack of facilities for religious practice but the exclusion of the Catholic majority from political and municipal government. Yet this policy, however repugnant to modern concepts of civil rights, was in accord with the broad European practice of excluding from power those who did not accept the established order in Church and State. The Penal Laws were not designed to force the Irish to become Protestants but rather to keep them politically subdued lest they might join with England's European enemies, especially Catholic France. It was only as Europe grew exhausted by the bloody and seemingly interminable Wars of Religion, and as the age of Reason dawned with the eighteenth century, that the concept of the pluralistic society came gradually to be accepted. In these islands the winning of Catholic Emancipation in 1829 marked a most significant step in the long road of liberal reform.

One of the most regrettable by-products of an exclusive preoccupation with grand designs in politics and religion is a distortion of the full life being lived in the era in question; the assumption is that everyone was sitting around in breathless anticipation of the actions of prelates or princes or politicians. This misconception derives partly from the coming of a greatly broadened participation in public affairs as recently as the second half of the last century, a process enormously accelerated by the instant communication and the centralisation of government of this present century. But to deal with previous centuries according to these modern criteria is to see the past in relation to the present, rather than in accordance with its own standards. Not everyone in Elizabethan Cork was solely preoccupied with the theology of the Reformation, certainly not the shoemakers. The tanning of leather was permitted only in certain towns, and in 1577 an act of Elizabeth granted to the Company of Shoemakers the right "to tan, curry and dress hides and leather except sheepfell and deerfell, provided they give security not to issue any leather insufficiently tanned and offer their work at reasonable rates." Why the industrious and honest shoemakers were forbidden to work with "sheepfell and deerfell" becomes clear when shortly afterwards the Company of Glovers were licensed to tan these materials as well as "horsehides, faunfell, kidfell and lambfell." These pieces of Tudor domestic legislation give an indication of what the citizens were wearing on their hands and feet—at least on fashionable hands and feet. They also indicate the existence of craft guilds in the city and the three industries of tanning, shoe-making and glove-making.

The accession to the throne of the first of the Stuarts, James I, in 1603 had important consequences for most of the

Irish cities. Initially they refused to proclaim him king mainly on the religious issue, and as a penalty for their disloyalty they were obliged to submit their Charters to the Court for revision. Cork's new Charter from James was granted on 10th March, 1608, and is a meticulously-worded document. One provision extended the boundary of the County of the City of Cork to three miles beyond the city walls, a most significant extension of municipal authority: "We will and ordain that our aforesaid City of Cork and all and singular the houses, edifaces, lands, water and watercourses, soil and foundation, standing, lying, being and extending from the outside part of the wall of the said City of Cork on all sides whatsoever for the space and circuit three miles according to the form of the Statute passed in our Kingdom of England, to be measured within one year after the date of these presents, to be measured to a great stone or other plain and remarkable sign to remain for ever." It was some-what over a year later, on Friday, 13th July, 1609, that the Mayor, Sir Dominick Sarsfield, accompanied by Sir Par Lane and Sir Edmond Fitzgerald, set out on their perambulation and the full text of their delineation of the new boundaries, full of place names so obviously derived from the Irish language, is given in Caulfield's Minute Book. The Corporation coffers were also to benefit to the tune of a "messe of herrings, five hundred herrings of, in, or upon such boat, bark or vessel in that year that shall take at least one thousand herrings." The King was to be paid "Twenty Pounds of Wax at the Feast of St. Michael the Archangel." Another provision of the Charter was not calculated to bring down blessings on the royal memory from harassed present-day citizens: "all and singular persons shall contribute according to the rate and proportion of the annual rent of their houses," so laying the foundation for the payment of rates on house valuation that still survives. Finally there came permission for two annual fairs within the city, "on the Morrow of the Feast of the Holy Trinity and the vigil of St. Matthew the Apostle, provided it be not a Sunday." Yet another indication of the trade of the city comes from the list of tolls imposed by the Corporation in August, 1609. Among the items carrying a toll of from 1d. to 9d. were: a barrel of grain, a barrel of meal, a barrel of oats, beef slaughtered, cow hide, tanned hide, deer hide, marten skin, fox case, mutton, pork, veal, a stone of wool, stone of flax, stone of butter, stone of tallow, a horseload of oarsboards, planks and poles, a hogshead of salt, a barrel of double beer, a barrel of herrings or pilchards, a salmon, twenty barrels of coals, a gallon of honey, a pound of wax. One item was more costly, "millstones brought in or out of the bridge, 3/4."

The middle of the seventeenth century found a political highlight in the arrival in Cork of that foremost of republicans, Oliver Cromwell. He had beheaded the luckless King Charles and initiated his Puritan regime by dismissing Parliament and putting the key in his pocket. With his Bible and his sword he had turned his attention to Ireland and he strode into Christ Church on the South Main Street in Cork denouncing alike Catholic Irish and Anglican English. Having stayed some while at Shandon Castle he sailed home from Youghal, leaving the details of the confiscations to be worked out by his henchmen in Ireland. The visit of yet another English dignitary was to have somewhat more impact on the city. Having been chased off the throne as much for his haughtiness as for his popery, James II sought the help of the Catholic Irish and landed at Kinsale in 1688. A plaque in the wall behind Acton's Hotel marks the house in which he reputedly stayed. Escorted by a mounted entourage he rode into Cork by Evergreen and down Barrack Street to be greeted by yet another Mayor, Dominick Sarsfield, and his dashing young nephew, Patrick, at the South Gate Bridge. As he went by it was noted that the haughty Stuart showed little appreciation of the cheers of the citizens and the green boughs strewn beneath the royal mount. James heard Mass at the Franciscan Abbey on the North Mall before riding off to fight and lose the Battle of the Boyne, so changing the whole course of Irish history. If the Pope had a Te Deum sung in Rome for the victory of William of Orange nobody wanted to know about it in Ireland; it was more convenient for tribal simplicities to see the moderate Dutchman as the embodiment of Protestant triumphalism and as the scourge of Catholic liberties. But whatever the politics, the wars of William and James were to have an important topographical effect on Cork. As part of the campaign to subdue Jacobite strongholds, the city was besieged by the Duke of Marlborough, the ancestor of Winston Churchill, in 1690. When the Duke's heavy guns battered down the old medieval walls, the small, enclosed life of the city was about to vanish. By the August of 1690 William himself had been severely rebuffed by Patrick Sarsfield at Limerick, and he was more than anxious to listen to an ambitious plan propounded by Marlborough for the capture of the important port of Cork. Indeed the Duke was first to display his military prowess at this engagement and his achievement laid the foundation for his subsequent career. The city was defended by the Irish commander, Colonel Roger McElligott, with a rather poorly equipped force of some 5,000 men. On September 17th 1690, Marlborough set out from Portsmouth with a fleet of 82 ships. He entered the Harbour on September 22nd, occupied the fort at Haulbowline, and on the following day landed at Passage West. Briskly proceeding through Glenbrook, Rochestown and Douglas, he came down Evergreen Street and took the Cat Fort. His force of 1,000 men was to be supplemented by 4,000 Dutchmen under the Duke of Wurtemberg, while ships with supplies arrived from Waterford. Marlborough placed a gun on the still extant tower of the Red Abbey and fired balls with devastating effect at the eastern wall along the present Grand Parade. Another gun on the tower of the old St. Finbarr's Cathedral took care of the western walls.

Those fateful events took place on the 24th and 25th September, 1690, and when Marlborough led the final assault through the swamp that is now the South Mall one of his staff, the Duke of Grafton, was fatally wounded by a musket ball which tradition relates was fired by a blacksmith defending a breach in the wall where now stands Old Post Office Lane. Grafton's Alley or street on the Mall recalls this episode. Tradition also states that the victims of this bloody interlude were buried in a mass grave in Christ Church Lane, and this seems to be confirmed by the excavations presently being carried out by the Archaeology Department of the University. Before leaving the seventeenth century and the grim episode at its close, it might be of some interest to record a more everyday hazard to life and limb than the cannon balls of the Duke of Marlborough. The Corporation Minutes of June 17th 1631, give the gory details: "Whereas there hath been in former times used in this city a very barbarous and incivil kind of sport upon Easter Tuesdays, May Days and Whitson Tuesdays, viz. tossing of great balls and hurling in the open streets with the small ball, great mischiefs have sometimes happened as the death of men and many wounded and maimed in those sports, and many quarrels have followed which were like to break out into a general tumult within the city. We, therefore, ordain for a bye-law that said tossing and hurling in the street shall not be used the days aforesaid, nor any other, upon pain of 40/."

Two major developments from 1700 onwards changed both the physical shape of the city and the life-style of the citizens. There was a continuing expansion both eastwards and westwards from inside the cramped confines of the old medieval walls. But as the new development areas were largely marshland with a proliferation of small channels of water, the expansion involved a very considerable feat of civil engineering as marshes had to be drained, arched and built over. The modern city centre was created piece by piece as the eighteenth century progressed and the perennial problem of flooding which affects the Cork of today is the legacy of building on reclaimed marsh. On the western side such areas as Pike's Marsh surrounding Adelaide Street, and Hammond's Marsh in Henry Street, were built over to provide town houses for merchants and professional people moving out from the old narrow lanes. In 1767 Henry Street was to see the erection of the first modern prestigious civic building, the Mansion House, now the Mercy Hospital, designed by the Sicilian architect and engineer, Davis Ducart, with its finely proportioned frontage, Italianate windows and Ionic doorway, matched inside by the delicate plasterwork of the Waterford stuccadore, William Osborne. A later section of this book gives a detailed account of the making of the Mansion House. Directly opposite, the Methodist community built their chapel and manse, while the great equestrian evangelist, John Wesley, had preached in the open air in the new street. While on a visit to Cork Wesley saw women filling their buckets with water from the river and in his diary on 17th April, 1756, he concluded that "the salt must affect the stomach and bowels of tender folk." The old Fenn's Quay, now Sheares Street, which had formerly been a tree-lined walk on its northern side, was also arched over, as was Grattan Street by 1790—both to become fashionable residential areas. The gracious tree-lined walk of the Mardyke had been laid out in 1719 to become a fashionable promenade on Sunday mornings when dandies and their dames strolled up to the Red House at its end to indulge in the new frivolity of drinking tea! But if high fashion and select residences were to be found in the expanding western areas, it was in the east that commerce found its new habitation. The Grand Parade, Patrick Street and the South Mall were all laid out by 1800 with a breadth and dignity sharply contrasting with the narrow passages of the old city. Patrick Street still follows the curve of the former channel and eighteenth century maps show Colville's Quay where now stand the premises of the "Cork Examiner." That portion of the Grand Parade now occupied by the City Library was Tuckey's Quay, while directly opposite was the original Mall, a small tree-lined walk alongside the open channel joined to the quay by a bridge on the site of the present Berwick Fountain. The new South Mall was built on what was originally called the Rape Marsh because the rape seed plant used for lamp oil grew there; later it became Dunscombe's Marsh with Morrison's Island lying behind. The names of these marshes and of others such as Copley's and Clarke's derive from the practice of the Corporation of leasing or selling such out-lying portions of property to private citizens.

Parallel with this unprecedented physical expansion the eighteenth century saw Cork take quite a dramatic step into the commercial life not only of Ireland but of Europe and the New World. Through their enterprise and expertise the merchants of the city were to create a wide-ranging commercial network that was to bring prosperity at home and fame abroad. The hub of this activity was the Butter Market situated at the foot of Shandon Steeple. The city became one of the major centres of the European butter trade and the Market became a hive of activity as the farmers from the rich Munster pasture lands brought in their firkins of salted butter to have it tested, weighed and packed for export from the quays to Liverpool, Rotterdam, Amsterdam, Lisbon, Seville, Malaga and Hamburg, and to the West Indies, Carolina, Georgia and Newfoundland. What would nowadays be called a butter technology was evolved with meticulous standards of weighing, branding and packing in oak casks and with the coopers as kings of the craftsmen. Alongside the butter trade there grew up the spin-off industries dealing with the procuring, the curing and the export of hides and tallow; throughout the north side there was a profusion of slaughter houses for pigs and cattle. In 1736

Lord Orrery found all of this distinctly distasteful, referring to Cork as "the slaughter house of Ireland, full of butchers, hogs and pigs." But to the merchant princes, as they came to be called, and to the coopers, the carriers, the farmers, the tavern-keepers, the shop-keepers and the other beneficiaries of expanding trade the butter and pigs meant a better life. The city was especially fortunate in that the quays came right up into the heart of the town and so Cork saw the masts of sailing ships from around the world bringing rum from Jamaica, tobacco from America and claret from Portugal, and sailing away with firkins of salted butter, with pickled pork, with salted herrings, with tallow for candles, with hoofs to make glue and with round gut sent to Venice to make sausages. Another lucrative trade was built up in victualling the sailing ships for the long weeks at sea; they put in on the outward or the return voyage from America, with Bristol as their home port. Cork acquired something of the tang of a great seaport, its local scene enlivened by the business, the colour and the bawdiness of men who went down to the sea in ships. It was during the Napoleonic Wars that the provision trade reached its high peak with British naval and merchant fleets taking on supplies for the armies in the Peninsular War and later campaigns. Whether apocraphyl or not, the cry of one Cork merchant must have caught the mood of the age, "if this be war let there never be peace,"

The most enduring signs of that upsurge of commercial life are the stately Georgian mansions that stand on the sloping parklands by the riverside from the city to the sea. Here the merchant princes lived sumptuously, bringing Italian and Flemish artists to decorate their ceilings and paint the walls of their drawing-rooms. They sent their sons on the Grand Tour of Europe accompanied often by a priest or clergymen as tutor; the names of many of the riverside mansions and the stone embellishments of gateways and walls bear witness to a strong Italian influence. However, the business community and the municipal authorities kept a sharp eye on practical realities and at the close of the eighteenth century a massive effort was set afoot to deepen the channel of the Lee from Blackrock to the city. This involved the building of what was known originally as the New Wall, later the Navigation Walk, extending from the present City Hall down to and beyond the present Ford

Factory. By the middle of the last century it had been extended to form the picturesque riverside walk of the Marina with its double line of trees and its captivating views of the sloping parklands of Tivoli and Glanmire, a scene enriched by the bright limestone of Blackrock Castle in the distance. When in 1842 the noted novelist, William Makepeace Thackeray, came into Cork by stage coach from Fermoy he was moved to write lyrically of the beauty of the entrance through Glanmire and Tivoli: "We arrived at the beautiful wooded village of Glanmire, with its mills and steeples and streams, and neat school-houses and pleasant country residences. This brings us down upon the superb stream which leads from the sea to Cork. The view for three miles on both sides is magnificently beautiful. Fine gardens and parks and villages cover the shore on each bank; the river is full of brisk craft moving to the city or out to sea; and the city finely ends the view rising upon two hills on either side of the stream. I do not know a town to which is an entrance more beautiful, commodious and stately. Passing by numberless handsome lodges and, nearer the city, many terraces in neat order, the road conducts us near a large tract of some hundred acres which have been reclaimed from the sea and are destined to form a park and pleasure ground for the citizens of Cork. In the river and up to the bridge some hundreds of ships were lying, and a fleet of steam-boats opposite the handsome house of the St. George Steam Packet Company. A church stands prettily on the hill above it, surrounded by a number of new habitations, very neat and white. On the road is a handsome Roman Catholic Chapel, or a chapel that will be handsome as soon as the necessary funds are raised to complete it." The funds were raised to give the city the beautiful church of St. Patrick, with its stately classical portico and its distinctive belfry.

Even though Thackeray's pen picture brings the story of Cork into the nineteenth century it will be of interest to have some contemporary glimpses into the city's life as the eighteenth century drew to a close. Irish historians have good reason to be grateful to that indefatigable traveller and that meticulous observer of the passing scene, Arthur Young. His "Tour of Ireland" published in 1780 contains a wealth of acute observations on social and economic conditions, particularly on matters agricultural which were his special interest. He wrote as follows on the city: "Got to Corke in the evening and waited on the Dean, who received me with the most flattering attention. Corke is one of the most populous place I have ever been in; it was market-day and I could scarce drive through the streets they were so amazingly thronged. I should suppose it must resemble a Dutch town for there are many canals in the streets, with quays before the houses. The best built part is Morrison's Island, which promises well. The old part of the town is very close and dirty." Young, one of those Englishmen with a taste for facts and figures, gives the following details of the city's exports for the nineteen years ending on March 24th 1773, based on information supplied by Robert Gordon, Surveyor General: Hide exports, £64,000; Butter exports £180,000; Beef exports £291,970; Candle exports £34,225; Tallow exports £20,000; Pork exports £64,000; Herrings £21,000. Seventy or eighty sailing ships belonged to Cork, and the average number of ships entering the port was 872 each year. There were 700 coopers at work in the city and in 1780 a total of 240,000 firkins of butter were handled. Eggs were selling at four a penny and a horseload of dung could be bought for eight pence. Labourers were paid 1/1 per day and "as much bread, beef and beer as they can eat and drink, and 7 lbs. of offal a week for their families." There was also a flourishing woollen trade, "the wool comes to Corke and is delivered out to combers who make it into great balls. These balls are bought up by the French agents at a vast price and exported." The wool came from Galway and Roscommon and the combers were earning from 8/- to 10/- per week making the balls of 24 ounces each. "Half the wool of Ireland is combed in the county of Corke." Mr. Abraham Lane had recently established a manufactory for the supply of army clothing. A domestic or cottage industry was "the making of knit-stocking by the common women about Corke, for eight or ten miles around; the yarn from 12d. to 18d. a pair and the worsted from 16d. to 20d. Besides their own consumption great quantities are sent to the north of Ireland." It was with especial relish that Young left Cork on September 22nd 1780, and met a man after his own heart at the lovely mansion of Coolmore, near Carrigaline. He was the Rev. Archdeacon Oliver, an improving landlord. Young went into ecstacies at the mere slight of the archdeacon's turnips:

"he began the culture of turnips four years ago and found them so profitable that he has every year had a field of them in the broad-cast method, and well hoed. This year they are exceedingly fine, clean, and well hoed, so that they would be no disgrace to a Norfolk farmer." There was no end to the agricultural delights of Coolmore—potatoes were being sown in drills, there was a field planted with 20,300 cabbages, and the good archdeacon was buying "great quantities of dung and soap ashes in Corke."

Though not relating specifically to Cork City one or two other little cameos of everyday Irish social life in 1780 are worth recalling. Young found that "dancing is very general among the poor people, almost universal in every cabin. Dancing masters of their own rank travel through the country from cabin to cabin with a piper or blind fiddler, and the pay is sixpence a quarter. It is an absolute system of education. Weddings are always celebrated with much dancing, and a Sunday rarely passes without a dance. There are very few among them who will not after a hard day's work gladly walk seven miles to have a dance." The game of hurling merited a mention: "Hurling is a sort of cricket, but instead of throwing the ball to knock down a wicket the aim is to pass it through a bent stick, the ends stuck in the ground. In these matches they perform such feats of activity as ought to evidence the food they live on to be far from deficient in nourishment." Regarding the simplistic notion that the mass of the Irish peasantry were living in enforced ignorance due to the restrictions of the Penal Laws, Young's assessment makes interesting reading: "other branches of education are likewise much attended to, every child of the porest family learning to read, write and cast accounts." Nor was Arthur Young content merely to record the facts of social and economic life; he addressed himself deeply and at length to the religious restrictions which prevented Catholics from taking part in the public life of their country; "the system adopted in Queen Anne's reign has failed; has not the experience in every age and every nation proved that the effect is invariable and universal?" He urged the Protestant ascendancy to form a partnership with the majority of their countrymen for the common good of Ireland. In doing so he was attuned to the rising spirit of Protestant patriotism then being so finely expressed in the Irish Parliament by Henry Grattan, whose name is commemorated by one of the old streets of Cork. It was a tragedy from which Ireland still suffers that the meeting of minds of liberal Catholics and Protestants so evident in 1780 was frustrated by extremists on both sides.

If the bucolic Arthur Young left some benign memories, yet another visitor to the city was full of tart comments and undisguised disapproval. Monsieur de Latocnaye was apparently a Royalist officer who fled from France to England in December, 1792. He published in French an account of a tour of England, and then he turned his attention to Ireland with his "Promenade d'un Francais dans l'Irlande." Part of his promenade was a best-forgotten visit to Cork. Before giving some excerpts from his observations it is worth recalling that the Gallic gentleman seemed well armed with suitable introductions to many of the best houses; as well as putting up at wayside inns, he stayed in the houses of deans and dukes and country gentlemen, including "some time in the island of Foaty with a spoiled child of fortune, Mr. Smith Barry. He has travelled much, is very courteous and reasonable, appears to be well educated, is good natured, and would be happy if he had only £500 a year instead of £25,000; but his riches have so surfeited him and disgusted him with the world that he has almost totally retired from society and lives a rather melancholy life on his island." The wandering Frenchman obligingly left a pretty detailed account of his bag and baggage which may be a useful guideline should the gentle reader consider taking to the roads: "For the information of future travellers on foot it is my pleasure here to give details of my complete equipment; a powder bag made out of a woman's glove; a razor; thread; needles; scissors, a comb carried in one of a pair of dress shoes; a pair of silk stockings; breeches fine enough to be, when folded, not bigger than a fist; two very fine shirts; three cravats, three handkerchiefs, the clothes in which I travelled. The sundries I divided in three, two lots going into the silk stockings which served as bags, the third packet containing my shoes." Such at the close of the eighteenth century was the outfit of one who was very literally a gentleman of the roads! Thus encumbered with his powder bag, his silk stockings, his dress shoes and his needles de Latocnaye descended on Cork. He had a "recommendation to the Bishop who received me very kindly, and this gave me great pleasure for I think it proves that all animosities between the two religions are at an end. He sent me to the Catholic Bishop, Dr. Moylan, who is an educated man and much respected in the country."

But apart from his episcopal encounters the Frenchman was not at all pleased with what he saw: 'I arrived at Cork, the dirtiest and dullest town which can be imagined. The people met with are yawning, and one is stopped every minute by funerals or hideous troops of beggars or pigs which run the streets in hundreds. And yet this town is one of the richest and most commercial of Europe. The principal merchants are nearly all foreigners, Scotch for the most part, and in the short period of ten years are able sometimes to make large fortunes. The dirt of the streets in the middle of the town is shameful, and as if that were not enough it would seem as if it were wished to hinder the wind and the sun from drying the filth, for the two ends of the street are terminated by prisons which close the way entirely and prevent the air from circulating. The climate of Cork is rainy in the extreme. It rains every day in life and the temperature of the air has perhaps influenced the character of the inhabitants. I have seen poor people obliged to collect water from roofs on a rainy day, or to take it even from the streams in the streets. All the time there is perhaps hardly a place which it would be so easy to supply with water as Cork by reason of the heights which suround it. There is even a spring or fountain about a mile away which is called Sunday's Well, which appears to me to have sufficient water for the supply of a public fountain in the centre of the town." This comment underlines a problem experienced by most cities in the eighteenth century, the supply of drinkable water, a problem which had to await municipal action in the following century. On his way into the city de Latocnaye had stayed a few days at Castle Martyr," one of the most beautiful and one of the best-cared for places not merely in Ireland but, perhaps, in Europe. The garden, which Lady Shannon finds pleasure in cultivating, is a charming retreat where flowers of every species are arranged with singular skill." Then to divest himself of the malodours of the city he "quitted Cork at last and took my way to Bandon." It must have been with some relief that he once again used the contents of his powder-bag and felt the caressing softness of his fine breeches and silk stockings!

Whatever it was that brought them to Cork, they still kept coming; more importantly they kept scribbling away, so enabling us to catch a glimpse of distant days through contemporary eyes. In the same year as Arthur Young's treatise, 1780, there was published in London "A Tour through Ireland wherein the Present State of that Kingdom is considered, and the most noted Cities, Towns, Seats, Buildings and Loughs described, interspersed with Observations on the Manners, Customs, Antiquities, Curiosities and Natural History of that Country." The author was Mr. John Windham who stated in his introduction that he had decided to see Ireland first before embarking on the traditional Grand Tour, "a task to be performed by our English gentry as soon as they are taken from school." He landed in Dublin, finding it "much greater than in general imagined. The greatest part of Dublin is very indifferent but the new streets are as elegant as the modern streets of Westminster. Lately has been added to it an elegant square called Merryon's square built in a superb stile. Near that is the square called St. Stephen's Green, each side being near a quarter of a mile, probably the largest in Europe." He came to Cork by boat from Dublin, landing at what was then Cove. "From Cove we were rowed up to Passage. Here all ships of burden unlade and their cargoes are carried up to Cork either on small cars drawn by one horse, or in vessels of small size, the channel higher up admitting only those of one hundred and fifty tons burden." He found the city "large and extensive beyond my expectations. I had been taught to think worse of it in all respects than it deserves. It was described as the magazine of nastiness and as the great shambles of the kingdom. But it is really as clean in general as the Metropolis. The slaughter-houses are all in the suburbs and there, indeed, the gale is not untainted. The island where the city stands is intersected with several canals either natural or artificial which, being banked and quayed in, bring up ships almost to every street. On the new quays there are some good looking buildings which they are obliged to weather slate." The people were "hospitable and generous; they are rich and deal largely in provisions; many of our fleets both of merchantmen and ships of war touching here to victual, which they do at a cheap rate. Yet to us the place was dear enough, not less than London." Some excellent examples of the kind of weather slating Windham saw can still be seen in the picturesque bow-fronted houses near the National Monument on the Grand Parade. He was obviously impressed with the bustle of trade: "I have not heard a bell in any of the churches too good for the dinner-bell of a country squire. But here is something infinitely better. Here is the busy bustle of prosperous trade and all its concomitant blessings. Except in the article of linen, its exports are more considerable than those of Dublin.

Whereas de Latocnaye was not enamoured of the stone prisons at both ends of the Main Street, Windham had a different view: "there are two gates, the north and south; though prisons for debtors they are beautiful buildings, the river Lee passing with its divided stream on the outside of each." What is now the School of Art and was then the Custom House is described as "a handsome brick building with angles, window-cases and door-frames of stone; it was erected at the expense of George I and is surrounded by a good quay, with cranes and all proper conveniences for landing goods, close to the north channel of the river." The city Exchange in Castle Street, on the site of the present Catholic Young Men's Society hall, was "small for such an opulent trading city, but a very neat building erected in 1708; it is supported by substantial pillars and opens to the north and west sides." The old St. Finbarr's Cathedral was "without the gate in a very pleasant churchyard, shaded with rows of trees planted uniform. It was rebuilt in the reign of the late king by a parliamentary tax upon coals imported into Cork. It is a spacious structure of the Doric order, but the tower near it is a mean spirical structure, low and poorly built. St. Mary Shandon stands upon a rising ground, is a handsome building with a high square tower. There is also another new church (St. Nicholas) within a hundred paces of the South Gate, much the handsomest in the city." It has been asserted earlier in this chapter that in regard to Catholic worship the harsher restrictions of the Penal Laws were of short duration and spasmodically enforced; Windham's observations reinforce that point, painting a picture of a vigorous and open religious practice. "It must too be observed that though the monasteries are destroyed the monks remain to this day, and have regular services in their distinct houses, as in the parish mass-houses, in all of which they have a succession of services on Sundays and holidays from early in the morning to late at night. Besides these eleven mass-houses there are four different meeting-houses belonging to the Presbyterians, Anabaptists, Quakers and French Protestants." By 1780 the Franciscans, Dominicans and Augustinians had resumed community life in the city. Windham paints a particularly interesting picture of Sunday Mass in what was then the new church of St. Finbarr South, still one of the most atmospheric in the city, with its splendid "Dead Christ" by John Hogan beneath the High Altar. "On Sunday morning early I stepped into one of their mass-houses and a spacious one it was. The priest had just finished the celebration of mass. On the altar stood six candles. A servitor came in after the priest had withdrawn and, kneeling before the altar, he entered the rails and snuffed out two of the candles; then he kneels again and snuffs out two more; he kneeled a fourth time and extinguished the fifth, the sixth he left burning. There were several elegant carriages standing before the door when I entered and a prodigious crowd of people in the street, as motly an assemblage of human creatures as I have ever seen. There was a multitude of beggars imploring alms in the Irish language, some in a high and some in low key. Some of them measured out tones as if singing but in accents the most unmusical that ever wounded the human ear." This reference to the use of Irish in the city streets should interest any reader pursuing the matter of the extent to which the language was still in common use in urban areas. Windham must have been in an ecumenical mood that Sunday morning in Cork for having observed Catholics at Mass in the South Chapel he went along to Christ Church in the South Main Street where "the service was performed with the utmost decency and propriety; they had a good organ and the singing was remarkably good."

These varied accounts show something of the living city as the eighteenth century drew to a close, a century characterised as the age of elegance and the age of reason. It was to end with revolution in America, France and Ireland. The French Revolution was to impress itself indelibly on men's minds and was to have profound influences on the thought and the political shape of Europe in the following century. But the elegance and the reason were made to look hollow as the mob perpetrated its obscenities in the streets of Paris, and when the benign though inept Louis XVI and his frivolous queen, Marie Antoinette, were carted to the guillotine a shudden of revulsion ran through Europe. As before and since, the easy slogans of armchair theorists had been translated by the mob into brutal realities. If Wordsworth was moved by the early revolutionary enthusiasm to pen the line, "bliss it was in that moment to be alive, but to be young was very heaven," it was Edmund Burke, a kinsman of the Cork pioneer of religious education for the Catholic poor, Nano Nagle, who gave to the world the memorable phrase "the age of chivalry is gone and the glory of Europe is extinguished forever." The impact of those tumultuous events in France reached out to a lane still standing off Patrick Street, to Carey's Lane in which was situated the old Catholic chapel of St. Peter and Paul's, later to blossom into the present graceful ediface built to a design by the younger Pugin and opened on 29th June, 1860. In his Diary for 1793 the Cork schoolmaster, John Fitzgerald, made the following entry for February 6th: "Very cold, wet weather, gloomy with rain. A funeral sermon by Dr. McCarthy at Ss. Peter and Paul's Chapel for the King of France." The preacher was the coadjutor bishop to Dr. Moylan and the text of the sermon is preserved at Maynooth Library. It was from France that the republican tradition first entered Irish political life and the Sheares brothers are commemorated by a street in which was the family town house, while their villa was out at Glasheen. Sheares Street and Grattan Street intersect, recalling the two main streams of modern Irish nationalism, the constitutional and the revolutionary.

The general alarm felt by the news of an attempted French landing at Bantry Bay, with Wolfe Tone aboard the fleet, prompted the Catholic bishop of Cork, Dr. Moylan, to issue a pastoral letter to his flock on Christmas Day, 1796. The text as given in the "History of Cork" by M. F. Cusack, the colourful and controversial "Nun of Kenmare," includes the following passages: "Loyalty to the sovereign and respect for the constituted authorities have always been the prominent features of the Christian character; and by patriotism and obedience to the established form of government have our ancestors been distinguished at times and under circumstances very different from these in which we have the happiness to live. For, blessed be God, we are no longer strangers in our native land; no longer excluded from the benefits of the happy constitution under which we live; no longer separated by odious distinctions from our fellow subjects . . . Germany, Flanders, Italy, Holland, to say nothing of their own, once the happiest now the most miserable country in the world, can attest the irreparable ruin, desolation and destruction occasioned by the French fraternity . . . Be not then, imposed on by their professions, they come only to rob, plunder and destroy. Listen not to their agitating abettors in this country who endeavour by every means to corrupt your principles . . . I shall conclude with this simple reflection: if the sway of our impious invaders were here established you would not enjoy the comfort of celebrating this auspicious day with gladness and thanksgiving, nor of uniting with all Christians on earth and with the celestial spirits in heaven in singing, Glory to God on high." Though the United Irish movement had some support in the city it is probably true to say that the majority of the Catholic community shared in the general revulsion felt at the news of regicide and mob violence coming out of France, a revulsion accentuated by the accounts of attacks on the persons and property of the clergy and religious.

This general survey of the history of Cork over eleven centuries has of necessity concentrated on the major highlights of local events as well as the impact on the city of the broader movement of national and European life. The passing centuries had woven many patterns into the fabric of the life of Cork and the year 1800 found it bigger and more prosperous than ever before, with its Butter Exchange bringing the thrust of commerce and its physical shape about to experience an enormous expansion in size and style. Yet the original outlines remained familiar, the encircling hills and the river Lee flowing in the valley; while a church dedicated to St. Finbarr still stood on the early monastic site. Irish and Normans, natives and planters had become moulded into citizens of a city which won the affection of them all. The next chapter will give a detailed account of the various activities of everyday life as seen through the eyes of the City Fathers.

EVERYDAY LIFE AND HOW THE CORPORATION MANAGED IT, 1700-1800

Chapter II

Every decent citizen is utterly convinced of one thing and that is that the Corporation is to blame for everything. This wholly laudable sentiment was to some extent shared by Mr. Thomas Browne, even though he was himself a member of that august body as well as having his name still commemorated by an old city street. The particular antics which aroused the wrath of the worthy Mr. Browne on the 8th December, 1773, was the proposal to build the first St. Patrick's Bridge. As he saw it the thing was preposterous on two accounts; it would increase the rates and the site was manifestly ridiculous. His motion of dissent regarding rates was a fine example of civic grumbling while it gives a detailed picture as to how the Corporation proposed to raise extra money: "I object to the applying for local taxes on wine, brandy, Geneva, oranges, lemmons, herrings, salt, balk, deal boards, wheel carriages, as the inhabitants too justly complain of the heavy taxes they already labour under." Why do Corporations have such a persistent hatred for citizens who elect to travel on wheeled contrivances? In 1773 they were penalizing carriage wheels while their successors of today have men prowling the streets waiting to pounce on the owners of horseless carriages. As regards the proposed new bridge Mr. Browne failed to see any reason why the existing North Gate Bridge was not adequate for the trade of the city; an extra bridge further down river would destroy the business life of the heart of the city, the North Main Street and Shandon Street, besides cutting off valuable stretches of quayside for the berthing of ships close to the very centre of activity. The building of a new bridge would be the ruination of Cork! On those issues he incanted a doomsday lament in the best traditions of all those who have seen change as the herald of disaster: "I am of opinion," he asserted, "that it would be of infinite disadvantage to a considerable part of the trade of this City, and would render almost useless about three fourths of the quays where colliers and other vessels generally lie; it would materially injure in their trade and properties all the inhabitants of Mallow and Blarney Lanes, the Main Street from the North to the South Gate, and all of the western parts of the City.." Yet what Mr. Browne saw as a recipe for commercial disaster was soon to become the main artery into the city, while the present gracious St. Patrick's Bridge, with the elegance of its colonnaded balustrade and the low curve of its three elliptical arches, represents the finest of the many works in the city that came from the hands of the architect, Sir John Benson.

The Browne incident illustrates a feature found in all cities, the tension between the citizens and the Corporation, between private interest and what is considered to be public good. That tension is sometimes acrimonious, often hilarious, but always healthy. For in the long run it is the Corporation that matters most in shaping the pattern of everyday city life. This was infinitely more the case before the present century which has seen national government take to itself such vast powers of decision in planning and the spending of public money. Previous to 1900 the municipal bodies of all cities in Ireland and Britain were more or less free to manage their affairs as they wished. Civic government fulfils a unique and purposeful role, at once a guardian of rights and traditions and yet charged with the task of making change and providing blueprints for the future. A study of municipal government in the ancient cities of Europe, and Cork is one of those, as well as in the newcomers in nineteenth century America and Britain would provide the full range of human folly and greatness, with greed and graft found side by side with vision and enterprise. A city is a microcosm of humanity and in running it the Corporation has the delicate task of reflecting the balance between order, beauty and the values of the market place. If part of a city's history is written in stone and story, yet another vivid chapter is contained in its municipal records. Cork is fortunate in that one of its nineteenth century scholars gave himself the monumental task of transcribing and publishing the Corporation Minutes from 1609 to 1800. He was Richard Caulfield and his appointment as Librarian to the University was one of the more notable acts of that institution in the last century. Considered purely as a social document, and leaving aside the larger religious and political issues arising from the fact that the spirit of the times saw fit to restrict membership of the Corporation to citizens of the Established Church, the Minutes provide a vivid contemporary account of the everyday business of administering the city of Cork. Written with the dry precision of such documents, and concerned more with factual narrative rather than literary flourish, there emerges a living picture of the things that concerned the citizens in their homes and at work and in the enormous amount of open-air street trading that was still a feature of city life until the opening decades of the present century. What were those things? There was the business of fixing and collecting tolls at the city gates, of regulating stalls for selling fish, fruit and vegetables, the building of bridges, the repairing of walls, the paving of streets, the lighting of public lamps, the collecting of dung, the apprehension of criminals and the winding of the public clock. Indeed, it was precisely because the Corporation entered so pervasively into so many aspects of the lives of the citizens that occasional flashes of conflict lit the sky. But if the decent citizen was convinced that the Corporation was to blame for everything, he must also have known that without it there would be nothing! Acting in the name of the citizens the Corporation gave order and shape to the life and labour of rich and poor, of butcher, baker and candlestick-maker.

One of the most marked differences between a city at present and in the eighteenth century is the matter of street lighting at night. In that respect the modern city is a wonderland of illumination. In the eighteenth century the coming of nightfall marked a very definite end to outside activity; the streets were pitch dark and the numerous potholes, open quays and sewers, beside the lack of an effective police force, made the night a time of hazard. Revellers coming from the theatre or the taverns sought the services of link-boys who earned a penny walking in front carrying flaming rush lights. Private houses often had iron holders over their front doors to hold similar torches to give light to visitors coming for a night of music or card-playing. Odd examples of these may still be seen in older residential areas. Beside the link-boys other creatures of the night were the town crier and the public constables. Swinging his lamp and armed with his cudgel, the town crier made regular rounds of the streets calling out the time and looking out for any sign of fire. As the citizen lay in bed and adjusted his nightcap he would be reassured to hear the cry, "two o'clock, all's well." The constables were generally feeble old men who spent the night in watch-boxes and were meant to protect the sleeping city from the attention of thieves and ruffians. More often they snoozed the weary hours away and should any formidable-looking ruffian appear they ran away as fast as their aged legs could carry them! The Cork Corporation considered the provision of public lighting at a meeting on 11th July, 1743 with the Minutes reading as follows: "The question being put whether shall lamps be erected in Shandon, Paul's, Peter's and Christ Church parishes and also in the parts measured without the South Gate. The members present being poled there appeared for the question nine, against it three and five who voted neither for nor against it, but in general for lamps being erected in the whole City and Liberties." Among members present at that meeting the following are still commemorated in city streets, Messrs Pembroke, Travers, Millerd, Browne and Smith. The whole city referred to in the Minute still in 1743 was broadly from Shandon in the north to St. Finbarr's in the south and from Grattan Street in the west to the Grand Parade in the east. Some progress in the matter of throwing light on Cork was reported on September 19th when "Henry Whetcroft and Thomas Mitchell were appointed to erect and maintain Lights in this City and Liberties." But the Corporation was not going to be rushed into action and the good citizens were left to spend the winter of 1743 in the dark. By June 22nd the following year the matter was ripe for further consideration with the record stating that "the persons appointed to erect and maintain Lamps have reported that the following number of Lamps are necessary, to wit, 114 in the parish of St. Mary Shandon, 65 in St. Paul's, 100 in St. Peter's, 133 in Holy Trinity and 26 in St. Nicholas and part of St. Bridget's." Having done its survey the Corporation got down to the little matter of deciding who was to pay for this projected burst of illumination. Some official or clerk had done his sums with punctilious exactitude; "ordered that for supplying lamps for the year next ensuing the sums mentioned to be raised on said parishes: £74.2.0 on St. Mary Shandon, £45.5.0 on St. Paul's, £65 on St. Peter's, £86.9.0 on Holy Trinity and £16.18.0 on St. Nicholas at the rate of 13 shillings for each Lamp." However, this neat bureaucratic arrangement was not to everyone's satisfaction; more particularly the gentlemen of St. Finbarr's were indignant at finding themselves left out in the dark. Accordingly, Messrs Austen, Harding Parker, Augustine Carre and James Piersy tabled the following amendment: "We protest against the above order because the parish of St. Finn Barry's is not mentioned in the said order, and the said parish ought to have Lamps and be lighted as well as the other parishes for the benefit of all the inhabitants." By July 26th, 1748, some at least of the lamps seemed to have been in operation for on that date Mr. Mitchell was empowered to "assign his office of one of the Lamp Masters of this City to Henry Duggan."

Yet there were vagabonds abroad at night as the Minute for 2nd November of that year testified: "The Constables of the Watch were about three or four o'clock this morning assaulted, wounded and falsely imprisoned in the execution of their office without any provocation by Robert Fitzgerald, a lieutenant in the Hon. General Ottoway's Foot." The fact that the culprit was a member of the garrison made it no less painful for the Watch. City lights again appeared on the Corporation agenda on 5th January, 1760, when some careful regulations were recorded as well as an indication that St. Finbarr's parish had its needs satisfied: "that no lamp be a greater distance than 23 yards from the next lamp on the same side of the street; and in lanes, courts and alleys no lamp shall be at a greater distance than 23 yards from the next lamp, and the parish of St. Finbarry's and suburbs be under the same regulations." Here is a good example of town planning, while the phrase "lanes, courts and alleys" evokes the peculiar atmosphere of an eighteenth century city. Perhaps the most grandiose entry relating to lighting occurs in the Minute for 28th October, 1772, and were there such a book as the "Compleat Lamplighter" it would assuredly find a place in it. "We do fix 800 Lamps with single burners and good wicks, and we fix 200 Lamps in the parish of Holy Trinity, 139 in the parish of St. Peter, 78 in the parish of St. Paul, 223 in the parishes of St. Mary Shandon and St. Ann and the suburbs belonging, 122 in the parishes of St. Finbarry and St. Nicholas and suburbs belonging, 38 in the Main Street on posts between the North and South Gate. That they be lighted on the 8th November at sun setting and continue lighting to sun rising to May 1st next; and every succeeding year they be lighted on 1st September, and they be lighted with good rape seed oil or good fish oil, or rape and fish oil mixed together; that the glasses of the said Lamps be kept cleaned and trimmed and snuffed when necessary, and we hereby fix that the sum of £1.5.5 (amounting to £856.13.4) shall be paid for maintaining each Lamp from 8th November next to 1st May, and that £1.5.0 be paid for trimming." The reader will recall an earlier mention of the Rape Marsh, the old name for the present South Mall. Further details as to who did what and for how much are contained in the Minute for 24th November of the same year: "£25.14.5 to William Wily, blacksmith, in full for Lamp irons and expense for erecting same; £2.3.4½ to Alderman Millerd, so much expended by him in marking out the places in the parish of St. Peter where the Lamps are erected, and painting 47 Lamp posts; £1.3.10 to Mr. John Jones for erecting 195 Lamps in the parish of Christ Church; £39.9.3 to Richard Burt, glazier, for reparing the Lamps; £26.2.0½ to Mr. Thomas Fuller in full for timber for the Lamp posts; £20.4.3 to William Rogers, tinman, in full for burners, oilpots and lanthorns, £17.11.1 to Andrew Dalton, carpenter, in full for making the Lamp posts; £7.9.10½ to Roger Ouldin, mason, in full for erecting the Lamp posts in the Main Street." Millerd Street, from where Alderman Millerd set out to "mark the places in the parish of St. Peter" can still be seen opposite the Mercy Hospital, off Henry Street. This splendid enumeration of the details of city lights is of interest in bringing out the mechanical aspects of the operation; equally it gives a realistic glimpse into the everyday working life of carpenters, tinmen, glaziers and blacksmiths. The nineteenth century was to bring the gaslights, with a wealth of nostalgia growing up around the lamplighter coming on his evening rounds with his long pole. Robert Louis Stevenson's poem captures that nostalgia with lasting effect. In this century electricity has turned night into day and made the city a fairyland of brightness at night, but the memory of the men who cleaned and snuffed and trimmed the lamps of eighteenth century Cork deserves a passing tribute.

Apart from the rather harmless matter of public lighting the Corporation had other more disturbing matters on its hands in April, 1753. The Minute for April 6th records attacks on country people bringing in their potatoes for sale: "whereas a riotous mob assembled in this City on Thursday, April 5th, to the great terror of the country people who supply the markets of this City with provisions, ordered that the Mayor issue a proclamation promising a reward of £10 to such person as shall convict the promoter of said riotous mob." But if the unfortunate country people were disturbed in selling their potatoes, at least they fared better than the luckless John Sullivan who ended up a few days later having his ear stuck on the gate of Shandon! The Minute reveals all: "whereas a most riotous and wicked mob assembled in this City on April 17th and cruelly seized one John Sullivan of said City, a porter,whom they carried through the streets of this City and unmercifully beat, wounded, bruised, and cut off one of his ears which they affixed to the gate of Shandon Church, and left said Sullivan in the street as dead." Whatever was the ultimate fate of the ear on the gate can only be a matter of speculation, but a piece of town planning was recorded on 17th September, 1753, concerning what is now the Grand Parade between Old Post Office Lane and Tuckey Street, then facing out over an open channel of water: "A petition preferred by the inhabitants living between Tuckey's Bridge and the Post Office setting forth that the quay opposite their houses is too narrow for carriages and dangerous for his Majesty's subjects passing in the night-time, and setting forth that 20 feet in breadth be added to said quay from the channel without prejudice thereto. Resolved that the inhabitants shall have such liberty as the Corporation can grant for enlarging said quay." To-day the City Library stands on that quay, while the old Tuckey's Bridge is the site of the Berwick Fountain. Then there was the question of parking, a little matter still troubling the descendants of the good citizens of 1756. What was the citizen to do if he or she wanted to pitch a stall in the street to sell fuel, faggots, straw, fowl, dead pigs, skins, wool, twigs, brooms or oysters? The Corporation was most indulgent; one could pitch one's stall for half an hour without paying what was termed petty customs. The Minute of 16th November, 1756 tells as much about the life of the traders in the streets as about the petty customs: "No fuel, faggots, straw, sedge, fowl, butter in baskets, eggs, which are drawn or carried through the public streets for the use of the inhabitants, in a moving posture, and not unladen or pitched in the public street in order to be sold there, shall be liable to pay for pitching or standing unless the same are really pitched in said streets and remain an incumberance there at least half an hour, or until sold. And also that no pigs killed in the country or hawked about the streets of this City on cars or horses' backs for sale, nor any leather, skins, wool, hoops, twigs, brooms, oysters, scallops, barley, oats and such like goods as are drawn in order to be sold before same shall be pitched, shall be liable to pay for standing in said streets, unless the same shall be actually unladen and pitched for sale, or remain an incumberence on said streets for at least half an hour." It appears, therefore, that the trader was given half an hour's grace as regards parking the goods provided they were not actually pitched for sale. The list of goods is itself most interesting, as is the evidence of a great deal of street trading carried out by people in from the surrounding countryside.

But as well as prescribing when the hawkers could sell or park their dead pigs, their faggots and their oysters, the Corporation had to attend to the maintenance of public buildings. The hub of civic and social life was the Exchange in Castle Street, standing on the site of the present Catholic Young Men's Society hall, a building described in 1780 by the English traveller, John Windham, as "small for such an opulent trading city, but a very neat building erected in 1708. It is supported by substantial pillars and opens to the north and west sides." The Exchange had an arcade of shops at ground level from which the Corporation drew rent. The spacious rooms upstairs were used by day for official municipal business, while at night they were often the scene of soirees and glittering grand balls where dandies in powdered wigs led their dames in the gavot and the minuet. And when their revels were ended they were taken home in sedan chairs to the North Mall or Dean Street and to the new fashionable streets such as Browne Street and the South Terrace. A leaking roof was utterly unbecoming to such pomp and circumstance and the Minute of 12th July, 1758, set about fixing things: "The Exchange to be new painted and whitewashed; the lead over the Council Chamber to be soldered; the leaks stopped; the cupola to be new painted. A new lead spout to be put up at the Meat Shambles. The windows, doors and rails of the Corn Market-house (situated in street of that name) to be painted, the slating new pointed. The North Meat Shambles to be repaired in the roof." A quick comment on that Minute would be that all Cork seemed to be leaking in 1758! The matter of widening streets came up again on 16th January, 1760, when the Corporation recorded agreement with Dr. Tuckey regarding what was then called Tuckey's Lane. He was at his own expense to pull down thirteen houses on the north side and "the Corporation is to pay said Tuckey £1000 for said ground in the following manner, to wit £500 on the execution of proper deeds of conveyance, the other £500 in six months afterwards, interest free." The city Courthouse bell (now the Queen's Old Castle) "which is cracked, to be taken down and exchanged with Nicholas Fitton, founder, for a new bell, allowing said Fitton six pence in the pound profit on the exchange." Then there was a matter which was to cause bother in the years ahead, the statue of King George I in the Grand Parade: "that £100 be paid Thomas Newenham as soon as an equestrian statue of his Majesty shall be erected in this City."

A wide range of civic administration was considered on 28th October, 1761, when a sub-committee on bye-laws made a number of recommendations. One of those concerned some sharp practice in selling wet straw, so making the commodity heavier in weight. This had nothing to do with feeding horses, rather it related to the common use of straw for bedding either made up in mattresses for the more genteel, or simply spread on the stone floor or in a garret room by the poor. A penalty was to be imposed on dishonest straw dealers: "a clause that Straw shall be sold in this City by weight, the same to be made up in bundles of six pound avoirdupois under a penalty of 2/6, and 2/6 for having same wet with intent to defraud." The tax on coaches and sedan chairs went to support the Workhouse and it was proposed " to make coaches, chariots, postchaises, chairs and sedans plying for hire in this City of Cork pay the same duties to the Workhouse of this City as are paid to that of Dublin." This is an early ancestor of that long list of iniquitous taxation which has afflicted the taximen and morotrists of Cork in this present century. The full story of sedan chairs and horse travel in and out of the city will be found in a later chapter. A simple clause to "prevent combination among workmen" gave a hint of incipient trade unionism, an issue which was to come forcefully to the fore in the industrial century to follow, with the tension between capital and organised labour. Lastly, there was the business of threatrical players posting up handbills without the Mayor's permission: "it is apprehended a suit is intended to be brought against the Mayor for preventing the players from acting in this City on account of their putting up bills without the Mayor's permission. In such case the Mayor's costs to be paid out of Corporation revenue." During the cold days of January, 1762, the streets of the city were infested by what were described as "certain shocking objects," namely beggars, and the Mayor was empowered to get rid of them as recorded in the Minute for January 8th: "that £11.7.6 be paid Mr. Mayor to enable him to punish and send away from this City all foreign beggars and strollers that in great numbers come from the country and other towns and infest this City, and to prevent several shocking objects as daily appear in the public streets to the great offence of the inhabitants and the public." This would appear to be rather harsh treatment of what today are politely called under-privileged people, but it must be seen in its context. In the eighteenth century, as for so long afterwards, the State in Ireland or Britain made no provision for social welfare for the poor, the sick or the unemployed. What provision there was came from a rate levied on the ratepayers of each local parish to provide for its own poor. Naturally, the sturdy ratepayers were in no mood to support other people's beggars as well as their own. Meanwhile, the Fire Brigade needed attention and the Corporation Porters had to be decently clothed, all of which was provided for on 26th May, 1762: "that 12/5½ be paid James Supple for repairing the City fire-engine £18.3.4 be paid to Mrs. Esther Holmes for clothing supplied to the Bellman and Exchange Porter; £7.17.10 to Eugene Swiney for printing work done from 1758 to 1761 and that said Swiney be no further employed by this board; £11.7.6 to Silvester Clarke for coal barrels." As well as doing printing work for the Corporation Eugene Swiney won himself a place in local history as the editor and publisher of one of the earliest city newspapers, "The Cork Journal." It was issued from his premises in Paul Street from 1753 to 1768. The one activity that has characterised cities all through the ages is the humble but necessary one of sweeping the streets, and the Corporation made the following arrangements on 16th June, 1762: "Whereas Messrs Wm. Lawton and Kevan Ivod have given a proposal for sweeping and keeping clean the Main Street from North Gate to South Gate, Castle Street before the Corn Market, the chair standings and Tuckey's Street when finished, and George's Street to the new Play House, that they will sweep said streets three times a week at least and carry away every heap, and for every heap neglected they will subject themselves to a penalty of 2/-, and they will do said work for a salary of £20 a year provided that they have a lease for seven years and the place be granted them where the dung is now kept by South Gate to lodge said sweepings in, leaving a passage to the slip and necessary house. That Alderman Wm. Harding be appointed to sweep the street called Mallow Lane, (now Shandon Street) from Newgate to Hillgrove's house, and that he may dispose of said sweepings as he shall think proper provided he carry away every heap as soon as swept up." The Corporation had not yet got round to the modern practice of having its own workmen, instead the work was put out on contract. It will be noted how important it was to specify that the heaps of dung, the product of a city full of horses, should actually be removed. This commodity, however, was itself a source of revenue to the collectors as it was sold to the owners of vegetable plots within and without the city walls. The reader will recall from the previous chapter that the writer, Arthur Young, noted in 1780 that Archdeacon Oliver of Coolmore, Carrigaline, had large quantities of dung carted down from Cork to cultivate his turnips. Clean streets three days a week—but what about the pavements? The Corporation had thought of everything as illustrated by the Minute of 21st July, 1762: "that Roger Oulden, mason and paver, proposed that he will new pave the Main Street from gate to gate between the two Gaols, also the Gate houses of the North and South Bridges, as far as the gates at the end of same at three pence the square yard; that he expects £7 every Saturday for the payment of his workmen whilst the new pavement is going on." From pavements to parapets, with a decision on 31st July, 1764, directing "the building of parapet walls of the height of four feet and breadth not exceeding two feet, on the several quays and on the edges of the several dykes and canals of the City and suburbs, having proper openings convenient for the shipping and loading goods and merchandise." A directive such as this might well have appeared in the municipal transactions of a European city that is presently celebrating the sixth centenary of its foundation, Amsterdam. It serves to corroborate the evidence of eighteenth century visitors to Cork who frequently compared the city to a Dutch one. Regarding the parapet walls by the riverside it will be noted by the reader that the present-day fine stretch of limestone parapet on the north channel of the Lee is one of the interesting architectural features of the city. That work was undertaken by the Corporation in the latter half of the last century. On December 13th of the same year there was more ado about street sweeping with "the Mayor appointed to sweep the street from South Gate to the Exchange; John Smith from the Exchange to the North Gate and Water Gate Lane; Alderman Bury to Castle Street, the Corn Market, Potato Quay and the Mall; Mr. John Travers to Tuckey Street and George's Street, and Mr. Moses Newson from North Gate Bridge to North Abbey." Lamps were again on the agenda on 30th July, 1766, when Mr. Norton Parr was to be paid 18/- for the following splendidly detailed activities: "lighting, cleansing, trimming, snuffing and maintaining each lamp." However, the Corporation did take time off from the more serious business of managing the everyday life of the city, and this meeting approved the motion that "£20 be paid Mr. Mayor for providing an entertainment at Blackrock Castle on August 1st next." Municipal frolics at Blackrock Castle formed a regular feature of Corporation life through-out the eighteenth and into the nineteenth century; indeed, they formed the subject of numerous satirical "squibs" from the pens of local wits. Boyle's "Freeholder" has some vintage speciments. The Castle again featured on 27th November, 1766, with a decision "that £104.12.3 be paid Messrs Dennis and Penrose for timber for the new building at Blackrock Castle." Originally designed as a fort to guard the river approach to the city in the early seventeenth century, the old Castle was to be burnt down and replaced in 1828 by the present fairy-like building in gleaming white limestone, designed by the Pain brothers, the rivals to Sir Thomas Deane in the upsurge of civic architecture which characterised the first half of the nineteenth century. A major problem of all cities before the present century was the supply of drinkable water; it involved not only the considerations of convenience and cleansing but the more important one of public health. It was on 22nd July, 1767, that the Corporation formed a committee "to carry out the act for supplying this City with water." By the 14th May of the following year there was agreement "with Nicholas Fitton, of this City, founder, for doing said work." Involved first with lamps, then with water, Mr. Fitton is still remembered by the names of two city streets. Mr. Fitton had advertised his goods and services as follows in "The Cork Journal" on Friday, 16th December, 1753: "Nicholas Fitton, Founder on Tuckey's Quay. Makes and sells all kinds of pewter, brass and copper work. Beds of all sizes which he hangs after the best and cheapest manner. He also makes all kinds of Water Engines for extinguishing Fires and supplying gentleman's houses and gardens, which he will engage to be as good as any made in England." John Wesley's observations, quoted in the previous chapter, pinpointed the water problems of eighteenth century Cork and their repercussions on gentle folk.

The year 1782 marked the flowering of a remarkable movement in Irish history when the Volunteers under Lord Charlemont and Henry Grattan seemed about to create a fusion of patriotic interest between Protestant and Catholic in a demand for Free Trade and Parliamentary independence. It was a moment of generous mutual feeling which was later to be frequently recalled by the great tribune of the people, Daniel O'Connell, and by the nationalist writer, Thomas Davis. The claim was to have the trade and manufacture of Ireland freed from the restrictions imposed by the London government at the dictate of British trading interests; coupled with that was the demand that the Irish Parliament in College Green, Dublin, should have full legislative powers in internal affairs. Reading the speeches and the literature of the time one is struck by the genuine and widespread strength of what historians call Protestant nationalism. A great many of the debates in the Irish Parliament found speakers denouncing the remaining civil restrictions of the Penal Code and advocating Catholic demands not as a matter of concession but as a matter of justice. Nor was the London government opposed to these more generous provisions. Its more spectacular gesture of conciliation to Catholics was the foundation of Maynooth in 1795 out of state funds for the education of the priesthood. Catholics were admitted to Trinity College to primary degree level, a concession not granted to Protestant Dissenters by Oxford and Cambridge until the passing of another half century of quite bitter controversy in England. The Volunteers and the Free Trade movement launched the first "Buy Irish" campaign with an insistence on having uniforms and ordinary daily clothing made in Ireland. Couched in memorable prose, the speeches of Henry Grattan portray a love for Ireland and an understanding of her problems that must be appreciated in the context of the times. Grattan Street in Cork bears the name of this patriot and gentleman, and at the end of Liberty Street may be seen a stone embedded in the wall bearing the legend, "the year of liberty, 1782." An echo of this fever of national feeling is recalled in the Corporation Minute for 24th August, 1782: "that 10 guineas be paid to the Mayor Elect for repairing the Market House loft, whitewashing and new glazing same, in order to fit it up for the reception of the Volunteers who are to be reviewed under Lord Charlemont on the 7th September next." By 18th March, 1791, a new name was appearing when dealing with the streets of Cork, for on that date it was ordered "that the three lots of ground fronting Patrick Street between the house of the late James Lee and the dwellinghouse of James Gregg be sold by auction for a term of 100 years." The deeds of this transaction may still lie in some city solicitor's office; their discovery would be most helpful in building up an authentic picture of the development of the modern city centre. On May 26th of the same year the Corporation laid down some very stringent and detailed town planning provisions for development taking place in Castle Street: "that the buildings to be erected to the front of said ground shall be so erected as to leave Castle Street 32 feet wide, and of equal height with the houses now building by Mr. John Shaw in said street, and the ground floor of equal height and uniformity with that of Mr. Shaw's houses, and that the lower part of the windows of the second floor shall range with Mr. Shaw's windows." The Corporation of the day was very fortunate in having in Mr. Shaw the very model of a maker of houses. It can only be regretted that its present successor did not have a similar model of good taste when the more recent constructions of glass and concrete were erected on the South Mall and on Lapp's Quay. A concern for a human dimension as regards height and a pleasing external appearance characterised most eighteenth and nineteenth century building. The citizens and their visitors still admire them precisely because they are pleasant to look at and show the skill of the craftsman, as well as displaying the quality of local stone. One hunk of glass and concrete looks as stark and lifeless as any other such hunk in any other place.

Apart from keeping a sharp eye on the details of the width of streets and the heights of windows, the Corporation took care that the citizens would not be exploited by bogus coal merchants. The Minute for 17th July, 1799, ordered that "all persons employed in the carriage of Coals within this City and suburbs after 31st July shall on or before that day register his name with the Mayor, from whom he will receive a badge with a number thereon, which shall be conspiculously worn at all times when such person shall be employed, and every such person shall on demand produce such badge and permit the number to be taken." A final entry must conclude this selection from the activities of the Corporation, one that involved national and international events of grave moment. When the danger of a French landing at Bantry Bay caused general alarm in the city in 1796 the Catholic Bishop, Dr. Francis Moylan, a prelate beloved by his people for his immense labours in the cause of charity and education, issued a pastoral letter warning his flock against what he saw as the danger of the unchristian principles of the French Revolution gaining a foothold among them. Whatever the appeal of the high calls for liberty, equality and fraternity, the news from France was of murder, pillage and rape, of the execution of her anointed royal personages, and of the exile of priests and religious. The earlier idealism had turned sour and throughout Europe there was foreboding and fear. The Minute for 30th December, 1796 recorded the presentation to Dr. Moylan of the Freedom of the City in a silver box: "the Rev. Doctor Moylan, in a Silver Box, to perpetuate our grateful appreciation of his pious exertions in promoting the peace and good order of the country at the moment of menaced invasion."

When Richard Caulfield published his transcription of the Minute Book of the Corporation of the City of Cork in 1876 he described it as "the proceedings of the municipal body, faithfully recorded as the events took place." In coming to write this chapter there was the problem facing most historians, namely what to include and what to omit in order to create an authentic picture. The reader will have seen the Corporation dealing at first hand with the multifarious matters involved in the managing of the everyday life of the city and its citizens. Something of the flavour of eighteenth century Cork has, hopefully, been captured in this account of how the citizens and their representatives went about the business of living and working, of buying and selling, and of giving their affection, their time and their talents to the place they called home.

Chapter III

HOW THEY BUILT THE MERCY HOSPITAL—THE MANSION HOUSE

The Mercy Hospital has won a place in the affections of the citizens of Cork since its Sisters of Mercy and its staff of doctors and nurses began ministering to the sick in 1857. But the history of the actual building dates further back and forms an interesting chapter in the civic and architectural story of the city. It was designed and built by an architect who has some other surviving works to his credit, while its original purpose was that it would be the residence of the Mayor and the scene for official functions, receptions and grand balls. The building, therefore, was intended to exemplify civic pride and dignity both in its exterior proportions and in the elegance of its internal fitments. The success of those two aims can still be seen at the Mercy Hospital as it stands at a picturesque bend of the river in Henry Street. The facade has a somewhat continental air, especially in the splendour and shape of its windows. The first and second floors have Venetian windows while the third floor displays two oval windows with cross-shaped astragals. Apart from their pleasing appearance from the outside, these windows were obviously designed to give a flood of light to an interior grand staircase. This still stands, a splendid affair in mahogany, with the main reception rooms opening off at different levels. These in turn still carry the finely-wrought stucco work of a Waterford stuccadore. The main entrance in the Doric style completes the attraction of this piece of eighteenth century architectural elegance. From its completion in 1773 it witnessed many nights of gladness, when claret flowed free, when the music of the minuet floated over the riverside, and when civic dignitaries in powdered wigs led their ladies to dance. And when their revels were ended they stepped out through the Doric door and sat themselves into Sedan chairs; then preceded by link-boys carrying flaming torches, they were carried by the chairmen to their houses in the South and North Main Streets, or over to the North Mall, or to Rutland Street and the South Terrace, or up to Dean Street.

This short chapter will show how it was that the Mansion House was built, with the details of the work of carpenters and stonemasons, the rates of payment for labour, and the business of buying green curtains and brass fireirons and pewter hardware and mahogany chairs. This kind of detailed study can have its own distinctive interest in putting flesh onto the bare bones of history, and in adding something more to the knowledge of a building than the customary facts as to the name of the architect, the style chosen and the date of construction. As was the case in the last chapter, it is to the local Cork historian, Richard Caulfield, that tribute must be paid for makin available the information on the building of the Mansion House in his Minutes of the Corporation of Cork published in 1876. What has been done in this chapter is that scattered references in the Minutes have been collected together to form a coherent picture of everyday work on the building. Before coming to that, however, something must be said about the site and the architect.

The decision of the Corporation in 1763 to choose Hammond's Marsh, or Haman's Marsh as it was sometimes spelled, as the site of the proposed Mansion indicated a significant new move in town planning. It marked that phase of development westwards and eastwards from the narrow old medieval city which laid the foundation for modern Cork. That development was a reflection of the growing prosperity flowing from the thriving Butter Market with its exports of salted butter, hides and tallow. Large numbers of English and continental ships were coming into Cork to be victualled, while many of the merchant families had wine depots in France, Spain and Portugal. The commercial middle class were beginning to look out over the battered old city walls and to seek more commodious residences than those afforded by the narrow streets and lanes where they and their forebears had been born and bred. From around 1750 to 1800 there took place a very considerable amount of what would now be called civil engineering as the many marshes to the east from the Grand Parade to the City Hall and to the west from Grattan Street to the Mardyke, were drained and built up. This was how Patrick Street and the South Mall were formed and very soon the centre of commercial and residential life moved out into those areas from the old South and North Main Streets. The development westwards saw Grattan Street and Sheares Street made from arching over small channels of the river. Hammond's Marsh became the modern Henry Street as part of that same process, though in selecting it as the site of the Mansion House in 1763 the Corporation unwittingly made an error of judgment for, in fact, the future thrust of the business and civic life of the city was to lie eastwards. So, within eighty years of its construction, the City Fathers had vacated it and moved down into the heart of the newer nineteenth century city centre.

In Ireland as in England the eighteenth century witnessed much activity in the building of elegant country houses, many of which embodied styles of architecture and furnishings borrowed from the continent, particularly from Italy. It was the grand age of Palladian buildings, of sweeping staircases in marble and mahogany, and of long galleries filled with oil paintings. The fact that it was the culture of the minority not only in Ireland, but in Britain and Europe, must not be allowed to detract from its value as an expression of good taste and fine feeling. In particular it gave to craftsmen in metal and wood and stone an opportunity to create objects of enduring beauty and to show the heights to which human creativity can reach. It is not without reason that historians refer to the eighteenth century as the age of elegance, while today most civilised countries lovingly cherish its surviving legacy of sculpture, painting and architecture. While Irish country house architecture was strongly influenced by English design, it also saw the work of some continental architects of whom the German, Richard Castle, is best remembered for his fine creations at Westport, Powerscourt and Carton. When the Corporation went about choosing their architect for the Mansion House their choice fell on Davis Ducart, an Italian about whom very little is known as to his exact place of birth or as to when and why he found his way to Ireland. It appears that he was originally a canal engineer, an occupation that was to be much in demand in the second half of the eighteenth century when canals were being built as a speedy alternative to the very poor roads for the movement of heavy goods. The Newry Canal, completed in 1741, attracted much notice throughout these islands as the first inland navigation in Ireland or Britain and it was in connection with it that Ducart first appeared on the Irish scene.

His earlier work as an architect was done in Limerick and it is significant that the city by the Shannon was then undergoing a physical expansion similar to Cork, with old walls being pulled down and new roads and bridges constructed. Ducart became the architect for the new Custom House which was begun in 1765 and finished in 1769 at a cost of £8,000. It was while he was engaged on this building that he secured the commission from the Cork Corporation. Before dealing more extensively with that, however, it might be of interest to say something of his other work in the Cork area. While engaged on the Mansion House he also in 1765 began work on the first of his country houses, Kilshannig House, near Fermoy, which he built for the banker, Abraham Devonsher. This is an elaborate creation with a splendid Doric frontispiece in the central block, while the rococo ceilings of the interior are in the style of the Francini brothers who had decorated Riverstown House. Most impressive is the grand circular staircase. Nearer to the city can be seen yet another of Ducart's creations, the very lovely house at Lota, now in the care of the Brothers of Charity. This was commissioned in 1768 by the Mayor of Cork, Noblett Rogers, and has many features of the Italian Baroque style, most notably in its front porch. The interior has many of the features still to be seen at the Mercy Hospital, a grand mahogany staircase with Venetian windows on the landings, and oval windows. Apart from his work at Limerick and Cork, Ducart was to build his finest country house at Castletown Cox, Co. Kilkenny, which he began in 1767 for Michael Cox who was to become Archbishop of Cashel. This incorporates all the characteristic features of the architect but on a much more elaborate scale than anything previously achieved. The splendid plaster work in the interior was executed by the same stuccadore who worked at the Mansion House at Cork, the Waterford man Patrick Osborne. Is it possible that some lesser houses in the Tivoli and Dunkettle areas of Cork were at least partly influenced by Ducart, as many of them have his characteristic lay-out of central block and wings, but it is not yet possible to make any definite attribution. Nor is there any certainty as to when he died, except that the evidence of his will suggests some date about 1785.

Having sketched in the significance of the site and the career of the architect it is now time to proceed with the business of building the Mansion House, and for that attention must turn to the Old Corporation Minute Book. The Corporation meeting of 13 August, 1763, was discussing the matter of petty customs on potatoes, fowl, butter and frieze cloth being sold at the shambles or stalls outside the South and North Gate Bridges. Having disposed of those everyday matters the City Fathers passed the following resolution: "that a Mayoralty House be built for the habitation of the Mayors of this City on the ground on Haman's Marsh, expenses out of the revenues of the City, and that Mr. Mayor, Sheriff Travers, Aldermen Newman, Wetherall, with those of the Court of D'Oly Hundred, be a committee for approving of a proper plan for carrying out same." The Mayor was Mr. John Smith. Doubtless there followed much exploration and negotiations as regards the site and the engagement of Ducart; so it was not until 27 November, 1766 that the matter again featured in the Minutes. By that time work was obviously in progress and the reading is as follows: "£176.3.9½ to Messrs Robt. and John Wrixon for sheet lead and scaffold ropes for the Mayoralty House; £200 to the overseers for building the Mayoralty House, to be laid out in the further prosecution of the work." Present at that meeting were Messrs. Travers, Harding, Owgan, Westropp, Millerd, Wrixon, Busteed, Swete, Franklin, Smith, Bury and Browne. Some of these gentlemen are still commemorated by street names in the city. It was on 24 March, 1767 that the matter again surfaced when it was "ordered that the Mayor, Mr. Sheriff Travers and Harding, Ald. Westropp and Mr. Browne, with those of the C.D.H., be a committee to examine the accounts of the gentlemen appointed to oversee the building of the Mayoralty House and report. That £200 be paid to the Overseers for buliding the Mayoralty House for the prosecution of said work." The meeting of 23 May, 1767 duly heard the report on the affairs of the overseers: "This day Mr. Sheriff Harding, Mr. Burgesses Browne, Baker, Izod, Wilcock, F. Carlton and Denroch, appointed to examine the accounts of the gentlemen appointed to oversee the building of the Mayoralty House, report that on a strict examination of the accounts produced by Henry Wrixon and William Butler, Esqs. they have fairly expended to 5 May inst. the sum of £2,822.0.1, for which they produced vouchers. And that they had received the sum of £2,900 from Francis Carlton, Chamberlain, and that a balance of £77.19.11 remains on their hands for carrying on said building: and also that £739.3.10½ remains due to James and Ebenezer Morrison for timber furnished to 4 May inst.; and that the sum of £203.10.3½ is due to Timothy Hughes, iron-monger, for sundries to 5 May inst.; and also £28.19.8 is due to Samuel and George Beale for sundries to 27 November, which report this Board doth agree to. That £450 be borrowed from Mr. Stephen Denroch at 5 per cent and that the Mayor execute a bond. That £200 of said sum be paid to the overseer for building the Mayoralty House; £200 to Messrs. James and Ebenezer Morrison past payment of their account for timber; and the remaining £50 to Timothy Hughes, ironmonger, part payment of his account. That Mr. Mayor in the name of the Board apply to the gentlemen appointed for building the Mayoralty House to request their further care in overseeing said work."

The Minutes mention the name of the architect for the first time on 29 May, 1767: "This day the Board took into consideration the agreement made by the committee for building the Mayoralty House of this City with Mr. Davis Ducart, and by an entry of 6 May, 1765, said Ducart on that day produced a plan of said Mayoralty House and reported that the same would cost about £2,000; said committee considered the plan and ordered that a sum not exceeding £2,000 should be expended in carrying it out, and that Ducart should be employed to execute it, to be allowed 5 per cent on the money laid out, the committee reserving a power to make said Ducart a further gratuity if they should think fit; and said Board is of the opinion that Ducart was not at liberty to expend any further sum than £2000, and he is not entitled to any more recompense for his trouble than 5 per cent on £2000; as it hath been reported to this Board by a gentleman of said committee that Ducart did not give due attention to the building of said Mayoralty House, whereby the Masons and Carpenters were often idle for want of his being in Corke to give them directions, that a larger sum than £2000 is expended and the same is not finished. And this Board is of opinion that Ducart when he gave the plan was conscious that it would cost much more and that his estimate was to induce said committee to go on with the plan." With these suspicions of sharp practice surrounding Ducart, it must have been with some relief that the members agreed to the harmless motion to pay Mrs. Esther Holmes £14.7.6 for clothing for the Blue Coat school and the Exchange Porter — doubtless that gentleman's sartorial elegance added colour to the corner of Castle Street.

By 22 July, 1767, the Corporation had come round to the matter of internal fitments with a list of requisites drawn up by someone with an eye for detail: "that Kitchen furniture, pewter excepted, four dozen of mahogany chairs with black leather bottoms and brass nails, fire-irons and fenders for the dining-room and parlour, be bought for the use of the Mayoralty House. That £200 be paid to the committee for building the Mayoralty House for prosecuting the work." On 16 October, 1767 the entry reads: "that £150 be paid the overseers of the Mayoralty House for further prosecution of same," while less than a week later on 21 October the matter of tables and chairs again appeared: "that 18 chairs and 3 mahogany tables be purchased by the overseers of the Mayoralty House for the use of said house." Obviously short of money, the Corporation went cap in hand to the North Infirmary for a loan as seen in the entry for 25 November of that same year: "ordered that £200 be borrowed at interest by the Corporation from the North Infirmary to be paid to the overseers of the Mayoralty House to discharge the debts due to the inferior tradesmen."

With the building apparently well advanced, it was early in the following New Year that the services of the Waterford stuccadore, Patrick Osborne, were secured to embellish the interior. Much of his work can still be admired and it is interesting to be privy to its beginning. The Minute for 22 January, 1768 deals with quite a range of interior decorating and furnishing: "Ordered that the overseers for building the Mayoralty House agree with Patrick Osborne for stuccoing the staircase, lobby and drawing-room of said house, and also with a proper person for erecting four marble chimney-pieces, two in the dining-room and two in the drawing-room; also for erecting a portico and proper entrance into said house; also for finishing all carpenters work that remains to be done, painting, and doing the outside stucco. That Ald. Millerd, Franklin and Mr. Browne be a committee to examine the accounts of the overseers for building the Mayoralty House, to inspect the tradesmen's accounts with regard to the prices charged, and to report." This entry conjures up a great deal of activity in Henry Street, with stuccadores, carpenters, painters and the makers of chimney-pieces all contributing their skills to the making of an imposing town mansion. But if a new building was tastefully going up, a more ancient ediface was on the

brink of falling down, as the Minute went to refer to "the dangerous condition of Skiddy's Castle" situated in the nearby North Main Street. Yet the Corporation was not found wanting in generosity despite the ups and downs of civic architecture, a point clearly proved by the vote of "£1.8.6½ to Richard Evans, Exchange Porter, for brooms and sand." Some more personal details as to who exactly was making the chairs is furnished by the entry for 14 May, 1768: "that £68.14.0 be paid to Richard Caldwell, cabinet-maker, for 66 mahogany and 24 oak chairs for the use of the Mayoralty House; £3.10.5 to Geo. Busteed for printing work; £100 to the overseers for building the Mayoralty House in further prosecution of the work." Mr. Osborne reaped the fruits of his artistry on 14 October, 1768 when it was ordered that £60.13.3 be paid Patrick Osbourne, the balance of his account for stuccoing the staircase and lobby of the Mayoralty House; £11.7.6 to Mr. Burgess Wrixon and Butler to buy a clock for the Mayoralty House." Another little matter attended to at that meeting might not altogether belong to the realms of history as regards the city generally: "3 guineas to Mr. Sheriff Kent for repairing several danger-ous holes in Castle Street."

On November 23rd, 1768, the stone mason had his reward and the matter of lighting the rooms was provided for: "£7.16.6 to Edmond Flaherty, mason, for work done; 10 guineas to the overseers of the Mayoralty House to buy seven globe lamps for the use of said house." By 16 Decem-ber of that same year the chimney-pieces were ready: "£50 to Samuel Daly, stone cutter, for two marble chimney-pieces for the Mayoralty House." Also to be paid in time for Christ-mas was the carpenter: "£3.10.0 to Owen Sullivan, carpenter, for seven weeks' work at the Mayoralty House." The Minute for 13 February, 1769, supplies the name of the clock-maker: "ordered that £5 be paid to Mr. James Aickin for a clock for the kitchen of the Mayoralty House." More details as to people come from the next entry of 3 March, 1769 when it was "ordered that £60 be paid to Charles Sweeny, joiner, for work done at the Mayoralty House; £8.5.10½ to Mr. George Graham for attendance as overseer at the Mayoralty House." A few days later, on 7 March, came another decision on the erection of the Doric front entrance: "that £11.7.6 be paid to the overseers of the Mayoralty House towards erecting the door-case and portico." Yet more information on the identity of the craftsmen can be gleaned from the entry of 5 July, 1769: "£1.8.10 to Timothy Lion and John Barry for Sawyers work for the use of the Mayoralty House." A more cosy and domestic item featured on 26 July, 1769: "£0.15.6 to Mr. Mayor, expense of a Green Curtain for the middle door of the Diningroom of the Mayoralty House." If the Corporation was determined that His Worship, the Mayor, was to be protected from draughts as he ate his venison and drank his claret, it was no less solicitous for the comfort of his nightly slumbers as the Minute for 8 August, 1769 reveals: "that four mahogany bedsteads with sacking bottoms, and four deal bedsteads with ditto be provided for the use of the Mayoralty House." A great amount of sitting around must have been anticipated as the entry for 1 September again reverted to the provision of yet more chairs: "that four dozen chairs be bought for the drawing-room at the Mayoralty House."

The finer points of fabric featured on 20 October following with "£0.18.8 to Joseph Harris for sixteen yards of green Camblet for a curtain for the door of the dining-room at the Mayoralty House." The stuccadore and the glazier featured on 28 November: "that £82.1.0½ be paid Patrick Osborne, in full, stuccoing the Drawing-room of the Mayoralty House; £60 to Richard Burt in part of his account for glazing-work at the Mayoralty House." Early in the New Year there were still more beds being carried into Henry Street, together with tables and curtain-rods. This assortment figured on 23 February, 1770: "£53.0.6 to Jonathan Wigmore for four mahogany bedsteads and five mahogany tables for the Mayoralty House; £2.3.4 to Samuel Bromel for four sets of curtain rods for the Mayoralty House; £92.2.7 to Timothy Hughes, in full, for iron and other materials supplied the Mayoralty House." Apparently the sixteen yards of green Camblet had run out as the entry for 14 August, 1770 ordered "that £0.18.8 be paid to Joseph Harrison, woollen draper, for 16 yards of Camblet for the Mayoralty House." Nor was that the end of the curtaining for the same Minute continues: "£8.5.0 to Mr. Mayor for four green window curtains for Mayoralty House." Yet more domesticity was attended to on 12 October, 1770 with an altogether splendid inventory of pots and pans, some for stewing, some for sauce, some for baking—all of this and still more curtains: "That Mr. Kent, City overseer, provide for the Mayoralty 4 large copper pans, 6 copper stew pans, 2 large copper sauce pans, 2 copper baking patty-pans, 4 dozen tin-fluted pans, a cross counter in the office, a shed in the yard, green paragon curtains for two of the bedsteads, and green paragon cutrains for two of the rooms." That splendid supply of hardware doubtless gave rise to many culinary concoctions as pies and stews and broths and tarts were later served to the Mayor and his guests. But the demands of the bedrooms continued to be served, too, as the entry for 9 November, 1770 indicates: "£4 to Andrew Dalton, Carpenter, for four deal bedsteads with sacking bottoms for the Mayoralty House."

It was not until almost a year later that the House was again on the Corporation agenda with an entry for 21 October, 1771 which reads: "that Mr. Mayor and Henry Wrixon ,Esq. do draw on the Chamberlain for £200 to buy chimney-pieces, finish the front, and decorate the Mayoralty House." Much later again, on 31 January, 1772, an item appeared which most probably relates to the work: "that £39.7.3 be paid Richard Gwinn for tyler work done, sworn before Ald. Bury and certified by Sober Kent, City Overseer: £58.8.9½ to Richard Burt, glazier, for work done." The authorisation for building the Doric doorway came on 30 April, 1773 with the entry: "that £69.8.2 be paid Mr. Mayor, Ald. Millerd and Henry Wrixon, Esq., for building a frontispiece of the Doric order to the Mayoralty House pursuant to a plan and estimate before the Council." On 10 August of the same year the Mayor was granted "£2.10.0 so much paid by him to Richard Navin, one of the constables, for a rate charged on the Mayoralty House." Interior decorating was once more provided for on 19 November, 1773: £21.15.6 to John Owen, upholsterer, for window curtains supplied the Mayoralty House; £2.18.6 to Edward Higgins for paper supplied the Mayoralty House.' On the following month, 17 December, provision was made for sideboards: "£10 to Richard Caldwell, cabinet-maker, for two mahogany Side Board Tables for the Mayoralty House." Then on 19 April 1774 the curtains were again attended to: "that £20 be paid to James Barrett for six window curtains for the Mayoralty House." The same entry indicated that the Mayor would have his law books at his elbow as he brooded over civic affairs surrounded by all that mahogany and shaded by his curtains: "£3.10.0 to Mr. Mayor for Bullinbroke's Abridgement, Vesey's Appendix, and Blackston's Commentaries for the Mayor's Office." More bills had to be met on 16 December, 1774 when the Corporation approved the following: "£0.10.6 to William Wily, whitesmith, for sundry articles supplied for the Mayoralty House; £49.8.1½ to Timothy Hughes, ironmonger, for work done; £46.17.11½ to Mr. Sheriff Fuller for timber supplied from 9 December, 1772 to 14 May, 1774." The entry for 5 May, 1775, shows a certain Mr. Izod in a bewildering variety of capacities—a most versatile man he was who could turn his hand to repairing a water-pipe, papering a room and burying the dead. The Minute reveals all: "for a year's pipe water paid Mr. Izod for the Mayoralty House, repairing the pipes, papering the parlour of ditto, and burying two poor men who died in Bridewell."

Trays for serving wine were on the agenda on 10 June, 1776: "£0.9.7 to Mr. Mayor for two large wooden trays bought for use of the Mayoralty House." For gentlemen with powdered wigs and laced cravats, no less than for ladies with elaborate hair-styles and rouged cheeks, nothing was more necessary than a looking-glass; such was provided for by the entry of 1 November, 1776 with the order that "two looking-glasses and two Gerandoles be bought by Mr. Mayor for the use of the Mayoralty House." Then of course it was desirable that the environs of the House be made to look as decent as possible and this was taken care of on 20 June, 1777 with "£12.10.8½ to Edmond Flaherty, mason, for repairing the Quay at the Mayoralty House." Many months later the looking-glasses were again in the picture when on 9 January, 1778 some more expenses were approved: "£30.9.4½ to Mr. Mayor for looking-glasses for the Mayoralty House; £2.10.2 to Caesar Fanning, Paper Stainer, for paper for the Mayoralty House." A few weeks later, on 21 January more tables were ordered: "£3.2.1½ be paid Thomas Cochran, cabinet-maker, for two mahogany tables for the Mayoralty House." That same meeting had to decide on a legal payment to the Lord Chief Baron, with the choice lying between a "suit of Black Velvet or 20 guineas." For some reason the City Fathers opted for the more prosaic 20 guineas. Nor was the Mayoralty House freed from that scourge of every decent citizen, the payment of rates, as noted on 8 August, 1778: "£10.14.5½ to Mr. Mayor, rates for the Mayoralty House." Further expense that reflects vividly on the time came on 3 September, 1779: "£3.14.1 be paid

Mr. Mayor for Pipe Water, Hearth Money, etc. for the Mayoralty House." Then the place needed to be painted and for that on 27 January, 1780, comes the entry: "£3.13.8 to William Stephens for painting the Mayoralty House." Whether in fact that job was then done is questionable in view of the entry for 17 August of the same year: "that the Mayoralty House be painted after 4 October, and that Francis Carlton, Esq. Mayor elect, oversee same."Not until 25 July, 1786 does the House again appear in the Minutes and then it is referred to by the name which passed into common usage—the Mansion House. "£15 to the Mayor for purchasing a ground seat opposite to the Archdeacon's in Peter's Church, the parish in which the Mansion House is situated, for the use of the present and all succeeding Mayors and their families during office." On 21 September of the same year there is the entry: "£18.18.7 to Sir John Franklin, sundry small expenses paid by him at the Mayoralty House,' the older title again being used. Just a week later on 28 September, Sir John the Mayor received another credit: "£4.11.0 to Sir John Franklin, one year's rent for the coach house belonging to the Mansion House"—at this stage the Corporation scribe seemed unsure of what exactly was the name of the place. A long gap ensues until the next mention on 19 September, 1789; the entry simply reads: "£4.3.4½ to the Mayor, expenses at the Mayoralty House" But he still attended to his routine duties of his Office at the Exchange in Castle Street, and that same meeting approved: "that three quarters salary at six guineas a year be paid to Mary Ballard for attending the Mayor's Office and Exchange." On 23 January, 1790 various sundry expenses were itemised: "£14.9.9 to Rowland Purcell, Esq., for Newspapers and small charges for the Mansion House during his Mayoralty; £6.17.4 to Edmond Roche Kinselagh, Esq. for stationery for the Public Office at the Mansion House." Nothing so recalls the homeliness and domesticity of the place than the news of smoky chimneys and of Mr. James Haly who came to cure them. That spot of bother featured on 5 March, 1790: "£15.8.6 to James Haly for curing the chimneys of the Mayoralty House of smokeing." The entry also deals with the Coach-house: "£4.11.0 to Thomas Owgan, Esq., one year's rent of a cellar used as a coach-house to the Mayoralty." Yet more money was paid out at the end of that month, on 30 March: "that £3.5.7½ be paid Mr. George Harris, late Church Warden, for the Minister's money and Parish rate of the Mansion House." On the following 6 July the entry reads: "£9.18.7 to George Barber for work done at the Mansion House." The following month brought a wealth of exterior decoration and interior furnishings on 30 August: "£60 for painting the Mansion House inside and outside under the direction of the Mayor, Mayor Elect and Sheriffs; 6 guineas for colouring and repairing the front of the Mansion House to William Mara; £15.5.8 to said Mara for whitening the inside of the Mansion House; £16.9.0 to the Mayor Elect for carpetting for two rooms for the Mayoralty; £40 for curtains for the beds and windows, repairing bedsteads, globes, etc. for the Mayoralty; £7.8.3 to James Fitzgerald for papering the Mayoralty House."

Yet another heavy programme of renovation was carried out in 1794 when the Minute for 12 November gives the details of work on the pantry, the closet that was boarded, the ridge tiles and the Banqueting Rooms: "£2.16.10½ to the Mayor for work done on the ceiling and walls of the kitchen, and passage leading thereto, ceiling and walls of back staircase and lobbies, whiteing the ceiling and walls of the pantry, sides of the Banqueting Rooms, the windows repaired and whitened of the Mansion House; £2.1.10 to the Mayor for repairing the roof of the Mansion House, upright slating, part of a boarded closet, and repairing the remainder, cleaning spouts, bracing part of them, pointing slates, mortar and ridge tiles." Two years later on 27 September, 1796 an entry records a more domestic item: "£11.16.8½ to be paid the Widow Campbell for cutlery ware for the Mansion House." In that fateful year of 1798 more domestic fitments were provided as noted in the entry for 27 September: "£14.6.3 to Charles Dickinson for kitchen furniture supplied the Mansion House; £4.18.0 to the Mayor for scarlet moreen curtains for the bedsteads belonging to the Mansion House; £15.15.0 for a variety of contingent expenses paid at the Mansion House by order of the Mayor by Mr. Kinselagh." Yet more chairs were to be brought in as approved on 20 September, 1799: "that six dozen Mahogany Chairs be purchased by the Mayor Elect for the Mansion House." The same entry mentions the clock: "£0.16.3 to James Uppington for repairing the Mansion House Clock; that a guinea be paid for engraving a Copper-plate for the use of the Mansion House.' The final entry brings the story into the early dawn of a new century, even if the matter is the old one of mahogany chairs: "£90 to Samuel Cox, cabinet maker, for six dozen mahogany chairs for the Mansion House." It was dated 28 March, 1800.

So it was that the Corporation, the architect, the masons, the carpenters, the glaziers, the sawyers, the painters, the stuccadore and the makers of chairs and tables and beds, of curtains and pans, came together to build and furnish a late eighteenth mansion that still stands by the riverside in Cork. Their story helps to highlight the everyday concerns and activities of a wide variety of craftsmen for whom the making of the Mansion House was a matter of personal importance and artistic pride. By a happy coincidence one of the Corporation members closely associated with the work has his name still commemorated by the street he built almost directly opposite, Millerd Street. Where it abuts onto Batchelor's Quay there may be seen the limestone street sign inscribed " Millerd Street, 1776." A visit to the Mercy Hospital will reveal the frontage almost exactly as the builders and the craftsmen left it; neither has the river changed, nor the swans, nor the old stone of the nearby Maltings and the Distillery.

Chapter IV

THE COMMERCE OF CORK—BUTTER AND GLASS

When the commercial and industrial expansion of any of the cities of Ireland or Britain is considered it is normally assumed that the matter is being seen in the context of the Industrial Revolution that was beginning to have such a dramatic impact on manufacturing and distribution in the early decades of the last century. Nothing so vividly underlines that impact than the expansion in population in what became the great industrial centres: Manchester in 1760 had between 30,000 and 45,000, by 1801 it had jumped to 72,000 and by 1851 it was over 303,300. The significant point about the commercial expansion of Cork is that it had nothing to do with the age of the machine and that it took place a century earlier than the age of steam and coal and iron. It was in the middle decades of the eighteenth century that the city rather dramatically emerged on the national and European scene as a hive of commercial activity and a chief centre of the export trade. Cork made its fortune and won its fame through the multifarious activities centred in the Butter Market at the foot of Shandon. There the prestigious Committee of Merchants directed the whole business of collecting the butter from the farmers and of having it weighed, graded, packed, branded and carted down to the quays to be shipped to Liverpool, Lisbon, Hamburg, Amsterdam and to the new lands of the West Indies and of Carolina and Georgia. The new wealth and the wider horizons infused an air of confidence and energy which the city still retains long after the demise of the butter trade. Other reminders of that era are many of the finely-proportioned mansions dotted along the riverside from Sunday's Well to Tivoli and from Ballintemple to Blackrock, built as the homes of the new merchant princes. The heavy classical portico of the Butter Market, designed by Sir John Benson, still stands despite the recent tragic fire which destroyed the interior. Not the least welcome reminder of other days is the Butter Exchange Band which still blows its trumpet in the shadow of the Market.

In seeking to present an outline of the economic factors which originated and sustained the butter trade this chapter will rely on two professional sources, the "Economic History of Cork City to 1800" by Dr. W. O'Sullivan, and an article in the journal "Studia Hibernica," 1971, by J. S. Donnelly of the University of Tennesse entitled "Cork Market, its role in the nineteenth century Irish Butter Trade." Having sketched the background this chapter will then make its own original contribution by reflecting the day-to-day affairs of the Butter Market through hitherto unpublished extracts from the manuscript Minutes of the Committee of Merchants. How then did Cork come to make its money in butter? It was partly a question of geography and partly a question of parliamentary legislation. The rich pasture land of South Munster provided the grazing and the cattle for milk, butter and a range of associated products. Following the end of the wars of William of Orange and James II there came a number of parliamentary acts designed to expand and regulate the potential for trade in butter. What Dr. O'Sullivan describes as "the most important and complete of all the acts hitherto passed" came into operation in 1721 requiring that public municipal weighhouses should be established in cities and towns exporting butter. Weighmasters were to be appointed under oath, the casks or firkins containing the butter were to be weighed and branded, and complete records of all transactions were to be kept. It was due to the thoroughness and flair with which this basic legislative provision was implemented that the Cork Butter Market was to achieve such prominence.

Two years later, in 1723, another act related specifically to Cork, giving the names of the gentlemen appointed as public weighmasters; "in order that the several regulations herein appointed may be strictly observed and well and faithfully executed in the City of Cork which is a place of great export, be it enacted by the authority aforesaid that Edmund Knapp of the said city, alderman, and Edward Hoare of the said city, alderman, and the survivor of them, shall be and are hereby appointed to be weighmaster and weighmasters of the said city." The fact that the worthy aldermen also happened to be members of Parliament for the city only proved that a mild self-interest could be profitably blended with civic progress! The name of Hoare was to be associated with a city bank as well as with Hoare's Quay on that stretch of Patrick Street on which Egan's the jewellers now stands. Mr. Knapp is still commemorated by Knapp's Square off Camden Quay. As the century advanced the Cork butter trade with England, Europe and America steadily grew; yet it was still greatly behind the city's major export, barrelled beef. But with the formation of the Committee of Merchants in 1769 the Butter Market became the hub of the commercial life of the city, with the merchants gradually assuming overall responsibility for almost all trading interests and, indeed, for a wide range of civic concerns such as deepening the river channel, arranging for new quays, and the provision of buoys and lighthouses. The Committee was a voluntary body consisting of buyers, merchants and exporters; whatever authority and prestige it acquired was to come from its effectiveness and finesse in managing what developed into quite a sophisticated business operation. The most vital consideration that went to make the Commitee so successful and respected at home and in the markets of Europe and the New World was the absolute reliability of its standards of grading the butter. In Liverpool, Lisbon and Jamaica, a firkin marked "Cork First" was accepted and found to be such without question. The scale of grading went from first to sixth, as will be described later.

The abiding principle of the Committee of Merchants was to use every means of human ingenuity to achieve two aims, first an absolutely fair deal for all concerned, second the highest possible standard of end product in the matter of the firkin of salted butter that left the Cork quays. In order to prevent corruption or the possibility of the butter trade falling into the hands of a clique, the Committee in 1780 resolved that it should consist of twenty one members, with ten "senior members" retiring at the end of each year, to be succeeded by ten "junior members" with ten newcomers. Of course previous members were eligible for election in rotation. The chairman was elected for only three months, so ensuring a rapid turnover in so important an office. A fine of 2/2 was imposed on members absent without sufficient cause from the weekly meeting. The actual daily operation of the Market involved, first, the public weighmasters who were salaried officials of the Corporation. The Committee appointed three butter inspectors sworn by the Mayor to act conscientiously and not to accept bribes. Their duties were to examine and classify the quality and weight of the butter brought in by the farmer, as well as to determine fraud in the packing. Some crafty farmers were in the habit of soaking the firkins in streams, so adding to their weight, before they packed their butter in them to bring to the Market. The next functionaries were the inspectors of empty casks. These casks were in almost all cases made in the vicinity of the Market by the kings of the craftsmen, the coopers. To endure the long weeks at sea in the great sailing ships and to preserve the state of the butter in the hot climate of the West Indies, the most meticulous attention had to be paid to the making of these casks as well as to the manner of packing them. The casks were made normally of American oak, and when the cooper had made each one it was taken to the weighmaster to be "tared," the technical term for the actual weight plus two pounds to allow for water seepage when packed with butter. It was this expertise in making and packing the firkins that made the Cork Market excel all others in Ireland or Britain in almost monopolising the trade to the warm climates of the West Indies and Brazil. In evidence before a Parliamentary Select Committee in 1826 an English merchant declared that only Cork butter was shipped from Liverpool to foreign parts.

Some statistics from Dr. O'Sullivan's work will indicate the scope of trade up to 1800 as compiled from the Custom House Books in the National Library, Dublin. With figures given per cwt. the following were the totals for 1787, a date chosen at random:

to England, 73,552 cwt.	to Spain, 2003
to Scotland, 209	to Antigua, 3371,
to Coastal Islands, 617	to Barbadoes, 4247
to Canary Islands, 100	to Carolina, 20
to Denmark and Norway, 191	to Jamaica, 9,815
	to Montreal, 36
to France, 12,622	to New Zealand 63
to Germany, 2171	to Newfoundland, 838
to Holland, 8000	to Nova Scotia, 1093
to Italy, 332	to St. Kitt's, 2,951
to Madeira Islands, 222	to Virginia, 40
to Portugal, 20,934	to West Indies, 5.440

The Donnelly article quotes figures for the nineteenth century, when in 1825 the given total of exports was 209,000 firkins, of which 77,000 were sent to Lisbon for re-export to Brazil and the West Indies. The Lisbon trade, a particularly lucrative one, was, however, to suffer a serious decline after 1842. In that year the Conservative Prime Minister, Sir Robert Peel, equalised the duties on Portuguese and French wines, so depriving Portugal of its accustomed lead on the United Kingdom market; it retaliated by imposing heavy import duties on all United Kingdom products. This included Cork butter; but the Committee of Merchants were not content to sit around nursing their misfortune. By the 1850s they had gained a firm foothold on the Australian market with 60,000 firkins being sent out in 1858. Meanwhile, the rapid rise in the population of Britain that accompanied the Industrial Revolution and the comparative rise in the standard of living that manifested itself from 1850 onwards created a new market for a greater variety of food; beer, cheese, bread and potatoes were being supplemented even among the working classes by more luxury items such as butter, tea, sugar and meat. Cork greatly benefitted by this market on its doorstep, especially when steam boats shortened the time at sea and made scheduled services more regular.

But from 1880 onwards a combination of international and local factors began to erode the dominance of the Cork Butter Market. Continental countries, especially Denmark and Holland, were establishing native butter industries and were more progressive than their Cork competitors in using mechanical processes such as refrigeration. Their butter proved more popular on the British market than the Irish product chiefly because it was less salty. Palates were becoming more refined and Cork was too slow in catering for the new genteel taste. Australia, too, by 1865 had become self-sufficient in its supply of butter, so robbing Cork of a good customer. Most of these unfavourable developments were outside the control of the Committee of Merchants, but what was less easy to understand or excuse was the growing volume of complaints in Britain about the dirty condition of the Cork firkins. This reflected not only on the farmers and the Market officials, but also on the local railway and shipping companies. Firkins were often clumsily handled or left on the quayside or on railway sidings exposed to sun and rain. The brown Cork firkins made of oak compared badly with the new marketing cleanliness of Continental competitors using a variety of pails, boxes and baskets. Failure to match quality to demand and poor presentation ended the proud supremacy of a great Cork enterprise. Many among the local brokers and exporters saw the writing on the wall; there were questions in the Commons and demands for an inquiry. When in March, 1884, Lord Chief Justice Fitzgerald gave his judgment on a submission it signalled the end of the Butter Market as it had been in its golden age between 1769 and 1870. The Committee of Merchants whose vision and energy had earlier served the city so well was replaced by a Board of Trustees. The Market continued on a local scale until 1925.

Behind this rather bald chronology of economic rise and fall there lies the more immediately human story of the people who made the Market, the merchants, the farmers, the buyers or brokers, the exporters, the inspectors of butter and casks, the coopers, the scalesmen, the clerks and the unskilled workmen, all of whom played their alloted part in an enterprise with ramifications ranging from a small farmer in Kerry to a merchant in the West Indies. Their story is best told in the surviving Minute Books, great heavily bound ledgers where the weekly transactions of the Committee of Merchants were faithfully entered by secretaries who dipped their quill pens in ink-horns and strove to write with a good hand. These invaluable Minutes, which have been preserved in the care of the late Mr. F. J. Daly and then presented to the city, form a unique record not only of the economic life of Cork but also of the trade and commerce of Ireland. They date from 1780 but the record on which this chapter is based began in 1793. The entry for Tuesday, the 9th of April, 1793, concerned arrangements for regular meetings at the "new Coffee House." That was the great age of Coffee Houses in Dublin, London and other cities, when artists, writers, politicians and businessmen met in them either for convivial evenings or to transact their affairs. Suffice to recall the erudite and boisterous company which gathered in London Coffee Houses in the days of Samuel Johnson, Oliver Goldsmith and Edmund Burke, an era of good company and good talk so finely portrayed by James Boswell in his "Life of Johnson." Doubtless the Cork Merchants exercised their eloquence no less freely than did their countrymen in London, but as well as the general news of the day they had to discuss the business of butter, the movement of ships and the management of men. The entry reads as follows: "That the two rooms this day taken possession of by the Committee of Merchants shall be their meeting place on all future occasions of business; that the Trustees for the proprietors of the new Coffee House are at their expense to provide all necessary furniture and conveniences and Coals; that the Treasurer shall pay out of the Inspection revenue for the use of the said Rooms at the rate of Twenty Pounds per annum to commence on the 8th day of May next. Samuel McCall, Pres., John Russell, Wm. Jameson, John Thomson." Throughout the eighteenth and for much of the last century there is always great stress on the provision of "coals and candles" not only for meetings but for a wide range of residential posts in society at large. In the age before gas and electricity the supply of heat and light was a matter demanding careful foresight. Among other members of the Committee that year were William Beamish, William Crawford, Charles Casey, George Shea, Charles Malony, Marcus Lynch, John Power, Rueben Harvey, Ebenezer Deaves, Charles Waggett, Thomas Cuthbert and John Lecky. One of the more significant features of the Committee throughout its history was that it scrupulously avoided any sectarian bitterness; its members were drawn from across the often sharp battlelines of creed and party in the common pursuit of the welfare of Cork. Catholics took their place alongside their Protestant and Quaker fellow citizens; this was very important in the growth of a Catholic commercial middle class at a time when they were prohibited by penal legislation from taking part in parliamentary and civic life.

By the 17th of June, 1793 the Butter Inspectors were seeking a little extra in their "Sallerys": "The Butter Inspectors, having petitioned for usual Gratuity for good Conduct over and above their Sallerys, ordered that the Treasurer do pay Mr. Mahony £5, Mr. Buckley £10, Mr. Jones £5." On August 5th there is reference to Thomas Prendergast as Hide Inspector and David Gorman as assistant Hide Inspector. This raises the matter of the extent to which the Committee was supervising the whole butter and cattle trade of the city, with its spin-off industries. Beef rivalled butter as a major export, with 109,052 barrels of two cwt.

being exported from Cork in 1776, representing 54% of total Irish export. Pickled pork also sustained a lively trade; both products were in steady demand in Barbadoes, Carolina, Georgia, Jamaica and Newfoundland, as well as in the European ports of Amsterdam, Rotterdam, Malaga, Lisbon, Seville, Le Havre and Hamburg. Indeed, much of the growing wealth of the rising Catholic commercial class grew from the European trade. Deriving from the provision trade there developed a market for hides and skins, with England being the best customer, followed by Holland. Some of the hides were cured in the numerous small tanneries in the Shandon Street and Blackpool areas, others were pickled. The melting down of animal hoofs provided tallow for candles and soap; much of this was exported to Bristol and Holland. Animal hearts and skirts were sent in bulk. to Scotland, while salted round gut went to Venice to make the skins of Bologna sausages. The fact that this proliferation of slaughterhouses, tanneries and storage was to be found chiefly in Shandon Street, Dominick Street, Blarney Street and the profusion of narrow lanes thereabouts and in Blackpool made it convenient for the Butter Market authorities to exercise a general supervision, if only because they were operating in the very heart of the area. But if the heart of the area was good for business the collective heart of the Committee had a soft spot for the needy as the entry for 20th September, 1793 indicates: "That the Treasurer do pay the Sisters and Daughters of the late David Moylan, formerly Hide Inspector, ten guineas on account of his Honest conduct." By the 11th of February, 1794, the Committee was bending its mind to the matter of improved navigational facilities: "a resolution for taxing the English and Irish shipping which arrived in this Kingdom for the purpose of erecting Light Houses on the Coasts of Ireland, and requesting that the situation of Cork Harbour may be taken into consideration."

Fear of what was called "combination" among workmen persisted among employers until the second half of the last century; a resolution of the Committe on 8th May, 1796, indicated that they were not standing for any nonsense in that regard, more especially if the nonsense were to be hawked up from Limerick. "The Committee of Merchants, having been informed that the Journeymen Coopers at Limerick have declined working from an inclination to force a revision of their wages, take this method of showing their disapprobation of such proceedings and most strongly recommend to the Master Coopers of this City not to employ any Journeyman who has been guilty of concurring in the above mentioned combination." Reverting to an earlier date, Wednesday, 9th November, 1790, it is possible to glimpse a vivid picture of Market officials out on the streets of Cork diligently counting the heads of cattle being driven in through the main entrances; the officials were to count all "Horned Cattle," to note the hour of arrival and the owner's name. These street-side calculators were Michael Riordan and Dennis Cussin, whose appointment was record- ed as follows: "Resolved that Dennis Cussin and Michael Riordan, appointed, to be paid each Sixteen Shillings and Three Pence per week, and one English Shilling each for a Boy to be employed by each to bring into the Bar of the Coffee House daily returns agreeable to the following instructions to be given to each of said persons; You are to keep an exact account of all Horned Cattle droved to this City, distinguishing whether Bullocks or Cows, and noting the Owner's name, the number of each drove and the hour of arrival, to be entered in a book that will be given to you, making such other remarks as may occur to you be necessary; and a copy of each day's entry shall be sent to the Bar of the Merchants Coffee Room by Seven O'Clock every afternoon, by no account to be later than Eight O'Clock." Messrs. Riordan and Cussin did remarkably well for themselves to secure a salary of sixteen shilling in 1790; a whole century later great numbers of labourers were still earning only as much. The slaughtering season began in October so it was in the late autumn that the bullocks and the cows became the vital statistics of the Committee of Merchants as they gathered in the Coffee House at seven o'clock in the evening.

On the 11th March, 1797, the Committee addressed itself to affairs more high and mighty when it met "for the purpose of taking into consideration the propriety of apply- ing to the Lords of the Admiralty requesting them to appoint a Convoy for Jamaica and the other islands, as many ships are now in this port waiting therefor." It was not only the war between England and France that moved the merchants to seek the protection of the Admiralty; protection against piracy made it a policy to have cargo ships go by convoy to the West Indies and America. New names attending a Meeting on 6th May, 1797, were Henry Bagnell, Richard Lawton, Dan Goold, Michael Busteed, Peter Mazier, Thomas Woodward. Among five "gentlemen of the Butter Trade" attending were Alexander McCarthy of Church Yard Lane and Andrew Drinan of Cove Street. Drinan Street, off Cove Street, recalls the latter name, while Waggett's Lane near the Market recalls a name from the earlier list. Both lists contain names prominent in the commercial life of the city down to the present day. On the 5th December, 1796, the Committee were again concerned with a convoy, writing to Admiral Kingsmill requesting him to delay sailing "for the coast of Africa, the Merchants are not fully prepared at present to dispatch the Ships now in this Harbour bound to the different Islands, and praying that the Admiral will be so good as to delay the sailing of the Convoy until Sunday next, at which time it is expected that every vessel now in port, some of which have just arrived, will be fully ready to proceed. Signed: R. Lawton, President, Marcus Lynch, Wm. Crawford, Michael Busteed, Ebenezer Deaves, John Thompson." In May, 1799 there were two resolutions regarding casks; that of the 16th directed that the Inspectors of Casks, who were paid fifty pounds per annum, were to see "that all casks, firkins and kegs be inspected both when empty and full," while on the 27th it was resolved that "three Labourers be apointed to attend the Weigh Houses for the purpose of turning on their heads all casks and firkins of butter which may come to the Market so as to drain effectually the pickle therefrom." The Meeting of 17th September, 1799, was attended by "the gentlemen of the Dry Calf Skin Trade" with names well known in local business, Richard Abell, John Forster, William Jameson, James Kely and John Meade. Jameson's Row on the South Mall recalls one of the dry calf skin gentlemen.

Simply because of the exigencies of space this chapter is forced to select its samples from the Minutes, but the entry for an early year in the new century—and what a tumultuous and utterly strange century it was to be—deserves quoting if only becaue it gives date and detail for a Mail Coach robbery by highwaymen. Meeting at the New Coffee House on 20 January, 1803, the Committee approved "that the sum of Twenty Pounds be paid to Cor. Keane in consideration of his distress, and his being discharged from the service of this Committee not from any complaint against him, but from his present incapacity to perform the duty that may devolve upon him. Resolved that the sum of Twenty Guineas be remitted by the Treasurer of this Committee to Messrs. Solomon Watson & Sons, Bankers at Clonmel, for administering to the immediate comfort of Moore, Guard of the Dublin Mail Coach, who was dangerously wounded in his brave defence of the trust committed to him, and through whose spirited resistance the Mail Bags for this City were rescued from the Banditti who made a desperate attempt to plunder them near Clonmel on the night of the 18th instant." Apart from the compassionate action by the Committee in matters financial, this entry evokes something of the excitement and the hazard of the Mail Coach as the Coachman and the Guard galloped through the night to bring the Bags to this city of Cork. Interesting to note that a few years later Clonmel was to be the centre of the nationwide horse transport enterprise of the "King of the Roads," Charles Bianconi. A further entry on this matter, 11th March, 1803, gives the Christian name of the intrepid Guard: "That the sum of £61.8.6 publicly collected by the Committee for the relief of William Moore, the Guard of the Mail Coach, be payable to his order in addition to the Twenty Guineas already remitted by this Committee." Echoes of the Napoleonic War that was turning Europe into a battlefield and giving to England a role she was again to assume in regard to Hitler are recorded on 24th May, 1803 when a meeting was called "for the purpose of adopting such measures as may best satisfy our determined resolution to support His Majesty's Royal Person and Government in the present contest with the French Republic. Signed, M. Lynch."

An undated entry for December of the same year refers to agreement with the Bankers regarding "hollidays;" these were fixed as "Christmas Day, St. Stephen's Day, Good Friday, the King's Birthday, every Monday in the months of April, May, June, July, August and September; every second Monday of the other months." On the 2nd February, 1804, there was another donation to reward a good deed: "The sum of Twenty Guineas be paid to Denis Flynn and assistants out of the fund of this Committee for their humane, meritorious and gallant exertions in saving the survivors of the passengers and crew of the ship, Sovereign, lately wrecked at Ballycotton." The widely-held assumption that Cork was prospering through victualling the English Fleet throughout the Napoleonic War must be revised in the light of the following petition addressed by the Committee to William Pitt, "First Lord of the Treasury and Chancellor of the Exchequer. The Memorial of the Committee of Merchants of the City of Cork. That the Provision Trade of this part of the United Kingdom has been declining for several years past, which progressive decay must inevitably lead to its final destruction if immediate measures for its relief be not resorted to. That the facilities which the Americans possess, and which are as obvious as they are numerous, for introducing into the Colonies in the West Indies, Newfoundland and the conquered settlements Salt Beef, Pork, Butter and Fish, have almost extinguished this branch of Trade, heretofore so valuable to the British American Colonies as well as to the United Kingdom. Average export during the American War was double what the same has been during the present War. That if this oppressive rivalry be permitted to the Americans in the West Indies your Memorialists' interests, and those of a numerous Body of Persons in this part of the United Kingdom, essentially dependent on the prosperity of the Provision Trade, must be eventually sacrificed." The foregoing draft appears in the Minutes for 15th February, 1805. Yet the Auditors' Report for 27th June, 1811, shows a healthy turnover for the year ending 8th May, 1811: Butter Firkins, 224,185; Kegs, 10,294; Hides and Skins, 16.069; Carcases of ox, cow and bulls, 24,585; Calf Skins, 117,880. A significant development not only in the commercial but in the architectural life of Cork was to be highlighted on the 15th September, 1813, for it was on that day that the Committee held its first meeting in the Commercial Rooms on the South Mall. They had commissioned the young local architect, Thomas Deane, to give them a building at once commmodious and dignified. For Deane it was the first commission in a career that was to have distinction in Cork, Dublin and Oxford where specimens of his work may still be seen, with the University Quadrangle at Cork ranking as probably the finest. The architect's work is covered more fully in the chapter on the nineteenth century city. The original facade of the Commercial Rooms can still be admired, forming the main frontage of the Imperial Hotel which the Committee engaged Deane to build to cater for the growing stage coach trade in 1816.

Moving forward to 1837 the Minute for the 24th August records the practical test of four candidates for the post of Assistant Butter Inspector, the names being Mr. M. Skiddy, Mr. B. Egan, Mr. C. Tivy and Mr. G. Barry: "This day the Sub-Committee appointed to bring the judgment of the candidates for office to a practical trial reported that:

Mr. Skiddy agreed with the judges in	15 casks
Differed one quality from them in	31 casks
Differed two qualities from them in	4 casks
Mr. Egan agreed witht the judges in	24 casks
Differed one quality	26 casks
Mr. Barry agreed with the judges	33 casks
Differed one quality	17 casks
Mr. Tivy agreed with the judges	20 casks
Differed one quality	24 casks
Differed two qualities	5 casks
Differed three qualities	1 cask

Resolved unanimously that Mr. Garrett Barry be now appointed to the office of Assistant Butter Inspector at the Salary of Sixty Pounds a year, and with a promise of falling into the next vacancy of full Inspector should his conduct entitle him thereto." Three years later, however, Mr. Skiddy found more favour with fortune as is told in the Minute for 14th July, 1840: "A vacancy having occurred through the death of Mr. Morgan O'Connell, deputy Weigh Master, and Mr. Morgan Skiddy having been summoned by the Sub-Committee, resolved that he be appointed accordingly at a Salary of One Pound a week. Resolved that Mr. G. M. O'Connell, son of Mr. Morgan O'Connell, be paid the sum of Twelve Pounds according to his request to defray the expenses of his father's last illness and internment. Resolved that the sum of £2.10.0 be paid to John Fahy, an old servant who was 26 years employed in the Butter Weighhouse and in such sums as the Treasurer may consider most advantageous for him." While on this matter of doling out pounds, shillings and pence an earlier Minute of 26th April, 1840 tells the tale of a man who had his fortune doubled! "Resolved that the Salary of Henry Sullivan, Clerk in the Hide Crane, be advanced from 1st May next to Eight Shillings a week instead of Four." The great age of clerks was then getting under way with a hitherto unprecedented demand for their scribblings and their sums in the mushrooming railway and steamship offices. Fortunately the era also saw the coming of the campaign for universal elementary schooling, a campaign that found a unique development in Ireland in 1831 when the Government established the National School system. These schools, together with the voluntary ones established by the emerging teaching congregation of brothers and nuns, brought the Three Rs to ever increasing numbers of young people. Clerkships in the railways, the shipping companies and later in the Post Office became highly prized as a means of social mobility from unskilled labour. Accuracy at figures and a good hand at writing became high educational priorities. In Cork the North Monastery, as well as being known for its later significant work under Brother Burke and his Technical School, became a great nursery of city clerks.

In May, 1839 the Export Merchants had elected the following fourteen gentlemen to the Committee: Messrs. Burke, Honan, Reeves, Morgan, Hardy, Lane, Whately, Evans, McNamara, Downes, Kelly, Carr, Hodder and McSwiney. The Hide and Skin representatives were Messrs. Murphy, Sugrue and Moore, while in January, 1840 the Agricultural Association was represented by Colonel Hodder of Hoddersfield near Crosshaven, J. Fitzgerald of Cloghroe, T. Barry of Rock Villa and Capt. Breton of Kinsale.

An intriguing manifestation of the interaction of butter and education came from a school book known as "Voster's Arithmetic," a new edition of which was printed in Cork in 1834 by John Connor. The original was by Elias Voster and the new edition had been "corrected, revised and improved" by William Gutteridge, a truly versatile man who proclaimed himself to be "a land and timber surveyor and a Teacher of Musical Composition." The book had an appendix described as "the Butter Trade of Cork," and was probably used in the numerous private schools then found in ordinary houses throughout the city. Readers were informed that "butter is now commonly classed in Cork in six different qualities, the 5th and 6th called grease and the 4th commonly called bishop's butter." The kind of problems set to knit the brows of Cork youngsters were nothing if not relevant to the trade of the city; perhaps the gentle reader might wish to tackle one of them: "A Merchant sends to Barbadoes 300 Firkins of Butter, weight 175 cwt. 2 qrs. 19 lbs. at 18.8d. per cwt. Pay for Duty and other Charges £11.0.10. His Correspondent at

Barbadoes sells the Butter at 6d. per lb., weight as above. Pays for Freight £24.17.1, takes 5 per cent for his Commission. I demand Loss or Gain, if £135 at Barbadoes are worth but £100 in Ireland? (Answer: £152.14.5 Profit.)"

Moving forward to the 20th October, 1851, there is an interesting entry recording bits and pieces of refurbishing and mention of a gentleman so publicly concerned with the passage of time in Cork: "Denis Murphy, for fitting up an Office in the Firkin Crane, £15.13.11½; Mr. Drinan, for lettering Divisions, £1.1.6; Mr. Mangan, for Winding Clock, £1.0.0; Mr. Mangan, for Painting and Gilding the Dial of Same, £0.16.0; Mr. Goodman, for Framing View (taken from Illustrated London News) £0.7.0; Harris and Beale, for cement furnished in 1850, £1.8.6." His winding, his painting and his gilding completed, and with £1.16.0 in his pocket, the worthy Mr. James Mangan doubtless returned to his Patrick Street premises well pleased with the Committee of Merchants. Quite a number of their more humble employees were probably no less pleased at Christmastide in 1875, as the Minute of 9th December records promotions and establishments: "That upon the close of the present year James Farrell, scalesman, be placed on the superannuation list and in consideration of his long service of more than fifty years under the Committee his full rate of pay be continued to him, the appointment of his successor being postponed until the opening of the ensuing season. That Denis Murphy and Cornelius Hogan, supernumenary employees, be appointed to the permanent staff af Fifteen Shillings per week each. That Patrick Dalton, James Condon, Maurice Connor, John McAuliffe, J. Callahan, D. Linihan, M. Deane, J. Driscoll be also transferred from the casual list to the permanent staff at the probationary pay of twelve shillings per week until the opening of the Season, to be thence-forward increased to the amounts allowed to the men similarly employed in the department where each may be located." A final entry from the Minutes ushers in a new age when tallow for candles would soon be merely a curiosity; on the 9th March, 1876 the Committee "determined that Gas to the extent of two jets be given free of cost to the resident watchman."

In having these extracts printed and published for the first time it is hoped that the reader will have gathered from them something of a living impression of the men and the enterprise which mattered so much to Cork from 1769 to 1876. The Minutes give the human story behind the statistics of butter and skins and hides. They also endow the old Butter Market site at the foot of Shandon with the names and occupations of real people for whom that place was the source of their daily bread and the scene of their labours and their skills. It must be hoped that with goodwill and imagination the site will be preserved for the city, possibly as a museum or exhibition of the crafts and skills not only of the Butter Market but of the nineteenth century city as a whole. In an area so rich in historical associations and so evocative of old Cork such a permanent exhibition would be a source of immense interest to the citizens and to their visitors.

Old Cork glass is today valued as an antique and the story of the industry can be found in two general studies of glass-making in Ireland, "Irish Glass" by M. S. D. Westropp, published in 1920, and "Irish Glass" by P. Warren, published in 1970 . Unlike the case of the Butter Market where the Minutes and some parliamentary reports, as well as pretty copious newspaper material, all combine to give an objective and detailed account of the enterprise, the material available on Cork glass-making is scrappy and generalised. It seems generally agreed, however, that the great age of Irish glass in Waterford, Cork, Dublin and Belfast began in 1780 when, as a result of the patriotic campaign of Henry Grattan and the Irish Volunteers, the heavy excise duty on the export of Irish glass was lifted. The winning of Free Trade led in 1783 to the founding of the highly-valued Waterford Glass House by George and William Penrose; this was to continue until 1851 when economic conditions forced its closure on its then proprietor, George Gatchell. Early in its history the Waterford factory had over fifty manufacturers, as they were called, at work, most of whom had come from England to follow their craft and teach it to Irish workers. This pattern was also to be found in Cork which was to have three glass-making enterprises between 1783 and 1841, the Cork Glass House Company, 1783-1818, the Waterloo Glass House Company, 1815-1835 and the Terrace Glass Works, 1818-1841. It was on 6th November, 1783, that Messrs. Atwell Hayes, Thomas Burnett and Francis Rowe petitioned the Irish Parliament for a subsidy to establish a glass manufactury in Cork. Within six months they advertised as follows in the "Hibernian Chronicle" on 6th May, 1784: "Thomas Burnett and the Glass House Company takes this opportunity of informing the public that they have now ready for sale at their Glass manufactory in Hanover Street, Cork, a great variety of plain and cut flint glass, with black bottles of every denomination, which for excellence of quality is equal to any made in England. They now flatter themselves that after upwards of two years' perseverance through a variety of difficulties they have established this useful branch of business on such a footing as must render the greatest satisfaction to those who favour them with their commands, not doubting the support of ther fellow citizens and countrymen. N.B. John Bellesaigne, next door to said Glass House, retails the glass of said manufactury only." Hanover Street, therefore, became the birthplace of Cork glass, a fact visibly proclaimed to the citizens by the erection in 1782/83 of the conical fire-house which was a landmark in the area until it was pulled down in 1915. In fact, there were two fire-houses, one for bottle and window glass and one for plate and flint glass.

Exactly what could the customer hope to buy on a visit to Hanover Street? The following items appeared in contemporary advertisements; fine globe lamps for halls, for one to five candles; bells and shades mounted with brass; hyacinth vases; flasks encased in leather holsters to be attached to saddles; baskets, sweet-meats and jelly dishes; wine glasses, water glasses, whiskey glasses, water bottles, orange glasses, jugs and ewers; covers for tarts; butter coolers, cruet bottles with silver caps containing flavourings to be added to food during meals; cut flower glasses, carafes, punch glasses, goblets, salts and salt linings, mustard castors, salad bowls; Grecian and lustre lamps; ice pails, scent bottles and candlesticks. By 1787 only Atwell Hayes remained in the business, Rowe having gone bankrupt and Burnet having retired. From 1812 until its closure in 1818 the business was owned by William Smith and Company. Public notice of the end of the enterprise came on 23rd April, 1818, with an advertisement in the "Cork Southern Reporter:" "To be sold with the consent of all concerned the old Hanover Street Glass House, Cork. The premises extend from Hanover Street to Lamley's Lane, and have a quay on the south side of the river . . . The glass cutting machinery is modern and of the best description, and has as a moving-power a steam engine lately erected. Apply to Pope and Besnard, Thomas Carey, or to Johnson and Swiney, South Mall." Was the steam engine in Hanover Street the pioneer of the Industrial Revolution in Cork?

Following the old adage that opposition is the life of trade the second city glass house appeared within a stone's throw of the original. The "Overseer" of 24th December, 1816, gave a description of the new venture: "Waterloo Glass House. By his forming the Waterloo Glass House Company, which is now at work, Mr. Daniel Foley is giving employment to more than one hundred persons. His workmen are well selected, from whose superior skill the most beautiful glass will shortly make its appearance to dazzle the eyes of the public and to outshine that of any other competitior. He is to treat his men at Christmas with a whole roasted ox and with everything adequate. They have a new band of music with glass instruments and they have a glass pleasure boat." Obviously, Mr. Foley had nothing to learn from modern techniques of commercial showmanship and salesmanship. His choice of name for the firm probably was inspired by the Battle of Waterloo, then and for so long afterwards one of the great talking-points of Europe. The glass house was situated on Wandesford Quay on the site now occupied by Messrs. Harte, just across the river from Hanover Street. To press home his opposition he had a retail shop in this street at No. 14. Business must have prospered for in 1824 he opened a retail shop at Lower Sackville Street, Dublin, now O'Connell Street. However, by 1830 Foley had retired, but the business continued from 1831 until its closure in 1835 under the ownership of his partner, Geoffrey O'Connell. This gentleman was in turn to go bankrupt owing to the introduction of heavy excise duties on Irish glass, and the "Cork Constitution" of 18th June, 1835, carried notice of "an auction for non-payment of excise duties of splendid cut and plain glass at the Waterloo Glass Works, Clarke's Bridge, until the entire of the splendid stock is disposed of, consisting of rich cut decanters, salad bowls, celery and pickle glasses, dessert plates and dishes, tumblers and wine glasses of every description, hall and staircase globes, side lights, water crofts and tumblers. After the stock is sold the household furniture of a house in Mardyke Parade is to be auctioned."

Finally, in March, 1836, the actual premises in Wandesford Quay were advertised for sale by William Marsh, auctioneer.

The third glass-making business was the Terrace Glass Works founded in 1818 by the brothers Edward and Richard Ronayne for making flint glass. It was situated on the South Terrace backing on to Union Quay, with its rear portion now occupied by Messrs. Haughton. Products were sold in a shop in Patrick Street and also in a Dublin branch at Dame Street. But for this, the last of the Cork glass-houses, the end had come when the "Cork Southern Reporter" of 14th September, 1841, announced that the premises were for sale including "steam-engine, tools and apparatus for turning for forty glass cutters."

Without a survey of the development of shipping and the railways this chapter must necessarily be incomplete as a picture of the commerce of Cork. But, then, this book cannot go on forever. Moreover, the writer must frankly confess that at the moment he has not the material to deal with them as amply as they deserve.

Chapter V

IN AND OUT OF CORK—A COACH AND FOUR

Speaking with all the authority of his position as Surveyor and Superintendent of Mail Coaches for the Post Office in London, Mr. Charles Johnson declared in 1832 that "let the road be the best that can possibly be made, no Mail Coach with seven passengers, beside the coachman and guard, can travel above 10 miles an hour." He made this statement when giving evidence before a Select Parliamentary Committee on Communication with Ireland, and was himself about to come to this country to make a survey of the Mail Coach system. Johnson's statement deserves a second reading not only to appreciate its significance in regard to the time in which it was made, but to realise the dramatic changes between then and now. It must also be recalled that in talking of the Mail Coach he was talking about the fastest thing then being moved on long journeys, he was implying the use of the best roads and the absence of floods, fallen trees and large potholes. The speed of ten miles an hour in 1832 was the same as had been reached in 1500, while it was considerably slower than that of Roman chariots. The point to be stressed is that in 1832, as in all previous centuries, the only means of transport on land for people and goods was by their own two feet or the four feet of an animal. For Pope and prince and peasant alike travel was slow, uncomfortable and costly; it was virtually impossible in winter except in a small number of relatively better tracts; it was rarely indulged in for pleasure, and because of the almost total absence of public transport the majority of people in Ireland and Europe never went beyond thirty or forty miles of where they lived in the course of a whole lifetime. In a material sense nothing so marks off the present age from all other centuries of human experience than the incredible speed and comfort of travel. Today every man is king of the roads and lord of the sky and master of the sea. The double decker buses moving through the city streets represent a man-made miracle; so does the motor car nosing its bonnet along the most remote country roads; so does the train stretching out across the length and breadth of the land. And today it is possible to have breakfast in Ireland and dinner in America.

Before moving on to a more general consideration of the development of transport a few more items of information relating to Cork will give a note of immediacy and bring out the cumbersome nature of carrying the mail. In his submission of evidence to the 1832 Committee Mr. George Freeling, Assistant Secretary of the Post Office, told the tale of a letter from London to Cork. Two routes were in operation, from London to Milford to Waterford to Cork, and from London to Holyhead to Dunleary (later Kingstown, late Dun Laoghaire) to Cork. "A letter leaving London on Monday night would arrive at Milford on Wednesday morning and would be at Waterford on Wednesday night. I think it would lie there the whole of Wednesday night and would not reach Cork until Thursday afternoon. It leaves London by the Bristol Mail and remains at Bristol for thirty or forty minutes till the Welsh Mail is ready, and generally speaking the packet sails as soon as it gets the mail in the morning. It never arrives at Waterford before the afternoon. It arrives occasionally at Dunmore at four, five or six. Then there is the time to convey it to Waterford where it lies all night. It departs for Cork by the Mail next morning and arrives, as I have before stated, at five in the afternoon." The cost of postage on this route was 1/3. A letter coming from London to Cork by Holyhead would leave London on Monday night and reach Holyhead about midnight on Tuesday. It would arrive in Dunleary on Wednesday morning, and if in time for the Day-Mail to Cork it would reach the city on Thursday morning instead of Thursday afternoon, as was the case on the other route. Cost of postage was 1/5. But things did not always work out quite so smoothly and Cork businessmen were often angry at the late arrival of the mail, as is demonstated by the following exchange from the Report: "Are you aware that the merchants of Cork have had very serious cause of complaint frequently from the mail not arriving till two or three hours after its time?" Without batting an eyelid the gentlemen from the Post Office conceded that such might have been the case in a very few instances and, of course, they had a perfect explanation for any little problem: "Two or three disgraceful circumstances have occurred such as coaches breaking, wheels coming off, and axletrees breaking."

Reading through this Report on transport in 1832 one is caught up in the manifold ramifications of carrying the mail; the whole operation was involved and widespread, and the officials were enormously concerned with all the matters of horses and carriages, of Post Office contracts, of charge per mile, of proposals to cut twenty minutes or even half an hour on certain stages of the route. What they did not foresee was that they were standing on the threshold of a whole new era, that a transport revolution was about to take place which would consign their horses, their Mail Coaches and their time-tables to the realm of history. The railway was to bring more fundamental and permanent change to travel than anything that had previously happened in human history; it was to bring an era of mass travel and of cheap travel; it was to bring speed and comfort; it was to change economic life by allowing great quantities of goods to be transported from port to city and from city to inland regions. Ireland and Britain, and then Europe and the New World, could be traversed for the price of a railway ticket. The puff of smoke was the symbol of the modern age of travel. The coming of the steam engine not only brought the train but also the steamship, it was to lead to the tram and the motor car, then to the aeroplane and, finally, to men and their machines journeying to the Moon. Even while the Report of 1832 was being compiled that whole new era of man-made miracles was being ushered in, having been inaugurated at Liverpool on 15th September, 1830, when George Stephenson drove his "Rocket" to Manchester on a scheduled rail service that had the basic rail terminus fitments in operation at both cities. Eight trains puffed out of Liverpool that day, cheered by a crowd of 50,000 spectators, with the "Rocket" carrying a highly sceptical Duke of Wellington in a special ornate coach. The fact that the Member of Parliament for Liverpool, George Huskisson, managed to get killed by an engine while walking on the line to stretch his legs during a stop for watering, did nothing to dissuade the Iron Duke of the conviction that the whole railway business was nothing more than new-fangled nonsense. By 1831 the Liverpool to Manchester line was carrying 1,000 passengers a day. As soon as 1834 the railway had come to Ireland when the Dublin and Kingstown Railway Company opened six miles of track to service the busy Holyhead sea route. In 1839 this line carried 1,341,208 passengers. A stage coach carried eight passengers, four inside and four outside, and it travelled at best at ten miles per hour. Such was the contrast between the old and the new. Of course the new of the 1830s is the old of today, and those who now feel a nostalgia for the golden age of steam had their counterparts in those who lamented the passing of the Mail and Stage Coaches in the middle decades of the last century. Today's oddity will make tomorrow's nostalgia.

If the coming of the railway marked the beginning of the end of the reign of the coach and horse, it can be said that all previous history belonged to it. But it was only in the second half of the eighteenth century that road travel improved somewhat from the primitive condition that had existed in all European countries for the best part of a thousand years. Even as late as 1762 James Boswell, who was to achieve lasting fame as the biographer of Dr. Samuel Johnson, took over four days to reach London from Edinburgh, spending four nights at inns on the way. But he accomplished his journey so quickly only because he went by post-chaise, a light carriage carrying only two or three passengers and costing one shilling per mile. Had he taken the more usual mode of transport, the stage coach, he would have been ten days on the road. Indeed, by 1800 the situation was only marginally improved. The making of a long journey was certainly something of an event, if not an ordeal, and not only timid souls sometimes thought it prudent to make their will before setting out. Apart from being pulled by a horse or horses in some variety of carriage, there was always the quicker alternative of riding on horseback; but the man on horseback in 1800 was going no faster than a man in Old Testament times. In most cases the roads were no better, and the only possible improvement was the availability of a change of horse every twenty miles or so at a post-house on a main route. For all the sophistication of theological thought in the Middle Ages and the artistic refinement of the Renaissance, travel remained primitive. Wooden waggons without springs exacted their toll as they lumbered at four miles an hour over every rut and rock of a narrow track which became a quagmire in winter time. These medieval whirlicotes were especially trying for grand ladies and elderly people. It was only after 1620 that suspension began to be used in the construction of some of these coachwaggons, and their radius of travel is indicated by the fact that all such vehicles coming into London came from a distance of only thirty miles out in 1637. However, from 1660 a long-distance stage coach service was in operation to Chester, Exeter and York, carrying only inside passengers.

In Ireland as in Britain all traffic passed along the highway, but it is important to realise that the name referred to the right of passage rather than to the road itself. With no overall supervision by central or local government, the roads were simply tracts depending for their condition on the interest of the landlords through whose areas they passed. There were various statutes requiring landlords and Grand Juries to keep the roads in repair and giving them power to requisition free labour from their workmen. But even when these were adhered to it was simply a matter of filling holes with stones rather than making a road with a proper foundation and a hard surface. Until well into the eighteenth century Lord Lieutenants passing through parts of Wales to catch the packet at Holyhead for Dublin would have their carriage carried on the shoulders of sturdy peasants when the weather was bad. The cartage of goods was even more tedious, accounting for the almost closed economies of most countries until the coming of the railway. Merchandise was carried either by teams of pack-horses or by convoys of high wooden waggons with wide wheels designed to cope with holes in the road. It was because the movement of goods was so slow and costly that most people used food, clothes and furniture grown or made in the locality. As late as 1760 there was no road for wheeled vehicles from the city where the railway age was to begin, Liverpool. And that man-about-the-countryside, Arthur Young, wrote that in the same year "the roads of Oxfordshire were in a condition formidable to the bones of all who travelled on wheels." In this regard the record of Ireland was wholly commendable, for in his "Tour of Ireland," 1780, Young remarked that "for a country so very far behind us as Ireland to have got suddenly so much the start of us in the articles of roads is a spectacle that cannot fail to strike the British traveller exceedingly."

The two names which are most remembered in connection with improved roads in these islands are those of Thomas Telford and John Mac Adam, both Scotsmen. Telford was also to make a reputation as a great canal engineer, but as a practical stonemason he pioneered the making of roads especially designed to carry wheeled transport, and between 1800 and 1818 he was responsible for over one thousand miles of road-making in Scotland. The son of a shepherd, he had set out at the age of twenty-five to seek his fortune in London, riding on a borrowed horse and carrying little else than his bag of tools. He was to become one of those many-sided men of genius thrown up by the early Industrial Reveloution who, despite the lack of formal education, learned their crafts on the job and applied themselves with diligence and flair to making a notable career. In 1816 the Government employed him to remake the great road from London to Holyhead, so much used by travellers to and from Ireland. This was finished in 1826 together with his masterly Menai Suspension Bridge. Among those working under him was the young Irishman, William Dargan, from Carlow, who was later to become the greatest Irish railway engineer and was closely connected with bringing the Great Southern Railway to Cork City. Telford had three stages in his road-making: first the surface was levelled and drained, then a solid pavement of hard stones was laid down, finally there came a layer of small stones about the size of a walnut. His workmen had orders to throw away any stone bigger than a hen's egg. The fact that this rather obvious process was regarded as somehow revolutionary is a pointer to road conditions at the time. With his roads, his canals and his bridges, Telford was a professional civil engineer in the way that title is now understood, and he became the first President of the Institution of Civil Engineers. John Louden MacAdam gave two familiar words to everyday language, tarmacadam and tarmac. He had his opportunity when in 1815 he became surveyor to the Bristol Turnpike Trust. He, too, levelled and drained the foundation and then added a ten-inch layer of small stones which was compacted into a slightly convex surface. His fame quickly spread and he was in wide demand to remake roads for Turnpike Trusts. By 1820 the words macadamize and macadamite had already been coined and by 1827 MacAdam was appointed Surveyor General of Roads for Britain. In this capacity he directed a vast programme of road-making, and in London pauper women and children found employment breaking paving stones into small pieces to macadamize the streets. Both of these pioneers died within a short time of each other, MacAdam in 1836 and Telford the following year.

The improvement in the roads from the closing decades of the eighteenth century led to the golden age of the coach and four in Ireland and Britain. In Ireland there were a great many Turnpike Trusts, each one responsible for maintaining a stretch of road. The Trust was composed of a group of local landlords and magnates who ran it on a private commercial basis, using their own labourers for maintenance. A turnpike and a toll house were set up at each end of the piece of road and tolls were collected at a stated rate per wheel and per hoof. Though long-distance travel was out of the question for the great mass of the ordinary people in the eighteenth century, there was, nevertheless, a good deal of traffic on Irish roads. Great quantities of linen were carted from the north to Dublin, while Cork merchants brought wool down from Ballinasloe in long convoys of heavy wooden trucks travelling at four miles per hour. Indeed, the business of cartage was quite a lucrative one. Of course the gentry travelled a great deal between their country seats and their town houses, as well as to hunts and horse races and grand balls. Then in the summer months the spas had their clientele coming to take the waters to cure their gout, with Mallow being a high point in the pursuit of health and hilarity until well into the last century. The roads to Cork were busy with the farmers bringing in their butter from all over the county and from Kerry, Limerick and Waterford, sometimes spending ten days on the return journey. So busy was the traffic up along Shandon Street, then called Mallow Lane, and in along Blarney Lane that the Butter Market at the foot of Shandon remained open twenty-four hours a day, seven days a week. Apart from people on horses or in carriages, there was the enormous amount of movement of cattle on the hoof to ports and markets and slaughterhouses. From about 1770 onwards the Irish tourist trade began to make its debut with the dreamy charms of the Lakes of Killarney beginning to lure the opulent traveller. One such early visitor, Richard Twiss, complained of being fleeced down there in 1775!

In Ireland as in Britain the first regular stage coach began running between the main cities from about 1750 onwards. In 1784 there was published the "Post Chaise Companion or Traveller's Directory through Ireland." But however good or bad the roads, or whether or not there were coaches for public transport, there was one constant traveller on the highway—the man on horseback. He might have been a farmer going to the market, a priest or clergyman visiting his flock, a lawyer going to the county court, a landlord's agent calling on tenants, a businessman going to Cork or Dublin. The man on horseback was the basic traveller down through all the centuries until the present one. The value of the stage coach was that it allowed people who did not own a horse or did not want to ride one to travel long distances. When in 1780 John Palmer of Bath persuaded the Government that he could carry letters quicker and more reliably than post-boys on horse, the stage coach entered a new and important phase as the mail-coach. Henceforward the stage coach was one which carried passengers only, while the mail coach carried passengers in addition to having a contract from the Post Office to carry letters and small packets.

This chapter has been a long time on the open road and it is about time to pass the sign post for Cork and see how the citizens managed the business of getting in and out and about. As regards getting about the city the story is a simple one—most people walked as they did in other cities. The place was still small even by 1800 and, except for professional people and gentry living in the suburbs of Blackrock, Douglas and Tivoli, most of the citizens lived and worked within walking distance of the main city area. Of course it must be realised that walking distance is a relative thing; today a few hundred yards from a parked car is often regarded as something of a marathon, whereas in the eighteenth and nineteenth centuries a walk of two or three miles was regarded as normal even by genteel city folk. Their country cousins thought nothing of skipping ten or twelve miles to the market town or to a cross-road dance on a Sunday night. Cork was especially small even at the end of the eighteenth century when it was only beginning to burst out from behind its old medieval walls with the building of the new shopping and fashionable residential areas from Patrick Street to the South Terrace. Yet even that small city had its public transport, the ancestor of the hackney cabs, the trams, the buses and the taxis. The Sedan-chair was especially suited to carrying passengers within the confined space of an eighteenth century city. Its body was like a smaller version of a telephone kiosk with two poles protruding out front and back. The single passenger sat inside and two chairmen in velvet suits and buckled shoes lifted the contraption and conveyed their fare to the place of destination. The bodywork was executed in style, each side window had its little curtain, and there was a padded leather seat. Sedan chairs were much used by fashionable ladies shopping in Castle Street and the South and North Main Streets. Their long dresses were thereby protected from the mud and potholes of the footpath, and from being splattered by dreadful gentlemen careering along on horseback without watching what they were doing! Having done her business with the hosier, the greengrocer, the milliner, the wine merchant or the jeweller, the grand dame gathered her skirts and sat into the chair, to use the usual term. As she was carried in stately dignity she fanned herself and waved a delicate, laced hand at her acquaintances. The chairs also plied for hire at night bringing home patrons from the Theatre Royal on the site of the present Post Office, or from municipal frolics at the Mansion House, now the Mercy Hospital, or from the taverns in the town. Indeed, they were in especial demand delivering inebriated gentlemen onto their own doorsteps.

This latter service did not escape the notice of John Windham who in his "Tour of Ireland," published in London in 1780, paints this little cameo of travel in Cork. "There are no hackney coaches here but there are plenty of chairs or sedans. Their fare is but four pence for carrying you from one end of the city to the other. Indeed, if they carry you through the gates they will demand sixpence, but this is an act of their own making. These vehicles are extremely convenient for the followers of Bacchus who has a great number of votaries in this city. This vice is, in great measure, owing to their richness and commerce which brings a great resort of sailors who, it is well known, are one and all devoted to that deity. One of the coffee-houses is conducted like those of London. The taverns are pretty good and very cheap; port wine is better here than anywhere else I have been, and porter is more common than in any part of England out of London." Moving around the city, therefore, was a matter of walking or riding or taking a chair, but the business of travelling outside the city and of coming to it from distant parts involved the stage and mail coaches. A mail coach service between Cork and Dublin was in operation by 1789 under the direction of Mr. J. Anderson of

Fermoy, but the account of a Cork citizen of the time records the hazards of the rocky road from Dublin: "he left Dublin by coach on a Monday morning and did not arrive in Cork until the following Sunday at noon, due to accidents, bad roads and bad weather." If those early travellers did not have to contend with such modern plagues as slow punctures and broken fan belts there were often such little matters as broken axle-trees, horses having to wade through three or four feet of water, and coaches which overturned at sharp bends. These long journeys involved changing horses at least every twenty miles at establishments known as post houses. Fuller details on mail coaches come from West's Cork Directory of 1809: the Dublin Royal Mail left the office in Patrick Street at 10 o'clock at night, while its opposite number came clattering into the city at the unseasonable hour of three o'clock in the morning. Fares for inside passengers were extremely high at £3.10.5 which included the carriage of 20 lbs. of luggage. Outside passengers paid £2.4.5 for the privilege of exposure to wind, rain and snow not to mention the possibility of falling off. Four passengers sat inside on padded leather seats; four also sat on seats on the roof and simply held on to iron bars to prevent themselves from falling. All passengers had to make ample provision to keep themselves warm with greatcoats, muffs, rugs and a hipflask of whiskey. Even for the wealthiest of passengers on the inside there was no privacy in the sense that the modern traveller knows it by train, bus or plane. Of necessity only a small quantity of luggage could be catered and passengers on the Dublin Mail were charged 2d. per pound of excess baggage. The Limerick Mail left Patrick Street every morning at six o'clock passing through Fermoy. Inside fare was £1.8.2, outside 19/6, with a luggage allowance of 14 and 7 pounds respectively. The Youghal Mail left at half past five each morning, the fare being half a guinea with no differential quoted for inside or out.

The stage coaches catered exclusively for passengers and travelled somewhat slower than the mail coaches, though by 1820 they, too, were making a steady nine miles an hour. As more operations went into the business there was cut-throat competition to reduce the time on the road even by half an hour on long journeys; indeed bye laws were passed forbidding coaches to travel two or three abreast on main routes. Many had fanciful names to suggest reliability and speed, such as Wonder, Perseverance, Diligence and Lightning. When the novelist, William Makepeace Thackeray, left Cork for Bandon in August, 1842 he did so in the "Skibbereen Perseverance." In 1809 the "Kinsale Diligence" left Scott's Hotel in George's Street, now Oliver Plunkett Street, on Tuesdays, Thursdays and Saturdays at one o'clock in the day; it stayed overnight at Kinsale and left for Cork the following morning at nine o'clock. The fare was 7/7. All coaches were resplendent in a variety of colours, with the Mail decked out in the royal livery of scarlet, maroon and black. There were highlights to relieve the tedium of the journey; one such was the arrival of the Mail at a Turnpike Toll-gate through which it had free passage. While some distance away the guard would sound his horn and this was the signal for feverish activity on the ground—the gate was swung open, the roadway was cleared of hens, and an excited knot of men, women and children gathered to wave and cheer as the Mail swept by with blowing horn and pounding horses. Nothing must hinder the Mail and generally it was absolutely accurate as regards time; indeed, in the cabins and farmhouses on the route it formed the only correct time check. Another point of drama was the arrival at the Coaching Inn for breakfast or dinner. Slowing down to enter the archway, the Mail came to an excited halt on the cobbled coachyard. Immediately there was a flurry of movement; the ostlers ran out to rub down the steaming horses and lead them into the stables where a fresh team was waiting to be put in harness; the baggage men were unloading luggage; the guard was handing over the mail bags; there was always a crowd of onlookers, some gathered on the balconies that ran around the three sides of the yard, some at the entrance, all full of curiosity to see who had arrived and to hear the latest news from the big city and the great world beyond the distant hills. At a time when newspapers were dear and always a few days stale, the coach brought a first-hand account of men and events.

Meanwhile, the passengers had dismounted and were moving smartly into the dining-room where service was brisk as only ten minutes could be allowed for breakfast and twenty minutes for dinner. With such a quick stop passengers often complained of being cheated by innkeepers who charged for a full meal and managed to serve only a portion of it before it was time to be off again. Perhaps the greatest moment of drama in the golden age of coaching came at the main coachyard in the city when the journey was about to begin. The blacksmith had shod the horses, the ostlers had watered and fed them, the four strong horses had been harnessed to the coach and were stamping their feet on the cobbles, the passengers were arriving with the friends who were seeing them off, four taking their place inside and four climbing up to the roof outside, all well muffled to endure the weather. Then the guard emerged and took his place on top carrying his long horn, known as "the yard of tin." The great moment came when the coachman strode out in his greatcoat and carrying his whip in his white-gloved hand. He climbed to his seat and then they were off on the great expedition. Among the onlookers none were more excited than the knots of small boys who dreamed of one day driving a coach, just as many of their grandsons were to dream of driving a train. The coachmen had great prestige and their names were household words along the routes they served. Scenes such as just described were witnessed daily in Cork at the yard of the Imperial Hotel and at the premises of Messrs. Mc-Lysaght and Healy, both in Pembroke Street; at Winthrop Street between Winthrop Avenue and the junction with Oliver Plunkett Street; at Conway's Yard in Oliver Plunkett Street; at number 22 Patrick Street and in Coburg Street. At any of these places the imaginative reader can recall the thud of horses hoofs and catch the farewell wave of passengers in a coach and four.

In the early decades of the nineteenth century two Mail Coaches left daily for Dublin from Winthrop Street. The Royal Mail left at 8 a.m., changing guard and dining at Clonmel at 3.30 p.m. and arriving in Dawson Street, Dublin, at six o'clock the following morning. At 4.30 p.m. a second Mail left for Dublin via Cashel and Abbeyleix, with an overnight stop. A stage coach left the Imperial Yard each morning at the crack of dawn, 5.55 a.m. for Limerick, passing through Mallow, Buttevant, Charleville and Kilmallock. Its opposite number clattered into Pembroke Street at 7 p.m. in the evening. The "Royal Cork Almanac" of 1827 gives details of shorter routes:

In and Out of Cork—A Coach and Four

1. The Youghal Regulator left Winthrop Street daily at 4.00 p.m. passing through Midleton and Castlemartyr. Inside fare 4/-, outside 2/6.

2. The Waterford Mail Coach left at 5.00 a.m. Inside 23/6, outside 13/4.

3. The Limerick Coach via Fermoy left at 7 a.m. on Tuesdays, Thursdays and Saturdays, arriving at Limerick at 4.30 p.m.

4. The Mail Coach for Killarney and Tralee via Macroom and Millstreet left every morning at 6 a.m. Inside 12/-, outside 3/6.

5. The Mallow Day Coach left daily at 2.30 p.m., arriving at Mallow at 5.30 p.m. Inside 4/-, outside 2/6.

6. The Lady of the Lake Coach for Killarney left Winthrop Street on Tuesdays, Thursdays and Saturdays at 8.00 a.m. Inside 12/-, outside 8/6.

7. The Macroom Car left daily at 2.00 p.m. Fare 2/6.

8. The Bandon Diligence left Miss Dowden's, George's Street, daily at 3.00 p.m. in winter and 4 p.m. in summer. Inside 2/11, outside 2/6.

9. The Fermoy Coach carrying six inside and ten outside left Mrs. Day's office in Patrick Street daily at 4.00 p.m., arriving at Fermoy at 7.00 p.m. Inside 4/-, outside 2/6.

In later years other additional points of departure were at the Grand Parade, Cross Street, Leitrim Street and George's Quay. Indeed, it was from George's Quay that the last of these old coaches and cars operated towards the end of the century, the Carrigaline Long Car.

Easily the greatest name in Irish travel was that of a man who became a legend in his own lifetime, Charles Bianconi, the "King of the Roads." His was a classic tale of rags to riches; it was also an illustration of the self-made man without formal training rising to the top through hard work and the use of his native wit, a feat greatly admired in the nineteenth century. With an adult relative he had come to Dublin from his native Italy in 1802, a poor sixteen year old boy who had not a word of English. Soon he was out on the Irish roads as a pedlar selling picture frames and religious objects. With a keen business sense he opened a shop in Clonmel and came to realise that there was a need for cheap transport between the country towns. His opportunity came in 1815 when the Government was selling off horses at the end of the Napoleonic Wars. It was in that year that he ran his first car between Clonmel and Cahir, a simple one-horse open car that carried six passengers. By 1832 his cars covered 1,800 miles daily and served 23 towns. Eventually he came to own 3,000 horses based at depots throughout Ireland. The country people found it hard to get their tongues round that strange foreign surname, so they called him Brian Cooney, but his cars were known as the "Bians" or the Long Cars. That precisely is what they were, long outside cars carrying twenty passengers. At 1½d per mile they were cheaper than the Mail or stage coaches and they were an especial boon to small farmers going to the market. Bianconi was among those giving evidence for the 1832 Report referred to at the beginning of this chapter, though it would appear that his Long Cars had not by then been introduced: "My car establishment travels daily about 1,800 miles and passes through the following towns: Ballinasloe, Ballyhale, Banagher, Borrisoleigh, Cahir, Cashel, Carrick, Clogheen, Clonmel, Cork, Dungarvan, Doneraile, Enniscorthy, Eyer Court, Fermoy, Fethard, Freshford, Kilkenny, Kildorrery, Limerick, Mallow, Mitchelstown, Nenagh, Rathcormack, Roscrea, Thurles, Tipperary, Urlingford, Wexford and Waterford. It is a car on two wheels with a seat on each side for four passengers, with a space between the passengers in which the luggage is put, as well as a very roomy boot for more delicate luggage, and they are drawn by two horses. I fear I cannot describe it to you satisfactorily enough. In the South of Ireland we have neither roads nor commercial intercourse to support coaches, and the farmer who lived twenty or thirty miles from the principal market towns should either walk or ride, and that took him one day going, another to do his business and a third to return. Now for a few shillings he purchases two days' time for himself and three for his horse, not to speak of the safety and comfort he enjoys by going by the cars."

His cars travelled only by day from five in the morning to eight in the evening, and never on Sunday. Bianconi's evidence bears out what a problem it was to travel even thirty miles to a market town. In due course he grew to be wealthy and came to play a prominent part in public life, being especially pleased to become Mayor of Clonmel. His home became a noted social centre where he entertained in the grand manner, his dinner table sparkling with the wit and wisdom of writers, politicians, clergymen, artists and scholars. Pride of place went to the Liberator, Daniel O'Connell, and as a devout Catholic Bianconi was always happy to help and welcome Father Mathew and Ignatius Rice, founder of the Christian Brothers. His interest in education was deep, leading him to support the Mechanics Institute in Clonmel and, more notably, to buy 86 Stephens Green, Dublin, and present it as the nucleus of the Catholic University which was to be presided over from 1852 to 1858 by the sensitive genius of Dr. Newman from Oxford. Among those who sat at Bianconi's table were Lord Monteagle, Richard Lalor Shiel, Thomas Wyse, M.P., Thomas Drummond, the most enlightened Chief Secretary of the century, Mr. and Mrs. C. S. Hall, and a host of English and Continental journalists who came to savour the company and survey the enterprise. As an employer Bianconi demanded high standards of performance but his obvious concern for the welfare of his men won him their lifelong loyalty; his introduction of a retirement pension scheme placed him ahead of his time in labour relations. One incident brought him particular relish and well illustrates his journey from rags to riches. As a pedlar he had gone up the drive of the lantern-style mansion, Longfield House, near Cashel, only to be turned away by the butler. Even then he resolved in some strange way that he would one day own that house. His ambition was realised in March, 1846, when as Mayor of Clonmel he bought it for £22,000 and became master of its 600 acre estate. The pedlar had come to sit in the drawing-room. Bianconi was greatly flattered when on 19 August, 1843, he was invited to read a paper on his enterprise before a session of the Conference of the prestigious British Association for the Advancement of Science then meeting in Cork, an event also attended by the young nationalist writer from Dublin, Thomas Davis. He told his erudite audience that having started twenty-eight years previously with one horse and an outside car doing a round trip of eighteen miles a day, he then had 1,300 horses and 100 vehicles, charging an average fare of $1\frac{1}{4}$d per mile. His cars covered 3,800 miles a day from Donegal to Cahirciveen and from Cork to Dublin. He then conjured up an astronomical feat of equestrian gastronomy—his horses annually consumed from 3,000 to 4,000 tons of hay and from 30,000 to 40,000 barrels of oats! The coming of the railway to Ireland might well have ended the career of the "King of the Roads," but using the canny principle of "if you can't beat them join them," he became a railway share-holder and used his cars as "feeders" on secondary roads to the new stations that were beginning to dot the country-side. He lived to a happy and lucid old age, still scrutinis-ing account sheets at the age of eighty-nine. It was on 22 September, 1875 that his horses came up the long drive at Longfield to bear away the stranger who had come so to know and love the roads of Ireland. The house is now in the care of the Irish Georgian Society.

Bianconi's cars gave good service to Cork; the follow-ing is their time-table for 1843 as set out in a notice signed by "R. Newsom, Agent, Patrick Street, corner of Princes Street:"

A Car starts every morning at 6 o'clock for:

	Arriving	Fare
Watergrasshill	7.40 a.m.	2s.0
Fermoy	9.00 a.m.	3.6
Mitchelstown	10.10 a.m.	5.0
Cahir	1.15 p.m.	8.6
Tipperary	6.35 p.m.	10.0
Cashel	3.25 p.m.	10.0
Holycross	6.00 p.m.	10.6
Thurles	6.30 p.m.	11.6
Clonmel	2.30 p.m.	9.6
Carrick	4.40 p.m.	11.0
Waterford	7.00 p.m.	12.0
Nine-Mile-House	5.00 p.m.	11.6
Callan	6.00 p.m.	12.6
Kilkenny	7.00 p.m.	13.6

Passengers for Dublin sleep overnight at Kilkenny. From whence a Coach proceeds next morning at 15 minutes before 6 o'clock for:

Carlow	9.00 a.m.	20 outside, 17 inside.
Dublin	3.45 p.m.	28 outside, 21 inside.

In addition to these longer runs the Bianconi office in Patrick Street had cars leaving every morning at 9 o'clock on the following shorter routes: for Douglas arriving at 9.20, fare 6d; Passage arriving 10.00, fare 6d; Monskstown arriving 10.15, fare 9d; Carrigaline arriving 11.00, fare 1/-. All passengers were advised that the establishment was "not accountable for any money, plate, or millinery whatso-

116

ever, or any damage occasioned by wet or friction. The Day Cars do not travel on Sundays or Christmas Days." As the Bians were open cars passengers had to be prepared to endure all that the weather had to offer.

An interesting contemporary account of Cork in 1842 has been left by one of the leading writers of the last century, William Makepeace Thackeray, the film of whose novel, "Barry Lyndon," may have been enjoyed by some readers. He had come by stage coach from Fermoy and describes his arrival in Patrick Street as follows in his "Paris and Irish Sketch Book:" As the carriage drove up to those neat, comfortable and extensive lodgings which Mrs. Mac O'Boy has to let, a magnificent mob was formed round the vehicle, and we had an opporunity of an once making acquaintance with some of the dirtiest, rascally faces that all Ireland presents. Besides these professional rogues and beggars, who make a point to attend on all vehicles, everybody else seemed to stop too, to see that wonder, a coach and four horses. People issued from their shops, heads appeared at windows. I have seen the Queen pass in state in London and not bring together a crowd near so great as that which assembled in the busiest street of the second city of the kingdom, just to look at a green coach and four bay-horses. Have they nothing else to do?" His comments on the beggars bear out evidence already quoted in the chapter on that subject, but Thackeray does seem a bit harsh in his reaction to a crowd gathering around the arrival of a stage coach. At least he did not have to endue the tribulations of his equally famous literary contemporary, Charles Dickens, who found himself travelling in a stage coach in America in March of that same year of 1842. Mr. John Forster in his splendid biography of the writer, a book which Carlyle compared to Boswell's life of Johnson, quotes the following letter from America: "We left Baltimore last Thursday the twenty fourth at half past eight in the morning by railroad, and got to a place called York, about twelve. There we dined and took a stage coach for Harrisburgh, twenty-five miles further. This stage coach was like nothing so much as the body of one of the swings you see at a fair upon four wheels and roofed and covered at the sides with painted canvas. There were twelve inside! I, thank my stars, was on the box. The luggage was on the roof; among it a good-sized dining-table and a big rocking-chair. We also took up an intoxicated gentleman who sat for ten miles between me and the coachman; and another intoxicated gentleman got up behind but in the course of a mile or two fell off without hurting himself, and was seen in the distant perspective reeling back to the grog-shop where we had found him. When we changed horses on this journey I got down to stretch my legs, refresh myself with a glass of whiskey and water, and shake the wet off my greatcoat."

The stage and Mail coaches and the Bianconi cars served the citizens of Cork and their visitors in the matter of long journeys outside the city, but what developments had taken place in internal travel? As was the case in other cities the growth in physical size signalled the end of the sedan chairs and in their place the horse-drawn hackney car provided the public transport in the city and immmediate suburbs. But whereas the coaches were gradually consigned to history by the coming of the railway in the 1850s, the horses and cabs ruled the streets until after the first World War. For them the railways were the greatest thing since the invention of the wheel, bringing brisk business as they conveyed passengers to and from the trains to their homes and hotels. Nineteenth century photographs of street scenes in Dublin, London or Paris show the amount and variety of horse-drawn traffic ranging from elegant private carriages to the substantial brewery cars known as drays. Unfettered by the pernickety regulations which are designed to aid what is ironically called the free flow of traffic in this present age, they filled the streets with the open-air vitality of men and horses. They also created an enormous amount of noise as iron shoes and iron wheels clattered over cobblestones or thudded over wooden paving. Cork was to witness and to hear all the sights and sounds of milk carts, bread vans, coal waggons, watering cars, fire brigades, of side-cars, inside cars and outside cars, of jarveys and jingles, of waggonettes, dog-carts, landaus, broughams, ladies phaetons, Stanhopes and Victorias. And for a short while a horse-drawn tram came up the South Mall from Albert Street en route for the Great Southern Railway station, and apart from the little matter of occasionally overturning in trying to negotiate the Berwick Fountain on the Grand Parade, it was known to reach its destination. The two most common hackney cars on the streets of Cork were the jingle or covered car and the jaunting or side-car, both drawn by one horse. The covered car gave protection from the weather and privacy with its oilskin canopy; its wheels were fully outside the body of the vehicle. On the side-car the passengers sat back to back with a "well" or boot for luggage between them. It was very light and pressed little on the horse, while its wheels were covered over by footboards on either side. This whole business of wheels gave rise to the following quizzical description: the outside car has the wheels on the inside and the inside car has the wheels on the outside. The side-car was regarded as being rather unsocial for conversation, while the fact that the passenger could see only one side of the roadway prompted a sharp-tongued writer to remark that it was well attuned to the Irish character which, he alleged, took a one-sided view of everything. That was no more than a point of view—but the Cork jarveys held it as a certainty that they could always tell whether a couple hiring a side-car were married or single; a courting couple always hudlded together on one side, asking the jarvey to move over on his seat to balance the car "for the sake of the poor horse," whereas married couples sat on either side in solitary dignity. The jarveys jealously guarded their place on the "stand," rising their whip at the sign of a possible passenger, or lounging against their cars with their red handkerchiefs loosely tied around their necks and their long coats flapping against their legs. They enjoyed the banter of making a bargain with a passenger, they would only ask the fare, "leaving any other little trifle to your honour on account of the wife and children."

These hackney cars were licensed and regulated by the Magistrates Court under bye-lays such as the following for 1839:

1. The cars must be numbered with legible figures at least 3 inches long.

2. The drivers not to quit the "stand" to solicit employment.

3. No driver to refuse to go with any person when required, unless the car is already engaged, which previous hiring the driver must prove if required.

4. The cars to be kept clean and in good order and the horse properly cared for.

5. Check strings to be provided which the drivers must hold in their hands.

6. Drivers must be able and careful, of decent apparel and civil in behaviour.

7. No one to sit with the driver unless with the consent of the person hiring.

Conviction of an offence against any one of those regulations made the driver liable to a fine not exceeding £5. The following were among the approved "stands" in 1839:

1. The Grand Parade from Mr. Lawson's southwards for 35 yards. This firm of gentlemen's outfitters is still in business in the city.

2. The Grand Parade from Mr. Babington's southwards to the statue of George II at the river end of the Parade.

3. The south side of Lavitt's Quay commencing 10 feet from the footway of St. Patrick's Bridge and extending westwards.

4. The south side of the South Mall from the west side of Chatterton's Buildings and extending westwards to the statue of George II.

5. The east end of Warren's Place (now Parnell Place) commencing at the corner of the quay next to Anglesea Bridge (Parnell Bridge) and extending northwards.

6. The lower part of the South Mall opposite Beamish and Crawford's malt store.

The reproduced page of Purcell's Commercial Almanac gives an interesting survey of places and prices at a time when the jarveys were in their heyday. One point is clear, public transport was costly. When it is recalled that even in 1900 servant girls were sometimes receiving a weekly wage of only 5/- it must have been something of an expedition to spend 6d on a hackney car in 1882—even if the passenger was deposited at such an exotic place as Panorama Terrace on Wise's Hill. In a series of regulations that most probably applied equally to Cork, the Dublin Almanac and General Register of 1841 gets down to such basic matters as "bags of oats" and "improper velocity" and the "violation of public decency:"

1. That the drivers of all such Carriages, Chaises, Jaunting Cars, Caravans or other vehicles aforesaid, while on their Stands, or in any other time or place, shall not molest, disturb, annoy, insult the Owners, Occupiers, Inmates or

Inhabitants of any house opposite to or in the vicinity of their Stands, or any passenger or other person whatsoever, either by riotous, turbulent or disorderly behaviour, or by abusive or improper language or gestures, or in any manner whatsover, in violation of public decency or morals, misconduct themselves towards or in respect to such owners, occupiers, inmates, inhabitants, passengers or other person or persons.

2.   That the horses or other beast or beasts used in drawing such Carriages, Chaises, Jaunting Cars, Caravans or other vehicles, shall not be fed in any street with Oats except in Bags, nor with Hay unless delivered out of the hand; nor shall any Hay, Oats, Nose-bags or any dirty or offensive matter or thing be kept inside any such Carriage.

3.   That the drivers of said Carriages shall not drive same with improper or unreasonable velocity, or violently abreast with each other, or with any other Carriage or Vehicle, or by any rivalry of driving or contention with each other cause any terror or alarm to the Public or the Passengers, or any person whatever, or damage or endanger any other Carriage or the Horse or Harness thereof, or any other article, matter or thing whatsoever."

This whole body of bye-laws, so detailed in its specifications and so blunt in its implications, must prompt one honest question: What on earth were the Dublin jarveys doing that caused such laws to be framed?

The world of coaches and horses was created and serviced by a wide range of skilled craftsmanship, by blacksmiths and whitesmiths, by ostlers and grooms and farriers, by carpenters, coachbuilders and painters. Fine specimens of these skills of hand and eye were to be seen in Cork in the Patent Carriage Works of Mr. James Johnson in Nelson Place, now Emmet Place. The whole operation is well described in one of the finest series of books to come out of the railway age, "The Official Illustrated Guide to the Great Southern and Western Railway," written by Mr. George Measom and published in London in 1866. Measom was commissioned to write a series of such guides for the principal railway companies of Britain and Ireland and each one is a most informative survey of the chief cities and towns on the routes, encompassing a historical review as well as commercial and cultural developments. Before describing what he saw at Mr. Johnson's manufactory, Measom gave some general comments on what was involved in making a coach: "The art of Coach Building holds a somewhat anomalous position in the world of industry. Essentially, and of necessity for its practical purposes, a mechanical art, it nevertheless includes so much of what is termed art par excellence that it may be justly to be considered more than a mere industrial manufacture, producing only things of mere utility, and to rank along with the goldsmith's work and the higher efforts of the potter, as an art manufacture. To produce a well-shaped body requires no small amount of artistic taste, proficiency in drawing and knowledge of perspective. Many carriage bodies are shaped as if they were portions of a gracefully moulded vase or tazza, and may compare with the best forms thrown by the potter's wheel, while the Coach Maker has this difficulty which the ceramic artist has not, that his 'vase' is made up of many parts each of which must be formed separately before it takes its place in the skeleton of framework which, when covered with panelling, constitutes the body of a carriage. A carriage, considered as to the work it has to do do, is a machine which is subjected to more highly destructive agencies than any other. Used upon roads of all degrees of roughness, at varying speeds and with loads limited only by the ability of the horse to draw them, it is at the same time exposed to all the vicissitudes of weather and the ruinous effects of dirt and dust, while it is expected to be equally easy to the passengers under all circumstances. A very eminent engineer used to say that, considering the way in which all these difficulties are overcome in a well-constructed modern carriage, it may fairly claim to be one of the most pefect machines in existence"

Obviously knowing what to look for, Measom was well pleased with what he saw at Johnson's. In the upstairs showroom, 90 feet in depth, "we saw among hundreds of others, all the production of Mr. Johnson, the beautiful Stanhope phaeton and landau. Here, too, we saw the model brougham weighing but $7\frac{1}{4}$ cwt. and in all respects one of the most perfect vehicles which we have seen. The price at which it is sold varies from 100 guineas and would astonish a London builder. We observed the landau, a carriage that has now become so fashionable, as well as the Elcho sociale, barouches and a great variety of the peculiar Cork cars, together with the American hunting-drag, the Norwegian cabriole, the Malvern, Cheltenham, Shamrock, and a variety of other dog carts, besides waggonettes, park phaetons and basket carriages. At the end of this department is the drying loft, and near to it is the body loft, paint shop, trimming shops and store room. On the ground floor is the smithy which is also well arranged, as well as the other workshops, with regard to light and ventilation. Our attention was particularly attracted in the lower part of the building and yards adjoining, by the enormous piles of timber consisting of tens of thousands of spokes and felloes, planks of ash and elm, in the process of seasoning. Mr. Johnson uses no timber in the construction of any vehicle that has not been at least four years on the premises. The rejected timber he consumes in a large furnace erected in the smithy for the purpose of heating the wheel tires, and which is capable of containing tires for ten or twelve sets of wheels at a time."

The carriage-making operations of this same firm were again noted in Strattan's "Dublin, Cork and the South of Ireland," published in London in 1892. The list of carriages was almost identical but there were many improvements in machinery in the workshops: "there are boring and mortising machines, circular saws, band saws and lathes. There are machines of Mr. Johnson's own invention. One in particular we noticed is patented for making wheel spokes. This machine turns out fifty in one hour, which is almost five times more than any other in existence. The numerous machines are driven by an eigh-horse engine. The forge is certainly a very fine one in which we have seen as many as twenty men employed. The body-makers work upstairs and there are boring and planing machines to facilitate their work. The painting is all done on the top storey. The uninitiated will be a little surprised to learn that each carriage will take a month, and not less than one coat a day during that time, to complete the painting alone. Everywhere men of the very highest skill are at work, and in all between sixty and seventy hands are constantly employed."

So it was that as the nineteenth century drew to a close the smiths and the carpenters of Cork were still busy with the craftmanship of the golden age of coaches and horses. They were not to know that the future belonged to the horseless carriage and to Henry Ford.

Chapter VI

THE SICK, THE POOR AND THE BEGGARS

When historians come to write about the present century they will draw up the balance sheet of its distinctive characteristics. What features will stand out? Probably the astonishing advance in technology, with the conquest of space as a highlight; the concept of total war, with its barbarity of death and destruction for the civilian population; the phenomenon of the former colonial countries achieving independent nationhood, a process in which Ireland played a conspicuous part; the rise of America and Russia to dominance as world powers; the development of the ecumenical spirit among the great Christian communities whose divisions were so much part of earlier history; the pervading influence of press, radio, cinema and television; the spread of affluence; the cheapening of human life through the cult of violence. Amid the catalogue of gains and losses one notable advance will deserve record, namely the marked growth in social concern for the more deprived members of the community, the old, the sick and the handicapped in mind and body. It is not that this concern was born only in the twentieth century—it is as old as Christianity itself—but that it is now a matter of public concern and public policy, involving national government and state finance. In previous centuries the care of the poor was largely a matter of Christian compassion and of voluntary local effort, even though Boards of Guardians and Workhouses had statutory existence in the nineteenth century. Indeed, it was that century which saw poverty in a more widespread and degrading state than possibly ever before. If the Industrial Revolution in Britain brought the enterprise, the new comforts and the new wealth of men and their machines, it also had its darker side in the hordes of rootless operatives crowding into the slums of the growing industrial centres, many of them exchanging the rhythm of country life for the hard taskmaster of the factory hooter. With no state assistance for unemployment or sickness, with overcrowding in badly ventilated city lanes, alleys and courtyards, with primitive sanitary conditions and with typhoid, cholera and consumption hovering in the air, the cities harboured a sad mass of human distress. In Ireland the plight of subsistence living was brought to a horrifying peak by the monumental tragedy of the Famine. This chapter will be concerned with the life and times of the poor of Cork in the 1830s, but it is important to realise that throughout the nineteenth century the great mass of the people of Ireland and of Britain lived in varying conditions of poverty. It was not somehow peculiar to Ireland. Nor was poverty the real problem, rather it was destitution. Before dealing with the local situation a glance at the conditions of the poor of London will give perspective and indicate how in a great city growing so rapidly in numbers and wealth there was the other world of the poor and the distressed.

Among the small band of middle class philanthropists, aided by a thin scattering of titled spokesmen, who set about alerting public opinion to the needs of the depressed classes was Sir James Kay-Shuttleworth who published his "Social Condition and Education of the People in England and Europe' in 1850. In this book he showed a keen perception of the problems of the Irish peasant, but his material on city life in the London slums is of especial significance in this work. With the cold evidence of statistics and personal observation he delineated that life with compelling urgency. He described a London lodging-house: "The parlour measures 18 feet by 10; beds are arranged on either side of it, composed of straw, rags and shavings. Here are 27 male and female adults, and 31 children, with several dogs. In all 58 human beings in a contracted den from which light and air are systematically excluded. The quantities of vermin are amazing. I have entered a room and in a few minutes I have felt them dropping on my hat from the ceiling like peas." The courts and alleys in which so many lived "are in the immediate neighbourhood of uncovered sewers, of gutters full of putrified matter, nightmen's yards and privies, the soil of which is openly exposed and never or seldom removed. It is impossible to convey an idea of the poisonous conditions in which these places remain during winter and summer, in dry weather and wet, from the masses of putrifying matter which are allowed to accumulate." Quoting from the 1848 issue of the Journal of the Statistical Society of London, Kay-Shuttleworth gave some figures from the parish of St. George's in the East End, this parish being chosen "not as being the worst of the metropolitan districts but as affording an example of the average condition of the poorer classes." The Statistical Society had visited 1,954 families with a population of 7,711 individuals and the following were its findings: "551 families containing a population of 2,025 persons have only one room each, where father, mother, sons and daughters live and sleep together; 562 families containing a population of 2,454 persons have only two rooms each; 705 families containing a population of 1,950 persons have only one bed each in which the whole family sleep together."

Quoting from the City Mission Report of July, 1848, the following picture emerged of Orchard Place in the East End: "Orchard Place is less than 45 yards long and 8 broad, and contains 27 houses. Resident in this court in 1845 were no less than 217 families consisting of 882 persons, of whom 582 were above 14 years of age." Quite a common practice was that some more enterprising individual would hire a room and then let portions of it to poorer tenants. In a first floor front room in Fletcher's Court the following were full-time residents: "a man, his wife and three children; a man, his wife and one child; a widow and her two children; a single woman aged twenty years." Nor were these conditions restricted to one depressed area; Kay-Shuttleworth felt justfied in stating that "in the back streets of Kensington and of Oxford Street I know from personal experience that the state of the poor is just such as I have described." He was one of the handful of influential civil servants who worked to influence national government to take an active interest in the relief of social distress. As a medical practitioner in Manchester in his earlier years he had experienced at first hand the conditions in the new industrial slums where so many of the inhabitants had come from Ireland. As a Poor Law Commissioner he brought a capable and compassionate mind to his work, but it was chiefly to education that he looked to create a community consciousness that would in time change society for the better. He is best remembered as the first secretary of the Committee of the Privy Council set up in 1839 to consider educational development in the sphere of elementary schooling. This was the predecessor of the Ministry of Education.

Moving from the back streets of London to those of Cork was simply a change of place. The scenario was the same, the poor were in their garrets. A detailed description of their conditions is contained in the Report of the

Parliamentary Committee of Inquiry on the Poor of Ireland published in 1835. Evidence was taken at a meeting in the parish of St. Mary's, Shandon, at which the Assistant Poor Law Commissioners met the following community representatives: Mrs. Coleman, Superior of the Convent of the Sisters of Charity—it was the custom at the time for nuns to describe themselves in public as married women; Rev. Mr. Daly, senior Catholic curate at the North Chapel— all clergymen then used the title of Mister; Mr. Edward J. Downey, clerk of the North Chapel for 23 years; Mr. R. Howell, a woolcomber; Mr. John Murphy, a coffin-maker and President of the Sick Poor Society; Mr. John Nagle, son of a tradesman; Mr. James Nolan, foreman maltster; Rev. Dr. Quarry, Church of Ireland Rector of the parish; Rev. Dr. Sloane, Presbyterian Minister. The Report stated that "as a means of relieving the wants of those destitute by sickness there is a society in the parish called the Sick Poor Society. The object is, by collecting 1d. a week, to provide a fund for the sick poor, and by visiting the houses to discover fit objects for relief. The Assistant Commissioners, being anxious to know the actual state of the sick, went round with the visitors of the Sick Poor Society. The entire number of cases which fell under the observation of one or other of the Assistant Commissioners was about 40. The following are not selected but taken nearly in the order in which they occurred, the conversations are given verbatim, notes of them having been taken at the time." The following eye-witness accounts exactly reproduced from the Report, portray the life and times of the poor of Cork with a vividness which needs no comment from this writer. The cases are numbered as in the Report.

1.   In a small room two women lying coiled up in corners, a mother and a daughter. A little straw under them and a single covering over each of them. A young woman attending them, a daughter, said she had just recovered from fever. She showed a few miserable black potatoes in a saucepan and said they had nothing else to eat. So struck were the Assistant Commissioners by the evident misery that they did not think of asking questions.

2.   A small room in a cabin; an old woman sitting in the corner, palsied and blind. Her husband, an old man, sitting on a bench. Nothing in the room but a little straw. Being addressed she said. "I'm badly off, I can't stir a step without

somebody to help me. I'm a prisoner here, my husband has nothing to do now. I'll just tell the truth, he cut a handful of briars and sold them to get something to eat." The husband was asked: "How do you support yourself?" He replied, "I do as well as I can one way or another." "How do you pay your rent?" "Sure, I owe 9/- for this place and I don't know how I will pay it at all." "Would you let your wife go to the House of Industry?" "Is it let her go away from me? Why, then, I wouldn't as long as I could do anything, even if I was forced to beg from the neighbours." He said this with tears in his eyes. "But if you went with your wife?" "Sure they wouldn't leave her in the same place as me, they'd put us asunder." "And is that the reason— you'd be better treated there." "It is the reason, Sir, she shan't go as long as I can get a bit for her."

3. A small room; a man, Terence Sullivan, lying on a bed. He said he was "dead in his limbs.' A neighbour attends him sometimes and shakes his straw. He gets 8d. a week from the Sick Poor Society and pays 6d. of it for his rent. Has only 2d. for himself. Has a son a labouring man, badly able to support himself and with a wife that wouldn't let him do much for the old father. He brings home an odd meal. A charitable woman in the neighbourhood sends him a bit of breakfast. He wouldn't go to the House of Industry, "because I'm afeared I couldn't make my soul there as I can here." 'The priest attends there regularly." "Well, maybe he do but I couldn't go there at all." "But the Society won't be able to give you assistance any longer." "Well, God is good, I'd rather take my chance and stay among the neighbours than go there."

4. A very small room, a young woman lying on a bed. She has swelling in her legs and pains all over her. Her father is a labourer and being handy gets something to do mending shoes. Does not like to go to the House of Industry without her cloak which is in pawn for 5/- "I was there and came home on account of a duty (a religious vow to perform) I had to do." "Were you badly used when you were there?" "Yes, there is very bad usage there, there is little to eat or drink and bad beds, and you see 'em all turning for lucre. I'd rather stay at home if I could."

5. An old woman, a beggar, her sister lying in a corner, a half idiot. She pays for the room. "I wouldn't go to the House of Industry." "Why?" "I wouldn't go there at all, at

all. I would not have my liberty and I'd rather stay among God and the neighbours and Christians and take my chance for a bit of vittles from them." "But you'd be better off there, you'd have something better to eat." "I wouldn't go there if I was sure of getting that box full of good vittles every day."

6. An old woman sick and bed-ridden, her daughter, a poor widow, attending her. She wouldn't go to the "good house" at all. She hadn't long to live and what would be the use? Daughter was asked "would you let her go?" "No, Sir, I wouldn't let her go among strangers while we can do anything for her. I'd rather go begging about the streets than let her go there."

7. A woman, sick, lying on a bed in a small room; nobody belonging to her. A poor family that has the room gave her the corner "for God's sake." "Would you go to the House of Industry?" "Hy'ah no, sure there would be nobody to bury me out of it. I wouldn't go there at all."

8. A young woman sick and almost blind in a small room. Her aunt supporting her by begging, but she's lying in bed sick now. A poor family owning the room giving them a corner for charity. "Would you go to House of Industry?" "No, Sir, I was never in such a place among strangers and I'd rather stay among the neighbours." "Why wouldn't you go there, you'd be better off?" "Well, Sir, I'd like to be able to go out to Mass, it's the only comfort now." "But the priest would attend you there and you would hear Mass." "Why, Sir, if you must know it (she said this with tears in her eyes) there's a little creature of a sister I have and she's at service, and she has nobody to look after her or care about her but me and if I went to the Poor House and she was out of place what would she do, she'd have no place to come to." "Yes," said the woman who owns the room, "that is the reason she would not go there." These people were once in comfortable circumstances.

9. An old woman, Nelly Mullins, supported by her daughter. Daughter does a little plain work sometimes; her husband is no help to her, she was obliged to leave him as he took to drinking.

10. A small garret, two women lying in corners. The woman on the Society's list whom we had come to see had gone out to get a halfpenny worth of milk. One of the women said that this person ought to be glad to go to the

House of Industry as she has nobody belonging to her. If she was able to be up one day in the week she was down six more. We waited a short time but we did not see her.

11. Margaret Crowley. Chief dependence on her aunt who begs. They get a corner for charity from a poor family. She wouldn't go to the House of Industry. "I'd like to be among the neighbours, I was never in any sort of strange place. I wouldn't like to go where there would be nobody but strangers to do a hand's turn."

12. Ellen Callaghan, an old woman, has the jaundice, says she is all sore inside. Has seven children. Her son, a young man, lying in a corner sleeping after being up the night before watching coals on the quay to earn 8d . to pay the rent of the room. She was asked if her son would go there. "If he'd like it himself I wouldn't begrudge him to go there. I'd rather have my liberty, 'tis sweeter than good living."

13. Timothy Lacy, an old man, described himself as an asthma, with the gravel and pains in his limbs. He speaks well and seems to have been in better circumstances. "Have you any daughter or anyone to attend you?" "I have a daughter but she's poorly herself and no assistance to me; she often comes to see me. I have a sister who goes about the country selling little things and from what she can earn she gives me a little, poor thing." "Wouldn't you go to the House of Industry?" "I wouldn't be let in there because I would be disturbing them with the cough." "Oh, that would be no objection. "Well, Sir, I'd go in there then."

14. A young girl, sick. No brother or father, mother out begging. They have a corner of a garret for charity from a poor woman who has two little children herself. "Would you like to go to the House of Industry." "No, Sir, unless my mother would be with me."

15. P. O'Sullivan, 56 years of age, a carpenter. A cripple for six years, his thighs broken. He could earn a pound a week when he was in work; his wife blind.

16. James Tobin, 79, a cotton weaver. "dead in his limbs." Confined four months; until seven or eight years ago he would earn 22/- or 25/- per week in his trade. His son, a better workman, can only earn 3/- now.

17. Michael Chilly, aged 21, a cripple which he has been since he was nine years of age. Became so from being neglected. He was in a garret where he is confined to his

bed but it attended by his mother. Is able to read and we found him with a book in his hand. He is supported altogether by charity.

The foregoing eye-witness accounts from a Parliamentary Report give a compelling impression of what the poet Grey called the "short and simple annals of the poor." Their recorded snatches of conversation convey an immensely strong feeling of family attachment and of trust in the goodness of their neighbours. The sense of patient endurance is no less obvious, with no strident calls for better things, and with a manifestly low level of expectation in the matter of material comfort. Obviously, too, they found strength from their religious belief and practice. Almost all shared a horror of the House of Industry or the Poor House, then situated on the area now occupied by the Victoria Hospital, and later on in what is now St. Finbarr's Hospital. Their personal dignity, even among the rags and straw, and the feeling of security from being among their neighbours, deterred them from the final severance of family ties which admission to the Poor House would bring. One of the woman voiced a fear that haunted the poor all through the last century, the fear of a pauper's grave. The Report also gave some general statistics for the city parishes of Cork, using the Church of Ireland parish boundaries as the bases of population. In Christ Church parish there were 1,251 distressed persons, of whom 400 were in extreme destitution; in St. Peter's parish there were 1,932 distressed persons, while St. Paul's had 462, St. Anne's had 5,189, and St. Finbarr's had 3,274 distressed persons and 1,858 described as destitute. In Picket's Lane in the latter parish there were 121 distressed persons living in 32 rooms. In house No. 19 in that lane there were 17 such persons in four rooms. In No. 12 there were 10 persons in three rooms; in No. 9 there were 16 persons in three rooms and of these sixteen there were fourteen with no bed of any sort. In the historic old Portney's Lane off the North Main Street, where the Spanish grandee Don Juan del Aquilla had been feasted after the Battle of Kinsale, there were 150 distressed persons living in 56 rooms. No. 3 had 21 such people in four rooms, No. 5 had 28 people in eight rooms of whom 14 had no beds. No. 17 had twenty distressed people in five rooms of whom 18 had no beds. In Roman Walk there were 314 distressed people in 94 rooms. These conditions of

1835 were to persist for many more decades, and, indeed, had only marginally improved by the early decades of this century. They were equally to be found in Dublin, Liverpool and London. No fairy godmother came to wipe the tears of the poor or to turn their rags to riches. It was only through the slow awakening of public consciousness and the pressure of social reformers that the community as a whole came to accept responsibility for its distressed brethren. That responsibility is now exercised by that instrument of community will which we call the State. Meanwhile a great and vital service was rendered by voluntary and religious organisations such as the Sick Poor Society and the St. Vincent de Paul Society and similar bodies inspired by the various churches. But it must be borne in mind that social reform did not figure as largely in public life in the nineteenth century as it has come to do in the present age; it was not a major issue in the political programme of O'Connell or of the Fenians or of Parnell. And even the emerging trade unions had to concentrate more on the basic right to be recognised and to secure acceptable rates of pay and hours of work.

It is not being entirely facetious to remark that any poor person in Cork who had his wits about him should have contrived to get himself arrested and put in goal. At least in 1817 he would have lived in comparative luxury in relation to those crowded into the garrets of the city lanes. Through the courtesy of the Deputy Keeper of the Public Record Office, Dublin, this writer has been furnished with a copy of the Rules and Regulation in Every Goal, House of Correction, Marshalsea, Bridewell, Penitentiary House, Sheriff's Prison and other Prisons throughout Ireland," together with "Observations on how these Rules are observed in the City Goal and Bridewell, Cork," dated 29th January, 1817 and signed by Boyle Davies, Inspector and Chaplain. It appears that meticulous care was taken in distributing regular rations of bread. The Rules state that "in all Prisons wherein any person shall be confined for any offence, the person or persons whose duty it shall be to deliver out bread or other Provisions to such Prisoners, or one of the said Persons together with the Keeper of the Prison, shall attend for that purpose four days a week, to wit, on Sundays, Mondays, Wednesdays and Fridays, and shall take care that the same is properly distributed according to the wants of the prisoners and that it is of good quality and proper weight, and that it is not more than twenty-four hours since any Bread which may be distributed has been baked. And such Person or Persons shall not suffer the Prisoners to commute the said allowance by receiving the value thereof in money, or in any other manner whatsover." Alongside this printed paragraph in the Rules is the handwritten observation of the Rev. Mr. Davies regarding procedures at Cork: "This Rule is strictly observed except in the last clause. The Prisoners sell their Bread for the support of their families as they are not allowed any other sustenance. Great care is taken that they shall not commute it for liquor. The allowance to each is 3/- per week. The convicts transmitted from other counties and cities I have been lately informed are allowed by the Governors for their maintenance 1/1 per day." So while the poor starved in their garrets the gentry in the Bridewell were protected by regulations from having to eat stale bread on four days in the week.

Apart from matters of diet the creature comforts otherwise provided looked like placing a prison cell in what the poor might well have regarded as the upper brackets of affluence. Rule six stated that "every room in every Prison in Ireland shall be daily scraped and swept, and shall be washed once in every week from the first day in April to the first day in October, and once in every month for the residue of the year, unless the contrary shall in any instance be expressly directed in writing by the Physician or Surgeon; and that three times at least in every year the inside of each of the Rooms, Cells, Halls, Passages and Places of every description in the Prison shall be whitewashed, once in the month of April, once in the month of July and once in the month of October. And that sufficient Prison Dresses, Bedsteads, Tickens for Beds and Blankets shall be supplied for such Prisoners as shall be in want thereof. And also that a constant fire shall be kept in the Common Halls of every Prison for ten hours every day from the first of October to the first day April, to wit, from the hour of ten in the morning to the hour of eight in the afternoon, and for five hours every day for the residue of the year, to wit, from the hour of twelve at noon to the hour of five in the afternoon respectively, and that every Prisoner shall be supplied with fresh straw once in every month."

Again the Rev. Mr. Davies made this observation: "This Rule is observed except in the last clause. Straw bedding has long been discontinued; canvas mattresses have been proved by experience to be much cleaner, much cheaper and more conducive to the health of the Prisoners." Those intrepid penal reformers, Elizabeth Fry and John Howard, would doubtless have been impressed by the slick sophistication of the sleeping arrangements at the Cork Bridewell, even if they fell short of the conditions endured by Daniel O'Connell when Sir Robert Peel had him detained in Richmond Prison, Dublin, during the Repeal Campaign in 1843. On that occasion the Governor gave over his residence and private garden to O'Connell, streams of visitors were invited in for dinner and a portrait painter came to record the Great Man undergoing his ordeal.

The Commissioners of Inquiry of 1835 whose Report has been so extensively quoted in regard to conditions in the North Parish in Cork, also held a session in the South Parish. Present were the Rev. Mr. John England, Catholic Curate; Mr. Edward Malony, Member of the Josephian Society; Very Rev. Theobald Mathew, Provincial of the Capuchian Franciscan Order; Rev. William O'Connor, Catholic Curate, Mr. Richard O'Kelly, member of the Josephian Society, and Robert R. Pearce, editor of the Cork Mercantile Chronicle. Unlike its detailed treatment of conditions in the North Parish the Report gives no indication of similar matter in the South Parish, but it compensated by sketching a most rivetting picture of the life and times of street beggars. Indeed, if a title were required for the following rather lengthy extract it might well be the "Anatomy of a Beggar." The Report stated that "the particular season of the year at which vagrancy most prevails is summer. From September, through the winter, the provision trade is more brisk, there is considerably increased circulation of money in Cork, a good deal of employment, and potatoes are cheap. Many of those whose wives and children beg through the spring months are in employment during the winter. They are chiefly women, scarcely ever an able-bodied man. Numbers of women having children are the wives of labourers who would be ashamed to beg themselves; some are widows and some never married; they are mostly infirm through age. It does not appear that any who during the week are able to earn a subsistence are seen begging on

Sunday. There is a much greater reluctance on the part of mechanics to allow their wives to beg than of labourers. (In 1835 a mechanic was any kind of skilled workman). The former being known as members of a body to each other they will almost perish rather than let them beg. Those labourers who go for work to England are never seen to beg their way here. The majority of vagrants are produced by the death of the husband or by his being out of work. The greater part of street beggars have grown up so; there are none who choose this way of life though they may prefer remaining beggars after they have commenced it. In some cases they are driven to it with feelings of the deepest shame and sorrow. The regular beggar-woman obtains about 3/- per week. There is a class, however, who sit in the street and beg from passers-by who get an average of 4d. per day. Many of those who go about obtain fragments of food and halfpence to the amount of between 3/- and 4/- per week.

Vagrants sometimes pretend to be cripples and usually encourage a miserable appearance in order to excite sympathy, but are scarcely ever known to produce sores on their bodies for that purpose. They sometimes have recourse to surreptitiously obtained recommendations. Witness remembers one instance of a child representing himself as an orphan coming to a shop-keeper three or four times successively. At length he was detained and threatened with punishment and in a short time his father and mother made their appearance. He said that these expedients are not at all uncommon but knows of no instance of their refusing to have sores cured, or to have the deaf and dumb and crippled children taken to the asylum for fear of diminishing their excitement to sympathy. The children of beggars frequently grow up thieves and pickpockets; they begin with stealing coal, potatoes and straw from carts and become gradually hardened. Beggars are extremely charitable to each other."

The evidence from the North Parish indicates the extreme reluctance of the poor to exchange the precariousness of the garret for the relative security of the Workhouse. One of the reasons given by the Report reveals a very human trait: "the reasons for their reluctance are that they do not like the confinement nor the diet. Outside they occasionally get bits of meat. The women are very fond of tea, they sometimes remain till the middle of the day without food for the purpose of collecting a few halfpence for tea. In the House of Industry they get but potatoes and porridge." But apart from the charitable activities of the Sick Poor Society, and the St. Vincent de Paul Society which was to be founded in the city in 1846, what other provision was made to bring relief to the sick, the poor and the beggars? The Report of 1835 was quite comprehensive in its survey of need and assistance and it stated that "the medical institutions at Cork are the North and South Charitable Infirmaries, the House of Recovery or Fever Hospital, the hospital to the House of Industry, the Dispensary and the Lunatic Asylum." This list of establishments might well have given the impression that the sick poor of the city were amply provided for, but the Report stated "that the fact was far otherwise. When it is stated that there are but sixteen beds in the aggregate for the reception of medical cases, and less than three times that number for surgical cases and casualties of all sorts, it is plain that with such very limited means but little can be done for the alleviation and cure of disease in a city with a population of more than 100,000. This very defective provision in point of intern accommodation in the two infirmaries has contributed to the extension of pauperism in a very remarkable degree. It has become the common expedient of the poor, in the absence of all other means, to apply as paupers to the House of Industry where they are no sooner received than they complain of being ill, and so contrive to get passed into the hospital belonging to it. Here, however, when once admitted they are sure of being well attended to." The reader will note the discrepancy between this statement and the earlier evidence showing an extreme reluctance to have anything to do with the House of Industry. One explanation may be conjectured; the sick poor in the North Parish were unable as well as unwilling to leave their rooms, whereas the poor here alleged to be almost flocking to the House of Industry were not so confined and were using their wits and their limbs to better themselves. The quality of the medical service rendered to the poor was, in the opinion of the examining Commissioner W. P. Barrett, M.D., entirely satisfactory. He stated that "nothing could surpass the neatness and order conspicuous throughout, or the attention paid by the medical officers to the cases committed to their care and skill." This judgment related to the House of Industry; a similar tribute was paid the medical gentlemen of the North and South Infirmaries: "it is only just to state that they discharged their duties with ability and zeal, receiving little or no compensation for their arduous services."

With the passion for thoroughness which characterised the nineteenth century Parliamentary Papers, the following estimate of the cost of maintaining a hospital of 140 beds for one year was included; it is given here not only as a commentary on 1835 but as showing the contrast with the conditions of the present:

140 Patients, diet 5d per day, or 7.12.1 a year	£1064.11.8
1 Porter and 4 Nurses at £20 each; 6 assistants at £15 each	190. 0.0
Resident Apothecary, £80; Steward £65; Matron £50	195. 0.0
Medicines £100, Coals (100 tons) £75	175. 0.0
Soap, Candles, £50; Wine, Grocery £50	100. 0.0
	£1724.11.8
Incidental Expenses	£75. 8.4
Total	£1,800. 0.0

The South Infirmary was characterised by "the praiseworthy manner in which it is at present conducted" and especially commended was the administration of its funds. There had been suggestions to unite the funds of both Infirmaries to support the new premises of the North Infirmary, but "who can doubt that the two Infirmaries are indispensable? Reckoning 60 Beds to the South Infirmary and 140 to the North, what are 200 Beds among a population exceeding 100,000 for medical and surgical cases and casualties of all sorts, omitting fever cases which are sent to the House of Recovery? In so large and opulent a city considerable aid ought to be derived from private contribution. The feelings of humanity and a due and enlightened sense of what is owing to society must ensure the accomplishment of so useful an object." This last sentence, inspired as it is by a compassion for the poor and a call to the wealthy to support their weaker brethren, must put a large question mark over many of the simplistic assumptions regarding early nineteenth century social attitudes. Many published works give the impression of a hard, unfeeling attitude to poverty; that such existed was certainly true, but to represent it as the whole truth is to violence to the social concern proclaimed in the passage just quoted. Nothing is more dangerous in history than using a hard fact to support a soft judgment. In a general comment on the two Infirmaries and the Dispensary the Report unearthed a practice which demonstrated that if the Cork poor were weak in body they certainly had not lost their wits: they had the habit of attending all three institutions, "taking the physic given at each upon the calculation that if one be good, three must be better." The Cork Lunatic Asylum was described as "intended for the protection and treatment of the destitute idiots and insane of the city and county of Cork, who are received upon the certificate of two magistrates." The Report observed that a "medical certificate is not required which appears to be a great omission." Because of the size of the county and city, and the indiscriminate admission "of all classes of the insane, the pressure of cases is always heavy and the number constantly accumulating in the house, for which there is no vent but death. No less than 40 of the inmates were huddled together every night into one apartment, littered down with straw, a practice which had led to the most disgusting consequences. In the yards, too, by day it was almost impossible to preserve order and quiet in such a promiscuous assemblage of persons in every stage and variety of lunacy. Neither was the want of proper separation the chief evil; for although it cannot be denied that occupation of some kind or other is of the very first importance in the successful treatment of insanity, yet the lunatics were left in general with little or nothing to do which could serve to engage their attention. Some sat moping about the day-rooms or in the corners, disgusting, drivelling objects who had survived the loss of every sense. But the greater part collected in the open yards were mere idle spectators of the follies and ravings which were being enacted before them by chattering, grinning idiots, or their more turbulent and contumacious bretheren who, although harmless from being confined in strait waistcoats, would still be threatening and vociferating."

Yet despite those lamentable conditions great improvements were being carried out by the then physician; "through his exertions additional wards have been built and a hospital for invalids was being erected at the time of my visit. A kind of fourfold distribution of the patients had also been effected and other judicious regulations introduced for their better management and treatment. The Keepers had been doubled in each yard and ward, by which excitement was abated and confinement and personal restraint dispensed with in many cases. At the same time female delicacy was respected and preserved by the exclusion of male Keepers from the female wards. Something, too, had been done with the view of finding employment for the lunatic patients. The cooking, washing and the needle-work which used to be attended to in the House of Industry are now performed in the Asylum, with painting, gardening, scouring and cleaning, and the patients are in some cases induced to work by promising them a small gratuity to be laid out in clothes or hoarded for them for the season of their discharge to supply them with the means of returning to the distant parts of the extensive county. In addition it may be stated that the greatest possible cleanliness was observable in the cells, wards and yards, and indeed in every part of the establishment." The salary of the Physician was £171 per annum, and some idea of his success lay in the fact that though the annual average of admissions exceeded one hundred, yet those cured or so relieved as to be removed by friends amounted to two-thirds, while only one fifth died in the Asylum. This stark outline of life in the Lunatic Asylum has its own pathos, but it also indicates a real awareness of something very much to the fore in modern mental treatment, namely the value of occupational therapy and the incentment to rehabilitation offered by work and personal savings. The Asylum was situated alongside the House of Industry on the site now occupied by St. Monica's Home for the Blind; with the building of the large new premises on the Lee Road in 1846, under the direction of the government, a better chapter was opened in the care of the mentally ill in Cork.

Going to the Dispensary for medicine and coming under the care of the Dispensary doctor was an integral part of the life of the poor of Cork and of Ireland generally not only throughout the nineteenth century but until as recently as a decade ago. The Report gives a fairly full picture of the Cork General Dispensary. The building was "three stories high; it has a very good and convenient room for dispensing medicines but a very bad one for the Physicians to prescribe in. There is a waiting place which is a long, cold hall, subject to a current of cold air; there is scarcely any furniture belonging to the institution, that in use is the property of the apothecary. There is an abundant supply of pure water and the sewers are tolerably good. There are no baths but there is a small garden and plot of ground attached. The medical officers who attend principally are a licentiate of the King's and Queen's College of Physicians, Dublin, four physicians possessing Degrees from Edinburgh University, a member of the College of Surgeons of London, and a graduate of the University of Glasgow. The medical officers are elected by the subscribers." Patients who felt the officers "to be harsh or to neglect their patients" could complain to a subscriber. The medicine was reported by the physicians present "to be of good quality and always in sufficient quantity; also the more expensive kinds as quinine and morphia. The medicines are supplied by Messrs. Harrington, wholesale druggists, who are subscribers to the institution of a guinea per annum." In addition to medicines there were various appliances available; " a stomach pump, suspended animation apparatus, electrifying machines, cupping apparatus; and the apparatus seem to be sufficient for all medical purposes required. Leeches are not supplied, they are found to be too expensive." In 1833 there had been 12,060 patients under the care of the Dispensary and on the visit of the Assistant Poor Law Commissioner in 1835 there were 419 patients, of whom one half were visited at home. Midwifery cases were not attended to. Who were entitled to relief? "There can be no difficulty in a poor person getting relief, because if not known to a subscriber they will be told at the institution where to get an order, and if the case is urgent it is always attended to under all circumstances." The sick poor attended daily, but if unable to do so they were seen at their homes, "if several visits were necessary in one day they would be paid."

The medical officers reported that cases of small-pox were few, which they attributed "to the preservation value of vaccination." The income of this charity was derived from Grand Jury presentments, subscriptions, donations and bequests. "None of the poorer classes subscribe." The Dispensary was established to "provide medicine and medical attention for the sick poor of the city, and it is now made to include the suburbs and approaches to the town as far as the lamps and paving may extend." The area was divided into districts, each with an appointed physician, and they "were obliged to visit in every case and to continue attendance upon the patients at their residences if the illness be such as to prevent personal application at the Dispensary." This entailed labour and loss of time on the physicians for "they receive no adequate remuneration, and two are not paid at all, while it is admitted that they have discharged their duties with much credit to themselves, and the Roman Catholic curate who has been seven years aiding the poor never heard any complaints against them." Yet the Assistant Commissioner was not entirely satisfied with the management of the Dispensary and he concluded with the following overall assessment: "this institution is effecting great good and affording most material relief to the numerous poor who get recommended to it, and we cannot but lament that a charity so deserving of public patronage is not more liberally supported or better managed."

This outline of the pattern of poverty in Cork reveals a situation that had a broad parallel in all the other cities of Ireland and Britain in 1835 and for many decades subsequently. A new dimension in destitution was to be reached in 1846 when the shadow of Famine fell across the city bringing disease to the poor and an influx of destitute people from the surrounding countryside. In trying to draw some general conclusions about society and the problem of poverty in the first half of the nineteenth century the first necessity must be to view things in the context of the times. That age was only beginning to grope towards a realisation of the magnitude of the problems of poverty, bad sanitation and inadequate medical treatment. Indeed, part of that groping was the collection of information from the Parliamentary Inquiries such as the one from which this chapter has been constructed. The very fact that such inquiries were set on foot indicates very clearly a growing awareness of the problems. But awareness did not automatically mean a solution, and it took a great amount of poor law and public health legislation to bring about change. This programme of legislation was inevitably piece-meal; it involved overcoming the resistance of vested interests, the creation of a climate of public opinion willing to spend money on public welfare, the prodding of local corporations into the necessity of tackling the inadequacies of slum living, the mollification of irate rate payers, the realisation that malnutrition and bad sanitation led to general disease as well as causing personal distress to their victims.

Certain fairly ingrained prejudices had to be overcome; among the wealthier classes there was sometimes found the old attitude that somehow poverty was the result of culpable indolence and a lack of effort on the part of the poor; there was also the conviction, voiced by both Catholic and Protestant spokesmen on social questions, that the poor had their place in society assigned to them by Providence. This was not used as a pretext to do nothing to assist them, quite the contrary, but it reflected the notion of a society with different and settled social orders. Yet, despite these ideas held in whole or in part by various sections of the community, there was a very wide circle of religious and voluntary effort to bring relief to those in distress, involving hospitals, asylums, homes for destitute men and women, poor schools for children, and societies to provide clothing and coal in winter time. In a sense throughout the nineteenth century society was only learning to recognise and come to grips with human distress in the cities; it was left to the present century to fashion a code of legislation and effective provision that gives support from the cradle to the grave. The era of the State as the main instrument in social welfare was chiefly advanced by the Budget of Lloyd George in 1906 when, amid a chorus of abuse, he introduced the old age pension. Charles Dickens had highlighted many problems when he wrote in 1854 that "they never will save their children from the dreadful and unnatural mortality now prevalent among them, or save themselves from untimely sickness and death, until they have pure water in unlimited quantity, wholesome air, and constraint upon little landlords to keep their property decent under the heaviest penalties."

FATHER MATHEW—SOCIAL WORK, TEMPERANCE

AND FAMINE

Chapter VII

Compared with other cities Cork is relatively impoverished in the matter of public monuments, yet there is a sense in which all Cork begins and ends with the Statue. For many generations it has been a meeting point for old friends and young sweethearts; it was from it that the trams rumbled off to carry excited children to Tivoli and Blackrock, while today people catch a bus at the Statue to go home to the multitude of new suburbs that mark the growth and prosperity of the city. It is at once a landmark and something of an open-air parlour for Cork. This affectionate regard of the citizens of today simply reflects the love and esteem in which the man it commemorates was held in his own lifetime, for Father Mathew was part of the folk tradition of the nineteenth century Cork. As the Apostle of Temperance his name was known and honoured throughout Ireland and across Britain and America; apart from his religious standing as a priest he was regarded in public life as an important social reformer, consulted and listened to by Government departments and public bodies, and sought after by many of the writers on Irish life who came from abroad to understand and explain the great issues of the times. He was the friend of Daniel O'Connell, and his Temperance Movement was regarded as a major factor in creating the sense of discipline and social cohesion which underpinned the Liberator's mass movement. Perhaps it was the heartbreaking tragedy of the Famine that revealed the full range of Father Mathew's compassion and his practical ability as an organiser, qualities which won the attention and respect of the highest Government officials in Dublin and London. The people of Cork were well aware of his greater role on the stage of Irish public life; they respected him as a national figure, but it was as the genial friar from the little chapel in Blackamoor Lane that they loved him. His affability, his simple dignity, his care for the poor and for the children of the poor, won for him a special place in the hearts of the citizens. But he was a man for all classes and for all creeds, a genial and cultivated man who loved to talk and make friends, and in time the modest friary tucked away in the lane behind Sullivan's

Quay became a meeting-place for a wide variety of people. Father Mathew was catholic in his friendships and they included Quakers, Dissenters and Church of Ireland clergymen as well as those of his own persuasion. Indeed, it was that ebullient Dissenter from the Old Presbyterian Church in Princes Street, Richard Dowden, who was treasurer for the fund to erect the Statue.

How did he appear to his contemporaries? One rather full first-hand picture comes from the novelist, Thackeray, the film of whose book, "Barry Lyndon," many readers may have enjoyed. In August, 1842 he had arrived in Patrick Street by stage-coach from Fermoy to attend a meeting and dinner of the Irish Agricultural Society at the Imperial Hotel. This, together with his impressions of the city generally, he describes in his book "The Paris and Irish Sketch Book" with the following passage on Father Mathew: "On the day we arrived in Cork, and as the passengers descended from the drag, a stout, handsome, honest-looking man of some forty years was passing by and received a number of bows from the crowd around. It was Father Mathew, with whose face a thousand litte print-shop windows had already rendered me familiar. He shook hands with the master of the carriage very cordially, and just as cordially with the master's coachman, a disciple of Temperance as at least half Ireland is at present. The day after the famous dinner at MacDowall's (Imperial Hotel) some of us came down rather late, perhaps in consequence of the events of the night before and there was the Apostle of Temperance seated at the table drinking tea. Some of us felt a little ashamed of ourselves and did not like to ask somehow for the soda-water in such an awful presence as that. Besides, it would have been a confession to a Catholic priest and, as a Protestant, I am above it.

The world likes to know how a great man appears even to a valet-de-chambre, and I suppose it is one's vanity that is flattered in such rare company to find the great man quite as unassuming as the very smallest personage present; and so like to other mortals that we would not know him to be a great man at all did we not know his name and what he had done. There is nothing remarkable in Mr. Mathew's manner, except that it is exceedingly simple, hearty and manly and that he does not wear the demure, downcast look which, I know not why, certainly characterises the chief part of the gentlemen of his profession. He is almost the only man, too, that I have met in Ireland who, in speaking of public matters, does not talk as a partisan. With the state of the country, of landlord, tenant and peasantry, he seemed to be most curiously and intimately acquainted; speaking of their wants, differences and the means of bettering them with the minutest practical knowledge. His knowledge of the people is prodigious and their confidence in him as great; and what a touching attachment that is which these poor fellows show to anyone who has their cause at heart—even to anyone who says he has.

Avoiding all political questions, no man seems more eager that he for the practical improvement of this country. Leases and rents, farming improvements, reading societies, music-societies—he was full of these and of his schemes of temperance above all. He never misses a chance of making a convert, and has his hand ready and a pledge in his pocket for sick or poor. One of his disciples in a livery-coat came into the room with a tray; Mr. Mathew recognised him and shook him by the hand directly; so he did with the strangers who were presented to him; and not with a courtly popularity-hunting air, but as it seemed, from sheer hearty kindness and a desire to do everyone good. When breakfast was done—he took but one cup of tea, and says that, from having been a great consumer of tea and refreshing liquids before, a small cup of tea and one glass of water at dinner now serve him for his day's beverage—he took the ladies of our party to see his burying-ground, a new and handsome cemetery lying a little way out of town, and where, thank God, Protestants and Catholics may lie together without clergymen quarrelling over their coffins." To be taken to admire a cemetery immediately after breakfast would not be everyone's idea of a picnic, but in purchasing the former Botanic Gardens of the Royal Cork Institution and turning them into a cemetery where Catholics could be buried with the full rites of their religion, Father Mathew especially endeared himself to the great majority of his fellow-citizens. Therein he lies in the spot chosen by himself and until recent times the place was known as the "Gardens," or more affectionately as Father Mathew's Cemetery. For some reason or other it was later thought fit to give it a more exalted patronage.

Theobald Mathew was born on 10th October, 1790, at the mansion of Thomastown House five miles west of Cashel. The mansion was owned by an ancient and wealthy branch of the Mathew family, but it was as an orphan that Theobald's father, James, was taken in and reared there. Here, too, he first settled with his young bride of sixteen years, Anne Whyte of Cappawhyte. There were to be twelve children in the family and in due course Theobald's parents were provided by the lord of the mansion with a commodious dwelling and a comfortable farm on the estates of Thomastown. The boy grew to be remarkably kind and gentle by nature and from the outset showed a great compassion for the many beggars who came to his father's home. When he was sent to school in Kilkenny he was a favourite with teachers and pupils alike, as much for his ready humour as for his attractive personality. He was a diligent rather than a brilliant pupil. He took the first steps to achieve an early ambition when in September 1807, he entered Maynooth to study for the priesthood. Within a year he had left, having incurred the disapproval of the authorities due to the fact that he had been dicovered giving a party in his room to some of his classmates. Still determined to pursue his vocation he entered the Capuchin Franciscan Order in Dublin where on Easter Saturday, 1814, he was ordained by the distinguished Archbishop, Dr. Murray. So it was that as Father Mathew he returned to the scene of his schooldays when he was assigned to the small Friary in Kilkenny. His biographer, John F. Maguire, describes those early days: "The fame of the young friar spread rapidly and his virtues were the theme of every tongue. His personal appearance was of itself sufficient to excite interest, and his manner harmonised with his outward form. In the first bloom and freshness of early manhood, graceful and elegant in his figure and carriage, with a countenance of singular beauty of expression, winning of speech, polished of address, modest and unobtrusive—the youthful priest was calculated to create the most favourable impression."

Father Mathew was already gaining notice as a preacher, even though his voice at that stage was somewhat thin and shrieking. But it was as a confessor that he drew large crowds to his "box." Indeed, it was this feature of his ministry that led to an episode which resulted in his coming to Cork. There was a certain tension between the secular clergy and the religious orders not only in Kilkenny but in many other parts of Ireland regarding what would nowadays be called lines of demarcation in the administration of the sacraments. The local bishop evidently felt that Father Mathew was trespassing beyond his sphere when on one Saturday evening he sent one of his priests with an urgent note for him as he ministered in the confessional. The young friar forthwith left his queue of penitents, declaring that he no longer had the necessary faculties. The bishop, Dr. Marum, later regretted his action but Father Mathew determined to leave Kilkenny for Cork shortly after that episode in 1814.

The Capuchin Friary in Blackamoor Lane behind Sullivan's Quay was certainly a humble place for the worship of God and the abode of its two friars. It had been erected by Father Mathew's predecessor, Father Arthur O'Leary, who had won considerable public distinction as a controversial writer on religious and other current issues. In particular he addressed himself to the question of religious toleration for his Catholic countrymen, achieving wide publicity in Ireland and England with his "Essay on Toleration, or Mr. O'Leary's Plea for Liberty of Conscience." His efforts were commended in the Irish House of Commons in 1782 during the debate on the Catholic Relief Bill when Henry Grattan spoke of him as "poor in everything but genuius and philosophy." Those words in an all-Protestant assembly reflected the wide range of friendship and respect which Father O'Leary had gathered not only because of his pen but also by his tireless labours among the poor of Cork. Among his Protestant friends in the city was a Mr. Joseph Bennet, a well-known lawyer, who frequently came to the little chapel in the lane to hear him preach. On one St. Patrick's Day the friar and the lawyer dined together after Mass; Mr. Bennet complimented the priest on a fine sermon on the National Patron and enquired how much the good Saint had sent him for his eloquence. "There's the box on the chair near you," said Father O'Leary, "turn it up and count it." On doing so his friend exclaimed in disgust, "Eighteen pence half-penny." The incident illustrates the reality of poverty. Father O'Leary left Cork for London in 1789 to work among the Irish emigrants at St. Patrick's Chapel, Soho Square, where present-day visitors may see a plaque to his memory.

When Father Mathew came to Blackamoor Lane his companion and superior was Father Daniel Francis Donovan who had brought the echoes of a wider world to the confined Chapel. Educated in France he had been the chaplain to a nobleman before the outbreak of the French Revolution; with the coming of the Reign of Terror his patron fled to England leaving the priest in Paris. Father Donovan was duly brought before one of the tribunals of the people and condemned to the guillotine, his calling and position in life being considered an affront to the sacred principles of republican liberty. He spent the night before his execution giving the rites of religion to his fellow victims and on the following morning was placed in the rude cart and dragged through the streets of Paris to the chorus and the spittle of the incensed rabble. He was just about to climb the grisly steps to his doom when suddenly an officer rode up and cried out in English: "are there any Irish among you?" Half choking with fright and excitement Father Donovan shouted, "Yes, there are seven of us." For the remainder of his life he wanted especially to comfort prisoners condemned to death and so on his return to Cork he became Catholic chaplain to the County Gaol. He often retold the grim tale of his days in Paris, garnishing it with his customary wit—"though my pate is nothing of beauty I would have felt mighty awkard without it."

It was among such men and such memories that Father Mathew began his ministry in Cork. As in Kilkenny he became particularly popular as a confessor and his biographer captures rather vividly the peculiar flavour of one brand of his penitents, the lamplighters of Cork:" "so soon as Father Mathew's fame spread abroad the lamplighters turned to his confessional, and these poor fellows whose clothes literally reeked with fish oil in every stage of decomposition, though most edifying and excellent Christians, were about the least savoury of human beings. At first these highly-flavoured penitents were almost too much for the jaded stomach of the young priest to endure, but he never in any way manifested the slightest repugnance to their close neighbourhood and ere long it became to him a matter of indifference." His first public enterprise was to open a school in Blackamoor Lane where poor children were taught the rudiments of reading, writing and arithmetic as well as industrial crafts. By 1824 there were

500 girls attending, with 200 older girls in the upper loft engaged in knitting and needlework in addition to their ordinary lessons. In this way they were able to add something to the meagre family income. Evening classes for working boys brought more life to the Lane. He formed a number of societies of middle class young ladies and men and these helped in teaching catechism and reading, as well as in visiting the poor and the sick in their homes. A particular object of his discreet care were those persons whom life had reduced from better days but who were yet ashamed to come openly for charity. One early shadow fell across his path in the death of his younger brother, Robert, in 1824. By then he had moved from the Friary to live in a rented house in Cove Street; the house stood until a few years ago with a plaque denoting its earlier distinguished occupant but has since been flattened to the ground by the Corporation in the great cause of parking cars. Robert was in his early teens when his parents died and his brother brought him to live in Cork. The young lad was anxious to join another brother, Charles, who went to sea on the African trade. Reluctantly, Father Mathew consented. But when the ship returned to Cork it did not bring the boy; he had died of sunstroke. Father Mathew took many years to recover from his grief and he erected in his cemetery a headstone inscribed as follows: "Sacred to the Memory of Robert Mathew, who died in the Bight of Benim, May 27th 1824, aged 16 years."

Meanwhile his qualities as a preacher not only drew large congregations to the little Friary but led to frequent requests for charity sermons in other churches. In Cork as in other cities in Ireland such sermons were a most necessary source of income for the work of maintaining schools and orphanages for the poor and for the building of churches. His biographer has left a portrait of his manner as a preacher: "it was utterly divested of religious or, more correctly speaking, sectarian bitterness. He was not a controversialist. He was not a deeply read theologian and with canon law he was imperfectly acquainted. Few men, however, were better Biblical scholars than Father Mathew. With the Sacred Scriptures he was intimately and profoundly acquainted."

It was in 1830 that he obtained the lease of the former Botanic Gardens from the Royal Cork Institution in order to provide a cemetery where the poor could be buried without undue expense and where the full rites of the Catholic Church could be performed. Hitherto only the burial grounds of the various churches of the Established Church in the city were available and there were occasional episodes involving religious bitterness when Catholic priests sought to exercise their ministry in them. By a sad irony the new cemetery was to be put in full use in 1832 when the city was struck by a virulent epidemic of cholera. Recalling that calamity Archdeacon O'Shea wrote in 1863 of Father Mathew's work in the parish of Ss. Peter and Paul's, of which he was then parish priest: "Amongst those who at that awful period took a conspicuous part not only in unwearied attendance by the bedside of the plague-stricken sufferers, but also in suggesting and practically carrying out sanitary and remedial measures for the relief of the sick in private houses and in the public hospitals, Father Mathew was ever foremost and always indefatigable—the centre and focus of the disease being a block of narrow and ill-ventilated streets and lanes in the immediate neighbourhood of my residence." Tending the sick and burying the dead were not the only tasks on hand; there were widows to be provided for, and orphans to be fed and clothed and sent to school and to work.

In providing for the young people who came to the Chapel and the day and night schools at Blackamoor Lane Father Mathew displayed that rare gift in an adult, to be able to see life through the eyes of the young, to enter into their simplicity and exuberance while leading them into the ways of maturity. Maguire paints this picture of simple tastes and healthy fun: "He knew that apples and oranges and nuts, cakes and sweet things, including toffee and bulls eyes, were to them the summun bonum of earthly felicity; and that these with an out-of-door holiday when they could run and shout and tumble and play all manner of wild pranks, were in their esteem preferable to all the fine clothes in the world. Accordingly, he made a reputation for himself with the young people of the city as a holiday-getter as well as a feast-giver." In appreciating all this work with the sick, the poor and the schools it must be borne in mind that the age differed radically from that of today. The State either in Ireland or Britain made no provision for any assistance to the sick, the unemployed or the poor; neither did it provide for compulsory schooling at any age. There were, therefore, whole fields of human concern which depended solely on the initiative and generosity of individuals and the corporate efforts of religious charitable bodies. The chapter on the sick, the poor and the beggars deals with that matter more fully, suffice to say that the State as the fairy godmother made her debut only in this century.

It was in 1838 that Father Mathew turned his hand to the movement that was to win for him the title of Apostle of Temperance. Himself a man of convivial instincts, fond of entertaining friends at his humble home in Cove Street where he always had a bottle of brandy in the cupboard, he was persuaded to espouse the cause of temperance not with the harsh rectitude of the puritan but with a deep compassion for a prevailing social evil. It was as a governor of the House of Industry, later the Workhouse, that he saw the end product of excessive drinking. Also on the board of governors with him was a friend who greatly influenced his decision to establish his movement, the Quaker shopkeeper, William Martin. A frequent visitor to the priest's house, he had for many years sought to interest him in the temperance question. Two other friends from outside his own religious persuasion had also tried to enlist his support, the Rev. Nicholas Dunscombe, a Church of Ireland clergyman, and Richard Dowden, treasurer of the Old Presbyterian Church in Princes Street, partner in the Brown Street firm of Messrs. Jennings mineral water manufacturers, wit, botanist, promoter of cultural societies, and Mayor of Cork. It was from this diverse quartet of a friar, a Quaker, a Protestant and a Dissenter that the Temperance Movement was born. The event took place on the 10th April, 1838, in the schoolroom at Blackamoor Lane when Father Mathew approached the table and in a loud voice said, "Here goes in the name of God." Before the small meeting he then signed the register as follows: "Revd. Theobald Mathew, C.C., Cove Street, No. 1." It was to be a momentous moment in his own life and a significant one in the religious and social life of Ireland. It was to bring him to England, to Scotland, to America; it was to enshrine his name among the great social reformers of the nineteenth century.

By January, 1839 there were 200,000 names on the roll of the Temperance Society, drawn not only from Cork but from the surrounding counties of Kerry, Waterford, Limerick, Clare, Tipperary and further afield. The newspapers in Ireland and Britain began to carry reports of the progress of the movement. Father Mathew had become a public personality and the object of widespread esteem and affection. Despite the lack of railways and the tedium of travel by foot and stage coach, great crowds began to converge on the little schoolroom in Blackamoor Lane and on the house in Cove Street just to see Father Mathew and to receive the pledge from his hands. The propagation of temperance was to involve much travel outside of Cork, with the first invitation coming from the bishop of Limerick in December, 1839. The scene was described by a local priest: "So great was the rush of the temperance postulants that the iron railing opposite the house of Mr. Dunbar, the Rev. gentleman's brother-in-law, in which he had stopped, carried away and a number of persons were precipitated into the Shannon. Fortunately, they were all picked up." In four days 150,000 people had signed the pledge. In reflecting on these high figures it must be kept in mind that the country's population was then at the eight million mark before the onset of the disastrous Famine. In that same month Father Mathew went to Waterford where the story of success was repeated with 80,000 new disciples. On a visit to Maynooth College he stayed as the guest of the Duke of Leinster; tributes were paid to his work in the House of Lords, while the diminution of court cases at Cork and the testimony of employers regarding the punctuality and reliability of workers gave solid evidence of the social benefits of the temperance movement.

A pen picture from the Russian travel writer, Kohl, shows Father Mathew about the year 1840: "He is not tall, he is about the same height and figure as Napoleon, well built and well proportioned. He has nothing of the meagre, haggard Franciscan monk about him. His movements and address are simple and unaffected, and altogether he has something about him that wins for him the goodwill of those he addresses." At the same period Mr. C. S. Hall, then noted as a social commentator, said "no man has borne his honours more meekly, encountered opposition with greater gentleness or forebearance, or disarmed hostility by weapons better suited to a Christian."

In 1841 he had a most successful tour of Ulster, despite the misgivings of his friends on the possible reaction to a Catholic priest. He glowingly referred to his reception as follows: "From the time I went into Ulster to my return to Drogheda I have received the greatest kindness at the hands of all persons and parties. At Clones there were two Orange flags raised there when I visited it and, instead of an insult, I thought this a very great compliment never having one or being honoured with one before, and when I saw them I called for three cheers for the Orange flag, and the Catholics and Protestants became the greatest friends from that day forward. I could have apprehended nothing save goodwill and kindly feeling from one end of Ulster to the other, and this was amply demonstrated by my visits to Lurgan, Lisburn, Belfast, Downpatrick, Derry and other places. The 'Prentice Boys' of Derry showed me the greatest kindness. Thousands of them came out to Moira from Belfast and other places, and actually detained me three days longer than I intended to have stayed."

But the march of temperance led to a decline in the fortunes of the distillers and brewers and to loss of revenue to the Government. Maguire gives the following figures to show the rapid decline in spirits: in 1839 duty was paid on 12,296,000 gallons, whereas by 1844 the figure was reduced to 5,546,483 gallons. Not everyone was amused and in 1843 a member of Father Mathew's own family engaged in the distillery trade in Cashel wrote that "every teetotaller has gained morally and physically by the movement, but my immediate family have been absolutely and totally ruined by Father Mathew's mission." Yet the lady novelist, Maria Edgeworth, saw him as "the greatest benefactor to his country, the most true friend to Irishmen and to Ireland." Though he was scrupulous in his desire to keep the movement free from involvement in politics he had the support and friendship of the great tribune of the people, Daniel O'Connell. Indeed, it was generally acknowledged that the superb discipline which O'Connell imposed on the great mass meetings of the Repeal Campaign owed an enormous debt to the temperance cause. It was, however, with some trepidation that Father Mathew heard that O'Connell, then Lord Mayor of Dublin, was to join the mass temperance demonstration in Cork on Easter Monday, 1842. The "Cork

Examiner" described the event: "Long before the time for starting, the vast area of the Corn Market (behind present City Hall) was densely crowded with various societies, each headed by its band of twenty or thirty musicians, the members dressed with scarfs, blue, pink or green, of Irish manufacture. At the hour of eleven the procession began to move slowly from the Corn Market over Anglesea Bridge, down the South Mall, along the Parade and up Great George Street, the Western Road and so through the route settled some weeks previously. When it had proceeded as far as the County Club it was met by the Lord Mayor of Dublin who came to join Father Mathew. Who could tell of the wild joyous shout that rent the very air as the two great men of Ireland, the political and moral emancipators of her people, met together. In a short time after, our own Mayor, Thomas Lyons, accompanied by several respectable gentlemen and merchants joined the procession."

On his return from a successful visit to Glasgow Father Mathew was the guest at a memorable evening organised to do him honour by Mr. Purcell, the stage coach proprietor, and held in the Theatre Royal, Dublin, on 26th January, 1843. It is simply to indicate the extent of the support the friar had that it may be mentioned that the patrons for the event included two dukes, four marquises, nineteen earls, ten vicounts, four Catholic bishops, thirty M.P.s, and a great number of clergy of all denominations. The chair was taken by the Duke of Leinster, ever active in promoting the welfare of Ireland, and among the speakers were Daniel O'Connell, William Smith O'Brien, M.P., and Thomas Wyse, M.P., then well-known as a promoter of popular education in Ireland. In June, 1843, Father Mathew accepted an invitation to address meetings in England where he was warmly received in Liverpool, Manchester, Salford, Huddersfield, Leeds and York. He then went to London where he spent several weeks working among the Irish poor; his English tour brought an estimated 600,000 people to take the pledge. One memory of it Father Mathew preserved until his death, a letter from the Protestant bishop of Norwich offering him the hospitality of his palace. In introducing the priest to a crowded hall the bishop said, "Men of Norwich, citizens of this ancient city, I appeal to you to receive this wanderer on a sacred mission from a distant country, receive him and give him a Christian welcome, for he has come on a Christian mission."

It was to celebrate his return from this highly successful English mission that his friend, Mr. William O'Connor a Cork merchant tailor, erected the picturesque Mathew Tower on the Glanmire hill opposite Blackrock Castle, with the foundation stone being laid on 30th October, 1843. The completed Tower became a well-known landmark, with its ornamental fountain and a statue of Father Mathew. Regrettably, even in that lovely and remote setting the hand of the vandal has left its ugly imprint and today the smashed fountain and the broken statue reflect poorly on the taste and appreciation of elements in the community.

It was in the autumn of 1845 that the shadow of the Famine first fell across the country. The dreadful scourge of blight had affected the late potato crop, then the staple diet of the majority of Irelands eight million people. To an extent altogether unimaginable to our modern age the failure of the crop in 1845, and again in 1846, created a disaster of massive proportions and of lasting extent. It was the dreadful end of one era and the awesome beginning of another; hunderds of thousands were to die of starvation and fever in mud cabins, in country lanes and in workhouse wards; death and despair stalked the land; the calamity of nature was compounded by the bewilderment of the authorities at national and local level. Those with the enterprise and even some meagre funds began to flee the country at first in their thousands and then in their tens of thousands, to seek food and work in the garrets of Liverpool, New York and Boston. Stricken by death at home and emigration abroad, the life of Ireland was to be terribly changed, changed with a stark reality for many thousands in their everyday life, changed in the patterns of population and outlook for the nation as a whole. The Famine was one of those great convulsions in human affairs which men instinctively recognise as both an end and a beginning. It entered into the folk memory not only of the historians, the social commentators and the economists, but of those countless persons and families who had a relative or a neighbour buried in a pauper grave or consigned to the sea from a coffin-ship in the Atlantic. It set in train that dramatic fall in the population which was to reduce it from eight to four million. And if it was largely responsible for creating that considerable Irish influence in Britain and America that is so remarkable considering the size of the homeland, it did so at a price that neither Ireland nor her emigrants could afford to pay. It is simply a matter of history that the Irish victims of the Famine gave enormous popular strength to the Catholic Church both in Britain and America; equally, their support for later national movements was significant; but they carried in their hearts a lingering sadness and a haunting memory of the great hunger.

How did it come about that the course of history was to be so dramatically changed by so simple a thing as a potato? Because the great mass of the Irish peasants were living at subsistence level and depending on the potato as the mainstay of their daily diet. They ate potatoes for breakfast, dinner and supper on almost every day in the year. True, most cottages kept a pig or two; but the fattened pig was sold to pay the rent. The woman of the house had her hens; these too, were sold with the eggs to pay the rent. Meat and eggs were a rarity for great numbers of the people. Nor did the peasants have access to the great variety of foods now available; the railway had not yet opened up the country for the movement of goods; besides many of the menfolk were not paid in cash by the large farmers and landlords, but rather by having potato plots free. So it was that potatoes were the staple daily diet; indeed, a great proportion of the womenfolk were incapable of cooking anything else. In good times the peasant was well satisfied with his potatoes; they were cheap and easy to grow; they yielded a plentiful return from even a small plot; and as a food they were satisfying and pleasant. Many Irish and foreign social commentators before the Famine noted the good health and high spirits of the great mass of the people. With his potatoes and his turf the peasant had the basic necessities of life cheaply and readily, it was subsistence living, but it was in many ways healthier than the life of the labouring poor in the emerging commercial cities of Britain or the rigours endured in the mining towns where boys and girls of five or six years were put to work at six o'clock in the morning crawling in the darkened pits.

Nevertheless, there was danger in having a vast peasant population depending on one source of food, especially on such a precarious source as the potato. Between 1817 and 1839 there had been some severe parital famines due to crop failure, each marked by starvation, fever and death. The most serious of these was in 1822 when an abundant crop rotted in the pits due to the wetness of the growing season. This disaster hit Munster and Connaught most severely and there were widespread efforts to alleviate distress; the people of England responded with great generosity with a collection of £200,000. But beyond responding to the immediate need there was no attempt so to change the economy that such an emergency could be avoided in the future. Society simply did not have an understanding of the nature of the issue nor the social and economic skills to cope with it. As in the case of the Great Famine, it was not malice, or even neglect, by the British Government or the authorities at Dublin Castle which was responsible, but ignorance and bewilderment in face of a calamity that involved not only the potato crop but the whole structure of Irish society.

Father Mathew was one of the very first public figures to alert the Government to the impending disaster in August, 1845. The Prime Minister, Sir Robert Peel, acted quickly by setting up a Potato Commission to examine and recommend measures; this consisted of one of the best known English scientist of the day, Dr. Playfair, together with Mr. Lindley and the foremost Irish scientist, Dr. Robert Kane, later first President of the Queen's College, Cork. The Commission failed to come up with any effective remedies for the blight, but in November, 1845, they warned that "one half of the potato crop of Ireland is either destroyed or remains in a state unfit for the food of man." In the same month the Government secretly arranged for £100,000 worth of Indian corn to be shipped to and stored in Cork from America. Reporting to the Secretary of the Treasury, Mr. Trevelyan, the Commissary General for Cork, Mr. Hewetson, wrote on 10th January, 1846: "Father Mathew, who is well acquainted with the country and the habits of the lower orders, gave me a good deal of interesting information." Again on 24th February Hewetson wrote "Father Mathew has been with me today. I gave him your letter to read, of course he felt gratified by your remarks. He fully agrees with me that the meal once ground, with the light corn sifted, according to the sample I sent you, is the proper meal for the classes who need it." But the full impact of the Famine was only to be felt in the autumn of 1846 when the failure of the potato crop was total bringing a new dimension of distress which the Indian corn could not meet. It is possible to feel the despair of Father Mathew as he wrote directly to Trevelyan on 7th August, 1846: "The hopes of the poor potato cultivators are totally blighted and the food of a whole nation has perished. On the 27th of last month I passed from Cork to Dublin and this doomed plant bloomed in all the luxuriance of an abundant harvest. Returning on the 3rd instant I beheld with horror one wide waste of putrefying vegetation. In many places the wretched people were seated on the fences of their decaying gardens, wringing their hands, and wailing bitterly the destruction that had left them foodless. I am well aware of the vast expenditure incurred in provding Indian corn but I humbly suggest a cheaper and more simple plan. If Goverment would purchase in America and lay up in stores in the several seaports of Ireland, a supply of Indian corn, unground, and sell it at first cost to all who will purchase it, it would soon be bought up by the country millers and farmers, and the unholy hopes of the corn speculators would be completely frustrated . . . I am so horror-struck by the apprehensions of our destitute people falling into the hands of the corn and flour traders that I risk becoming troublesome."

The Government had embarked on a programme of public works to put money into the pockets of the peasants to enable them to buy Indian corn. Though many of the projects were ill-conceived, Father Mathew wrote to Dublin Castle that "the measures of the Government to provide remunerative employment are above all praise, yet they have not been accepted with gratitude." In November, 1846, he again wrote to Trevelyan, with hot anger at the abuse which had grown up about the public works programme: "It afflicted me deeply to find the benevolent intentions of Government frustrated and the money so abundantly distributed made a source of demoralisation and intemperance. Wherever these benevolent works are commenced public-houses are immediately opened, the magistrates with a culpable facility granting licences. The overseers and pay clerks generally hold their offices in these pestiferous erections; even some of these officers have a pecuniary interest in those establishments. It often happens that the entire body of labourers after receiving payment, instead of buying provisions for their famishing families, consume the greater part in the purchase of intoxicating drink. The same deplorable abuse takes place on the different railway lines."

No more pitiable picture of the effect of the Famine in Cork City exists than that found in Father Mathew's letter to Trevelyan of 16th December, 1846: "The present exorbitant price of bread stuffs, especially Indian corn, places sufficient food beyond the great bulk of the population. Men, women and children are gradually wasting away. They fill their stomachs with cabbage leaves and turnip tops to appease the cravings of hunger. There are at this moment more than five thousand half-starved wretched beings from the country begging in the streets of Cork. When utterly exhausted they crawl to the workhouse to die. The average of deaths in this union is over a hundred a week. I deplore the abandonment of the people to corn and flour dealers. They charge 50 to 100 per cent profit. We are establishing soup shops in all parts of the city to supply the poor with nutritious and cheap cooked food."

Further details of the soup kitchens are to be found in a letter to Trevelyan of 4th February, 1847: "The soup kitchens are affording very great relief. We are in a deplorable state in Cork from the influx into the city of more than 10,000 foodless, homeless people, young and old, from several counties around us. I am in horror whilst I walk the streets, and I return to my besieged dwelling in sadness and hopelessness. The workhouse has been closed and there is no refuge for these miserable creatures. As I have been much through the country latterly I can assure you, and with great pleasure, that agriculture has not been neglected; the quantity of wheat sown has been as large as usual. I would gratefully accept from you one of your improved querns, as a model for the instruction of our mechanics." Great attention was paid to detail, not only in regard to better querns but to the ingredients of the soup: another letter in the same month stated that, "we find beans, peas and biscuit the best ingredients to add to the liquor of flesh meat. Occasionally and always on Friday we use salt fish. If this latter were given twice a week to the inmates of the different workhouses it would be a great advantage to our, I may term them, infant fisheries. I am delighted with Lord John's measures (Lord John Russell, Liberal Prime Minister) and I shall have no apprehension about the future fate of the Irish people when they come into operation." On the following month, the 4th March, yet more details of soup-making found their way to Dublin Castle: "to encourage our soup committees to give gratuitous food to be consumed on the premises, I have presumed to give them the three boilers you so considerately presented to me. Mr. Bishop has promised to give me a very fine copper cooking apparatus with which I expect to be able to rival Mr. Soyer. My chief anxiety is to teach our unhappy people to manage to advantage their scanty means. The potato deluge, if I may so term it, during the last twenty years swept away all other food from amongst our cottagers, and sank in oblivion their knowledge of cooking. I am full of hope and rely with unbounded confidence in the mercy of God."

The mercy of God must, indeed, have seemed the last resort in that cruel early spring of 1847. The number of deaths in the Cork workhouse in the last week of January was 104; it had jumped to 128 in the first week of February; by the second week of the month it was 164, giving a morbid total of 396 in three weeks. From the end of December, 1846 to the middle of April, there were 2,130 deaths in the workhouse. In one day in April there were 36 burials in the poor section of Father Mathew's cemetery. In the same month 300 coffins were sold in a single street in the course of a fortnight. Maguire's biography captures the moment with chilling exactitude: "In meal and coffins and passenger ships was the principal business of the time. The Cork Patent Saw Mills had been at full work from December, 1846 to May, 1847 with twenty pairs of saws constantly going from morning till night, cutting planks for coffins, planks and scantlings for fever sheds, and planks for the framework of berths for emigrant ships."

Precisely because of the enormous human suffering of the Famine it left a legacy of understandable bitterness not only in the hearts of the Irish at home but especially in the folk-memory of those who sought a better life in America. Simply because he happened to be Prime Minister in 1845/'46 Sir Robert Peel incurred much of the odium, a process contributed to by those seeking for convenient villians or who have failed to make a dispassionate assess-

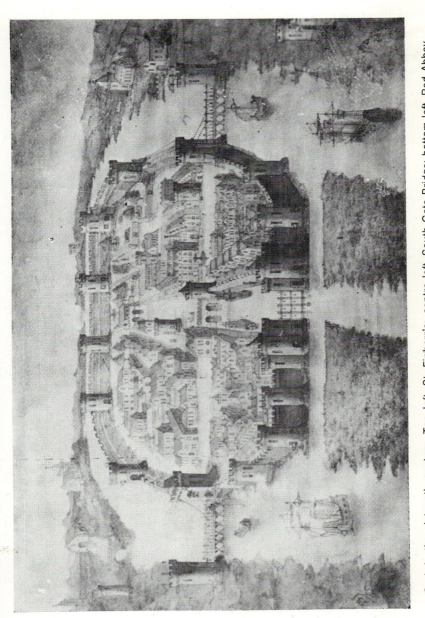

Cork in the sixteenth century. Top left, St. Finbarr's; centre left, South Gate Bridge; bottom left, Red Abbey. Centre, South Main Street with Christ Church; North Main Street with St. Peter's Church and Skiddy's Castle. Top right, Franciscan Abbey on North Mall; centre right, North Gate Bridge; bottom right, Shandon Castle.

North Gate Bridge, 1796. Note apple woman and beggar, stage coach with guard blowing horn, sedan chair being carried, and cupola of Exchange in Castle Street through prison arch. Drawn by Nathaniel Grogan, 1740-1807.

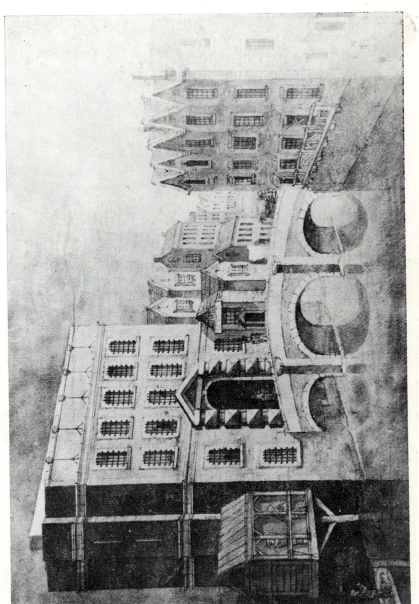

South Gate Bridge, 1796. Drawn by Grogan.

Castle Street with Exchange, 1796. Drawn by Grogan.

Old Blackrock Castle which also served as a lighthouse. Replaced by present structure in 1828. Drawn by John Fitzgerald about 1790.

Patrick Street at the turn of the century. From the Lawrence Collection, National Library, Dublin.

St. Patrick's Bridge, with the Dominican Church, Shandon and St. Mary's Cathedral on the skyline.

Lawrence Collection

The Grand Parade. Lawrence Collection.

The Coal Quay Market. Lawrence Collection.

The Butter Market. Lawrence Collection.

The leafy splendour of the Mardyke. Lawrence Collection.

The old City Hall, with the former metal Parnell Bridge. Lawrence Collection.

Holy Trinity Church with Parliament Bridge. Lawrence Collection.

"The Marriage of Strongbow and Eva," by Daniel Maclise, 1854. By courtesy of the Director of the National Gallery, Dublin.

Shop in Patrick Street with a dramatic comment on the history of travel. Photos courtesy of Messrs. Browne, Thompson.

Crawford School of Art. Photo by author.
Former premises of Royal Cork Institution.

University College, Cork. Photo by author. Designed by Sir Thomas
Deane, 1849.

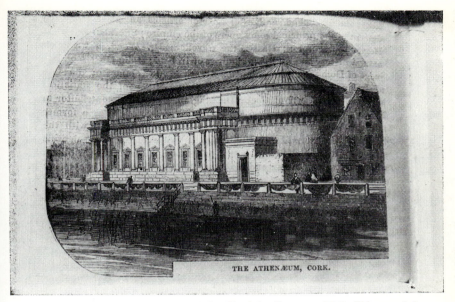

THE ATHENÆUM, CORK.

The old Opera House. Designed by Sir John Benson, 1856. This quartet of line drawings is from "The Great Southern and Western Railway" by George Measom, 1866.

THE IMPERIAL HOTEL, SOUTH MALL, CORK, THE PROPERTY OF MR. CHARLES COTTON.

The Imperial Hotel, South Mall. Designed by Sir Thomas Deane, 1811.

THE CARRIAGE MANUFACTORY OF MR. JAMES JOHNSON, NELSON PLACE, CORK.

Making carriages in Emmet Place, 1866.

A PORTION OF THE GROUND FLOOR OF THE PREMISES OF THE QUEENS OLD CASTLE COMPANY, CORK.

Out shopping, 1866.

FARES FOR HACKNEY CARRIAGES.

Fares within the Borough.	s.	d.
From St. Luke's Stand, and *vice* *versa,* to		
Ashburton & GlenviewTerrace,	0	6
Barracks Gate	0	9
Carrigmore, Mr. Donegan's Gate,	0	6
Montenotte Terrace or Road, extending to Mr. Goulding's Gate :—		
For Two Persons	0	6
For more than Two ..	0	9
Sunday's Well, St. Vincent's Church :—		
For Two Persons	1	0
For more than Two ..	1	6
From Summer Hill Stand, and *vice versa,* to		
Ashburton, Glenview Terrace,	0	9
Barracks Gate	1	0
Carrigmore, Mr. Donegan's Gate	0	9
Montenotte Terrace or Road, extending to Mr. Goulding's Gate	1	0
Or from any Stand to		
Beale's Hill	0	6
ClarenceTerrace,SummerHill,	0	6
CollegeRd.,BoroughBoundary	0	6
Panorama Terrace,Wise's Hill,	0	6
St. Luke's Cross :—		
For Two Persons	0	6
For more than Two ..	0	9
Southern Road, Borough Boundary	0	6
Sunday's Well Road, Panorama Terrace	0	6
Turner's Cross	0	6
Western Road, Borough Boundary	0	6
Or from any Stand to any place within the Borough..	0	6
With the following exceptions, to		
Ashburton & Glenview Terrace,	1	0
Ballyphehane Road, Borough Boundary	0	9
Blarney Rd., Borough Boundary,	1	0
Barrack Gate :—		
For Two Persons	1	0
For more than Two ..	1	6
Barracks, inside Gate :—		
For Two Persons	1	3
For more than Two ..	1	9
Blackpool Bridge, corner of Spring Lane, by York St.,	0	9

Fares within the Borough.	s.	d.
Botanic Gardens, St. Joseph's Cemetery	1	0
Borough Boundary, Blarney Road	1	0
Borough Boundary, Bally-phehane Road	0	9
Borough Boundary, Commons Road	1	0
Borough Boundary, Glasheen, upper and lower..	0	9
Borough Boundary, Middle Glanmire Road	1	6
Borough Boundary, Old Youghal Road	1	6
Borough Boundary, Silver-spring	1	3
Carrigmore, Donegan's Gate,	1	0
City Gaol	1	0
Coleman's Cross, Sunday's Well Road	0	9
Commons Road, Borough Boundary	1	0
Denroche's Cross	0	9
Fair Field, by Fair Hill :—		
For Two Persons	1	6
For more than Two ..	2	0
Fair Hill..	1	3
Fair Lane,end of Peacock Lane,	0	9
Friar's Walk, Saunder's Nursery,	0	9
Glasheen, upper and lower, Borough Boundary	0	9
Goulding's Bone Factory ..	1	0
Middle Glanmire Road, Mr. Donegan's Gate..	1	0
Middle Glanmire Road, Borough Boundary	1	6
Montenotte Terrace or Road, extending to Mr. Goulding's Gate	1	3
Myrtle Hill Terrace	0	9
Old Youghal Road, Borough Boundary	1	6
Peacock Lane, end of in Fair Lane	0	9
Queen's' College	0	9
St. Vincent's Church, or Coleman's Cross	0	9
Saunders' Nursery, Friar'sWalk,	0	9
Silverspring, Borough Boundary	1	3
Spangle Hill	1	0
Sunday's Well Road :—		
Panorama Terrace.. ..	0	6
St. Vincent's Church ..	0	9
City Gaol..	1	0

In the foregoing and following, one stoppage allowed, not exceeding five minutes.

Hiring a cab, 1882. Purcell's Commercial Almanac.

"Newsom's Café de Paris,
A Cup of Coffee in Perfection."

This delicious Coffee is prepared from selected berries of particular descriptions of Coffee, in such proportions as to obtain great strength and a peculiar richness of flavour.

The Café de Paris is roasted on scientific principles by steam machinery, and after being ground, packed into canisters by a process which preserves the essential properties of the berry, and it will be found to retain, for an indefinite period, that delicate flavour and aroma necessary to produce

A Cup of Coffee in Perfection.

[IRISH.]

Tá an cophuíde veaṫblasta so ulmoiġṫe uaó ṫoġ caonna áiriġṫe ve fopo cophuíde fa leiṫ aca con-mearġṫa ṫne ċeile aiṫ nóṫ a ċuṫan bṫeiṫ neaṫc aṫuṫ ṫoṫaó.

Rostaṫ an **Café de Paris** le ṫalmṫor aiṫ an nóṫ iṫ aṫuse caiṫ taṫeṫ a meiṫc siaċṫaṫ a n'áuṫuṫve ṫcáin aiṫ fluṫe fa leiṫ e cim luaċ na ṫcaoṫua a buan-coṫainc cuṫṫa bṫeaġ bṫuoṫṫiaṫ aṫuṫ ċum an veaġblaf álunn so fioṫ-cuiṫmeao aca maċcanaċ cum

Cupan Cophuíde so ṫleaṫa maṫ ṫa con.

Ce Café délicieux est un choix spécial des meilleurs grains mélangés de manière à obtenir une grande force unie à une délicatesse d'arome toute particulière.

Le Café de Paris est grillé d'après des principes scientifiques au moyen d'une machine à vapeur, et, après avoir été moulu, est mis dans des boîtes de fer blanc par un procédé propre à conserver les qualités essentielles du grain. On trouve qu'il retient indéfiniment ce goût délicat et cette finesse d'arome nécessaires pour faire.

Une Tasse de Café à la perfection.

Prepared by Newsom & Sons, Merchant Coffee Dealers. Cork

FARES FOR HACKNEY CARRIAGES.

Fares within the Borough.	s.	d.
From St. Luke's Stand, and *vice versa*, to		
Ashburton & Glenview Terrace,	0	6
Barracks Gate	0	9
Carrigmore, Mr. Donegan's Gate,	0	6
Montenotte Terrace or Road, extending to Mr. Goulding's Gate :—		
For Two Persons	0	6
For more than Two ..	0	9
Sunday's Well, St. Vincent's Church :—		
For Two Persons	1	0
For more than Two ..	1	6
From Summer Hill Stand, and *vice versa*, to		
Ashburton, Glenview Terrace,	0	9
Barracks Gate	1	0
Carrigmore, Mr. Donegan's Gate	0	9
Montenotte Terrace or Road, extending to Mr. Goulding's Gate	1	0
Or from any Stand to		
Beale's Hill	0	6
Clarence Terrace, Summer Hill,	0	6
College Rd., Borough Boundary	0	6
Panorama Terrace, Wise's Hill,	0	6
St. Luke's Cross :—		
For Two Persons	0	6
For more than Two ..	0	9
Southern Road, Borough Boundary	0	6
Sunday's Well Road, Panorama Terrace	0	6
Turner's Cross	0	6
Western Road, Borough Boundary	0	6
Or from any Stand to any place within the Borough..	0	6
With the following exceptions, to		
Ashburton & Glenview Terrace,	1	0
Ballyphehane Road, Borough Boundary	0	9
Blarney Rd., Borough Boundary,	1	0
Barrack Gate :—		
For Two Persons	1	0
For more than Two ..	1	6
Barracks, inside Gate :—		
For Two Persons	1	3
For more than Two ..	1	9
Blackpool Bridge, corner of Spring Lane, by York St.,	0	9

Fares within the Borough.	s.	d.
Botanic Gardens, St. Joseph's Cemetery	1	0
Borough Boundary, Blarney Road	1	0
Borough Boundary, Ballyphehane Road	0	9
Borough Boundary, Commons Road	1	0
Borough Boundary, Glasheen, upper and lower..	0	9
Borough Boundary, Middle Glanmire Road	1	6
Borough Boundary, Old Youghal Road	1	6
Borough Boundary, Silverspring	1	3
Carrigmore, Donegan's Gate,	1	0
City Gaol	1	0
Coleman's Cross, Sunday's Well Road	0	9
Commons Road, Borough Boundary	1	0
Denroche's Cross	0	9
Fair Field, by Fair Hill :—		
For Two Persons	1	6
For more than Two ..	2	0
Fair Hill	1	3
Fair Lane, end of Peacock Lane,	0	9
Friar's Walk, Saunder's Nursery,	0	9
Glasheen, upper and lower, Borough Boundary	0	9
Goulding's Bone Factory ..	1	0
Middle Glanmire Road, Mr. Donegan's Gate..	1	0
Middle Glanmire Road, Borough Boundary	1	6
Montenotte Terrace or Road, extending to Mr. Goulding's Gate	1	3
Myrtle Hill Terrace	0	9
Old Youghal Road, Borough Boundary	1	6
Peacock Lane, end of in Fair Lane	0	9
Queens' College	0	9
St. Vincent's Church, or Coleman's Cross	0	9
Saunders' Nursery, Friar's Walk,	0	9
Silverspring, Borough Boundary	1	3
Spangle Hill	1	0
Sunday's Well Road :—		
Panorama Terrace.. ..	0	6
St. Vincent's Church ..	0	9
City Gaol..	1	0

In the foregoing and following, one stoppage allowed, not exceeding five minutes.

Hiring a cab, 1882. Purcell's Commercial Almanac.

ment of the awful event in the context of its own times. The documentary evidence available in the Peel Papers in the British Museum, highly confidential personal letters and directives relating to cabinet discussions and orders to government officials in Dublin, dispels the simplistic notion that Peel just sat back and let the Irish starve. On the contrary the Papers reveal his deep anguish at the unfolding tragedy and his business-like energy in seeking exact information and in devising remedies. It was from Belgium that the first reports of potato blight came in the summer of 1845, and Peel was to express concern early in August when news came that it had struck the Isle of Wight, but as yet there was not a word of danger from Ireland. But when in September the blight was confirmed in parts of this country Peel was immediately alarmed and took swift action. The constabulary were instructed to send in detailed reports in all districts; as the blight was not as yet widespread these reports were naturally confused. Peel moved to enlist scientific aid and appointed a three-man Potato Commission to make immediate on-the-spot examination and recommendations to the government. Dr. Lyon Playfair had a reputation as a chemist; Dr. John Lindley was professor of botany at London University and had made Kew Gardens a world centre of botanical study. It was he who, in an article published in August, 1845, alerted opinion to the dangers of the Belgian blight and its results, "there is hardly a sound sample (of potato) in Covent Garden market." Again in September he raised the alarm about Ireland, "where will Ireland be in the event of a universal potato rot?" The third member was the Irishman, Dr. Robert Kane, who features elsewhere in this book as the first president of the University at Cork. He was probably the most noted scientist in the country while his book, "The Industrial Resources of Ireland," published in 1844 had been hailed as a masterpiece. But the Commission failed to diagnose the cause of the blight or recommend an effective remedy. Peel then took two vital decisions, one long-term and one for immediate action. He decided he would introduce legislation to repeal the Corn Laws which prohibited the importation of foreign food, especially grain, into the United Kigdom. This meant that he adopted a cheap food policy; but he well knew that it could also involve political suicide for him as the predomin-

antly agricultural base of the Tory Party had relentlessly
set their face against such a policy, seeing it as a betrayal
of their vested interest. His more immediate action was
also quite radical, acting on his own initiative and without
the approval of the mandarins of the Treasury, in November
he ordered £100,000 to be spent in buying Indian corn in
America and shipping it to Ireland.

In her fine study, "The Great Hunger," the late Mrs.
Cecil Woodham-Smith comments on this action: "His purchase of Indian corn proved the decisive factor in relieving
the distress of 1845/'46, but the subsequent value to Ireland
of Peel's boldness, independence and strength of mind
was unfortunately outweighed by his belief in an economic
theory which almost every politician of the day, Whig or
Tory, held with religious fervour." That theory was known
as laissez faire, of which more shortly. Meanwhile a board
of Relief Commissioners had been appointed, including
Robert Kane of whom Peel said "he has written on the
industrial resources of Ireland, but, mainly, he is a Roman
Catholic." They had a four-point plan to implement, first, to
form local committees of clergy, landlords and prominent
citizens; second, to co-operare with the Board of Works in
creating employment through the making of new roads;
third, the erection of new fever hospitals, and, finally, the
sale of Government corn in an effort to keep down the price
of other foodstuffs. But even if Peel's measures were alert
and even radical they were constrained by the need to
operate within the economic climate of the times, a climate
technically known as laissez faire. This laid down the
cardinal principle that a government must not on any
account interfere with the supply and demand of food; to
do so woud interfere with the free operation of the laws of
supply and demand, it would break the framework of commercial life and go against the course of nature. It was the
stress of the Famine that confirmed Peel in his conviction
that this accepted economic wisdom was no longer adequate to the needs of society either in Ireland or in industrial
Britain; his purchase of American corn had violated the
theory, but his decision to smash it by legislation to repeal
the Corn Laws aroused the wrath of the Tory backwoodsmen and by 1846 they had driven him from office, an
eventuality he had fully foreseen. O'Connell and the majority
of Irish members heartily joined to defeat Peel, while his

Famine policies were denounced as alarmist and excessively expensive. The Whig government of Lord John Russell introduced a more extensive programme of public works of which Father Mathew approved. By March, 1847, some 734,000 men were employed on relief work while in July of the same year the Temporary Relief Act resulted in three million persons becoming eligible for food rations from state funds. By the late harvest of 1848 the immediate horrors of the Famine had abated but an exhausted and demoralised country was faced with the herculean task of picking up again the threads of normal life. Many factors had compounded the natural disasters of the potato failure; there was the inherent danger of a vast peasant population subsisting almost exclusively on one type of food; there was the baffling obstacle of distributing relief in a country not yet opened up for transport by railways; there was the frustration caused by an economic theory and systems which prevented plentiful supplies of other foodstuffs existing in the country from being diverted to the immediate use of those in need; finally, there was the element of human inadequacy due to an absence of the skills and experience needed to cope at government and administrative level with so unprecedented a disaster.

The death of the bishop of Cork in April, 1847, the scholarly Dr. Murphy noted for his magnificent collection of books and his encouragement of Irish language scholars, resulted in an acute public embarrassment for Father Mathew. Enormously to his credit and satisfaction he was elected by the priests of the diocese as their first choice to fill the vacant see. As Rome normally acted in accordance with local assessment it was now publicly assumed that he was about to become bishop of Cork. The prospect did not call forth from him anything of that public display of humility sometimes produced by such events; he was frankly pleased, feeling that the new status would enhance his temperance work, and in the streets he joyously accepted the good wishes of his fellow-citizens. He knew that the General of the Capuchins in Rome, the venerable Cardinal Micara, was a firm supporter of his work. In this regard it is interesting to find Father Mathew's name linked in Rome with that of two other distinguished men of Cork, the Rev. Francis O'Mahony, better known as "Father Prout" and author of "The Bells of Shandon," and John Hogan the sculptor. In a letter from London on 20th May, 1847, O'Mahony told Father Mathew of a meeting with the Cardinal: "I left Rome as above stated, but had previously ordered a full bust of the IRISH CAPUCHIN ROBED IN THE HABIT AND COWL OF HIS ORDER to be executed by Hogan; and although Cardinal Micara was laid up in bed with the gout when the present arrived in the Barberini Convent, I had the satisfaction, in calling next day, to find it placed conspicuously in his reception-room, with the inscription as follows: Frater Theobaldus Mathew, Ordinis Capuccinorum; Temperantiae in Hibernia et ubique Terrarum Propugnator." One detail displeased his Eminence, Father Mathew was depicted without a beard. Even though O'Mahony explained to him that Capuchins in Ireland then managed to do their work without a hairy appendage the statue was, nevertheless, sent back to Hogan for the necessary dressing.

But in June the decision of the Holy See ended the episcopal prospect when Dr. Delany was announced as the new bishop. Father Mathew felt the blow but, as his biographer states, "if the wound bled, it was internally." In seeking to ascertain the cause of the adverse decision the following considerations were popularly advanced: he was not a theologian, he was in considerable financial difficulty due to his work for charity, he was totally prodigal in giving away everything he had, while many feared that as a bishop he would be lost to his work and forced to become an administrator. One source of financial embarrassment was his new church of the Holy Trinity. The Blackamoor Lane premises were increasingly seen as too small and it seems he was offered a site on Sullivan's Quay where the Fire Station recently stood; deeming the price too high he went against the wishes of his committee and purchased the then Charlotte Quay site for the present lovely church. The marshy land involved unexpected expense in laying a foundation, while the lack of money forced considerable modification of the design by the Pain brothers, among whose other works are the County Club and Blackrock Castle.

In May, 1847 came the death of O'Connell, adding yet another sombre touch to the darkening Irish scene. Writing to his son, John, Father Mathew said, "few have known longer or more intimately, or have more honoured and loved your great and good father." Meanwhile for some time influential friends were casting about for some means of ensuring that he would have an independent source of income not only to maintain his work but to give him peace of mind. It was due to this solicitude that in June, 1847, the Prime Minister, Lord John Russell secured for him a royal pension of £300 per annum. There was universal satisfaction and Father Mathew was deeply pleased. In the summer of 1849 he arrived in America, being received in a tumultuous welcome by New York City Council on the 2nd of July, He was to stay in the New York for two years, expressing gratitude for the enormous generosity of all classes and creeds in contributing to Famine relief in Ireland, and also incessantly busy in travelling vast distances to spread the cause of temperance. The diary of his friend and secretary, Mr. O'Meara, reads as follows for Sunday, 2nd December, 1849, with Father Mathew just recovered from an illness in New York: "Father Mathew said mass at half past six o'clock this morning in the Bishop's private chapel, which was crowded. Immediately after gave pledge; when he had breakfast proceeded with the Rev. Mr. Gartland to Gloucester, five miles across the river to attend the dedication of a new church to which the Rev. Mr. O'Donoghue of Waterford is appointed pastor. Father Mathew preached the dedication sermon, delivered in his usual good style despite his illness. After the ceremonies he administered the pledge. The weather became severe and extremely cold, and snow fell heavily throughout the entire day. After dinner returned to the Bishop's, and remained administering the pledge until eight o'clock. Several came." It might be appropriate to point out here that until much later in the last century Catholic priests, as well as Protestant clergymen, were styled "Mister" unless they possessed a doctorate in theology. This usage had nothing to do with penal laws and was not regarded as in any way derogatory, it was simply the existing custom. The use of the term "Father," together with the wearing of the Roman collar, was part of the Italianate influence heralded by such other manifestations as the hymns of Father Faber and the more florid devotional practices such as outdoor processions.

In Washington the members of Congress rose as he entered to be given the honour of a seat on the floor of the House. And when the President of America, Mr. Taylor, entertained him to a grand dinner he was seen to abstain from wine in honour of his guest. He returned to Ireland in December, 1851, his hair almost white and his former robust frame visibly shaken. During the following two years he suffered frequent fits of apoplexy and in 1854 he was advised to go to the warmth of Madeira. On his return in August, 1855 he went to stay wit his brother and sister-in-law at Lehenagh. His mind was often clouded by a deep melancholy while his step had grown feeble. Knowing that death might be close he invariably shook hands with the adults and kissed the children at his brother's house before retiring each night—it was a gesture entirely in keeping with the warm humanity of the man. Feeling that he ought not to impose on the kindness of his family he decided against their wishes to go to live in what was then considered the recuperative climate of Cobh. For the few months between the autumn of 1856 and his death in the following December he was often to be seen shuffling slowly along the street, his hand leaning on the shoulder of a little schoolboy. The voice that had sounded so often and so far was now a whisper, and the strength that had sustained the multitudes was now no more.

It was on the 8th of December, 1856, in the sixty sixth year of his age that Father Mathew died peacefully, having indicated at the last moment that he wished to be buried beneath the cross he had erected in his cemetery at Bally-phehane. Kneeling at that hallowed spot one feels the influence of this man of God who so made himself a man of the people. His story embraces much of the history of Cork and not a little of the history of Ireland. To both he brought honour at home and distinction abroad. It is only fitting that the Statue should stand revered in Patrick Street, for Father Mathew went about doing good in Cork; he breathed our air, he walked our streets, he fed our poor and buried our dead. He will be remembered as long as men cherish Christian benevolence and the warmth of human compassion.

It was on the 10th of October, 1864 that a vast assembly of 150,000 people gathered to witness the unveiling of the Statue. The distinguished Cork sculptor, John Hogan, had been commissioned to execute the work, but on his death the task fell to another Irish artist, Mr. Foley. The bronze cast was made by Mr. Prince at his works in Union Street, Southwark, London. The unveiling was performed by Father Mathew's lifelong friend and biographer, Mr. John Francis Maguire, founder of the "Cork Examiner" and then Mayor of Cork. Yet another old friend was treasurer for the fund, Richard Dowden of the Old Presbyterian Church in Prince's Street.

An interesting hour or two might be spent retracing the scenes of the great man's life. The shell of the old Friary in Blackamoor Lane still stands behind Sullivan's Quay. A few paces way is the dismal car park where until recently his house stood. A short walk over the picturesque limestone bridge, Parliament Bridge, brings the slender graciousness of Holy Trinity Church into view. At the Statue itself it is possible to board a bus for Ballyphehane where the cemetery and grave may be viewed. So it is possible to retrace the scenes made memorable by Cork's most illustrious citizen of the nineteenth century.

Chapter VIII

THE FIRST NATIONAL EXHIBITION, 1852

On the face of it nothing seemed more foolhardy than the decision of a small group of Cork gentlemen to set about organising an Industrial Exhibition. The year was 1852 and the times were not propitious. The country was only feebly gathering its strength from the prostration of the Famine, hundreds of thousands had died in thatched hovels, in workhouse wards and on country laneways. The more enterprising were still crowding the emigrant ships to find food and opportunity in the cellars of Liverpool, New York and Boston. The extent of that flood of emigration and the depth of human suffering it involved were poignantly illustrated in a letter written to the Secretary for the Home Department by Mr. Edward Rushton, Stipendiary Magistrate of Liverpool, on 21st April, 1849. He stated that "between the 13th day of January and the 13th day of December, 1847, both days inclusive, 296,231 persons landed in this port from Ireland. Of this vast number about 130,000 were emigrating to the United States, some 50,000 were passengers on business, and the remainder were paupers, half naked and starving and becoming immediately on landing applicants for parochial relief." (Quoted in Parliamentary Papers, 1849, Vol. XLVII) There was paralysis in agriculture and the stark reality of bankruptcy faced very many of the landlords. Underlying the whole tragedy a deep malaise affected the country, a feeling of hopelessness, a loss of confidence. The collapse of the Repeal Movement, the death of Daniel O'Connell, the abortive failure of the Young Ireland rising, had all contributed to leave the people confused and leaderless. And if the City of Cork had escaped the worst horrors of the West Cork countryside, and of the whole western seaboard, yet the carts had been busy bringing the dead from the Workhouse to the communal pauper grave at Carr's Hill on the road to Crosshaven. It needed a deep practical patriotism and something of a reckless optimism to set about creating an Industrial Exhibition from the shambles of the Famine. But something akin to a miracle of the spirit stirred the people of Cork in 1852 and they gave Ireland its first Industrial Exhibition.

The second half of the nineteenth century became an age of exhibitions in Europe and America. The phenomenon was a visual reflection of the profound changes that were taking place in industry, invention, trade, commerce and travel as the wheels of the Industrial Revolution gathered speed. The great factories with their tall chimneys billowing smoke became the symbols of the new age of men and their machines, just as the Gothic spires of the great cathedrals had symbolised the Middle Ages. Men began to change their mode of working and their place of living more rapidly than ever in the thousand years beforehand; instead of their hands alone, they were using machines to make a vast output of manufactured goods from pins to iron ships; instead of the immemorial rhythm of tilling the soil, there was the new living to be gained by working in a factory. And the cities began to grow with bewildering rapidity, bringing the extremes of a new commercial middle class and the great hordes of rootless operatives, living and sleeping within earshot of the factory hooter. One might borrow the words of Charles Dickens and say that it was the best of times and it was the worst of times. It brought new wealth and new poverty; it marked the beginning of the end of a society based primarily on the land; it ushered in the industrial society in which we now live. With a change so sudden and so pervasive men took time to adjust to the opportunities and the problems of the age of the machine. But with the aid of coal, steam and iron a vast range of new products was coming into the shops and the homes of the people, and because of the new techniques of mass production goods were cheaper. The various industrial exhibitions were designed as shop windows in which to display the hardware of the Age of the Machine.

Perhaps nothing so caught the imagination of Britain, Ireland and Europe as the Great Exhibition of 1851 held in Hyde Park, London, and housed in a building whose very name struck the right chord, the Crystal Palace. Two hundred and fifty four designs had been submitted for the exhibition building from architects from many parts of the world, but it was Joseph Paxton, the head gardener of the Duke of Devonshire's estate at Chatsworth, who was to win the distinction of creating a building which dramatically exemplified the new techniques of the age. Paxton was typical of the self-made man of many parts so often found to the forefront in the nineteenth century and so admired by his contemporaries. A good Irish example was Charles Bianconi. Like Stephenson and Brunel, Paxton was also in the tradition of useful knowledge acquired by direct observation and experiment rather than from formal schooling. As gardener, engineer and railway promoter he was very much a Victorian man of affairs. In fact, he sketched the outline of his Crystal Palace on a piece of blotting paper while attending a meeting of railway directors at Derby. It took him a month to draw up the blueprints and only seventeen weeks were spent by the workmen in erecting the colossus of iron and glass. The building rose like a giant mushroom, with nearly a million feet of glass fitted onto an iron frame of thirty-three hundred columns and twenty-three hundred girders. It was 1,848 feet long, 408 feet wide and 68 feet high. It was not only the design and the material that were significant, it was also the process by which it was built. Prefabrication had shown how time could be saved on the job. The driving force behind the Great Exhibition was Prince Albert who presided with unflagging stamina over numerous committees and brought an eager and informed mind to all the technical details. He was ably assisted by a civil servant, Henry Cole, who was later to devote his life to assembling that most comprehensive repository of human achievement, the Victoria and Albert Museum. As the preparations went ahead there was a plentiful lack of enthusiasm from the press: the lordly "Times" scarcely concealed its scepticism.

The idea for the venture grew out of a modest exhibition held by the London Society of Arts and its purpose was to be to "present a living picture of the point of development at which the whole of mankind had arrived." Cole was to describe it as "a festival of human skill," designed to demonstrate the manufacturing prowess of Britain but also intended to display the progress of all the civilised nations of the world. Nor was it to be merely a celebration of human ingenuity, it also had a strong moral purpose as an invitation to all peoples to work in peace for the betterment of mankind. And the world and his wife came to see the wonders of the Crystal Palace with its thirteen thousand exhibitors, half of whom were foreigners from France, Germany, America and even Russia. From the opening by Queen Victoria and the Prince on 1st May, 1851, to the closing in October just over six million people had gone to Hyde Park. There had been forebodings in London that the massive swarm of working-class people from the industrial north and the foreigners from the Continent might lead to political agitation or mob violence on the streets; after all never before had six million people congregated in an English city in so short a time. But there was general relief at the good order and good humour of the milling throngs. It was the Great Exhibition which finally marked the arrival of the Age of the Railway, with the cheap rail excursions transporting incredible crowds from the four corners of Britain. The era of mass travel had begun and for the first time in history the ordinary person could see the world for the price of a railway ticket. The event also enhanced the career of the "father" of tourism, Thomas Cook. He organised savings clubs for working men and their families, arranged for special terms with the railway companies, and brought 165,000 persons to London from the provinces.

Among the many Irish people who went to the Crystal Palace were three citizens of Cork, Mr. Daniel Corbett, merchant; Sir Thomas Deane, architect and patron of the arts, and Mr. John Francis Maguire, founder of the "Cork Examiner" and Mayor and Member of Parliament for the city on many occasions. A great deal of what follows in this chapter is based on Maquire's book entitled "The Industrial Movement in Ireland as illustrated by the National Exhibition in 1852." Printed and bound by Messrs. George Nash of 10 Prince's Street, Cork, it is a remarkably detailed survey not only of the Cork Exhibition but of the whole state of Irish industry and agriculture in the middle of the nineteenth century and is a primary source book for economic historians. Maguire gave to Cork a wide diversity of talent and a deep commitment to build up the industry of the city and of the country generally. The "Examiner," which he founded in 1841, was of the greatest significance in creating a sense of Irish values through its extensive reporting of the O'Connell Repeal Movement and its highlighting of personalities and events which displayed the genius of the people. In its editorials it examined the great issues of the day with critical insight and with something of a compulsion to arouse the people to a realisation of their own potential. Maguire was the close personal friend of the best-loved citizen of his day, Father Theobald Mathew, whose biography he wrote. His name can be seen on the plinth of the Statue in Patrick Street. In tracing the origin of the Cork event he gives the chief credit to Corbett for "the entire and exclusive merit of the inception of an idea which has been so practically and successfully carried out."

Mr. Corbett had mooted the idea privately to a few friends in November, 1851; a private meeting was convened in the office of the Mayor, Mr. James Lambkin, on December 1st, and this led to a public meeting in the Courthouse on 15th December, 1851. Corbett's original proposal was the modest one of an exhibition of the local industry of the city and county, but at a meeting of the Munster Exhibition Committee held at the Royal Cork Institution in Emmet Place (see relevant chapter) it was decided to extend its scope to include all Ireland. This was done on a motion proposed and seconded by two gentlemen who were untiring in promoting the material and cultural progress of the city, Colonel Beamish and Sir Thomas Deane. Messrs. Beamish and Crawford have been brewing stout on the South Main Street since 1792 and have entered largely into the commercial life of the city over that extended span of time. But not content with quenching the thirst of their fellow citizens, both families have honourable records in the civic and artistic life of Cork. The original Mr. Beamish lived at Beaumont, Blackrock, while Mr. Crawford had his residence nearby at Lakelands on the Mahon Peninsula. Both joined in giving the then fishing village of Blackrock the site of its Catholic Church in 1826, while the Minute Book of the Royal Cork Institution from 1826 to 1850 shows members of both families involved in a wide variety of cultural activities. At the end of the last century the Crawford private library at Lakelands was one of the finest in the country, while the name is still associated with a technical school, with the School of Art and with the University Observatory. Frequent reference to the architect Sir Thomas Deane has already been made. In proposing their motion for a National Exhibition both Beamish and Deane were prepared "to share any personal responsibility in the event of failure." Deane also undertook to go to London to seek exhibits from Irish artists residing there, including his fellow-townsman, Daniel Maclise. Uncertainty over money caused "fear and trembling," as Maguire puts it, with more ambitious plans being unfolded for more space, more exhibits and a better building. But the "good sense and patriotism" of the country responded magnificently, including the Lords Lieutenant Claredon and Eglington who "contributed munificently towards the funds of a then scanty exchequer." Nor was Cork neglected by the creator of the Great Exhibition; Prince Albert, in a letter of good wishes to Sir Robert Kane, President of the then Queen's College, sent a cheque for £100. Joseph Paxton figured in the published list of subscribers with a contribution of £5.

What were the objects of the exhibition? Maguire enumerates them succinctly as "to display to the country its own resources and capabilities; to inspire confidence, to remove doubt, to awaken interest in what materially concerned the welfare of all classes, to induce every person who entered the Exhibition to resolve on doing as much as possible to give employment, diminish poverty, lessen taxation, promote happiness and elevate the moral and physical condition of the mass of the people by the practical encouragement of native industry." Those objects seem as relevant today as they did in 1852. The one supreme object of the Exhibition was that the people would see Irish goods and so "buy Irish." Maguire elaborated as follows as to why he wrote his book: "I was anxious," he states, "that a noble display of Irish capability should not pass away like a transitory vision, full of beauty and hopefulness and promise, but also shadowy and vague from its limited duration. I deemed that what I saw of Irish genius, Irish capacity, Irish energy and Irish improvability was worthy of record." He dealt with the recent tragedy of the Famine, leaving the country with "its staple food blackened and rotted by some mysterious agency which science cannot fathom, its people mowed down in tens of thousands by the two-edged sword of famine and pestilence, its labourers driven to the Workhouse, its cities and towns filled with the demoralised wrecks of its population." Yet even that awesome visitation had one hopeful result in that it showed that "it would be the worst madness to confide any longer in the potato." A second deduction equally held true, 'that agriculture, alone and unassisted, is not equal to the emergency, and that the aid of manufacturing industry must be called in if this people is to be rescued from destruction and this ancient nation saved from utter extinction." Written in the aftermath of tragedy these words bear the intensity of the times in a manner rarely captured by the distant prose of a history book; they are also a blueprint for a programme of industrial expansion that had to await a native government for its fulfilment. It was to match words with action that Maguire and his associates set about the practical business of organising the 1852 Exhibition.

The venue was to be the old Corn Exchange which stood by the riverside on the site of the present City Hall, and the organisers were fortunate in having an architect of the calibre of John Benson to design and execute the adaptions and additions that were necessary. "A large gallery or transept was erected running across the southern extremity of the Corn Exchange Hall in a parallel direction to the quay. It was 300 feet in length by 30 in breadth." But with the prospect of so many exhibits it was realised that more space would be needed and this led to the erection of a distinct new premises, called the Southern Hall, which became the focus of the display area. It was situated in what is now the Fire Station section of the Corporation yard. Maguire gives the details of who did what and when: "On Saturday the 10th April, 1852, Mr. Benson was informed at a meeting of the Committee that it was found necessary to obtain further space, and after a very brief consideration he laid before them in pencil the design of this beautiful hall. On Wednesday, the 14th April, the first carpenter was put to work upon the site. It was to be erected in the space at the rear of the Corn Exchange which had been previously filled with sheds, and was to form a continuation of the original building. The space covered in by the Hall is 177 feet in length by 53 feet in breadth. The roof is of a semi-circular or dome-like shape and fifty feet in height. The roof consists of fourteen ribs spanning the hall in a full semi-circle, resting upon pillars of cast-iron. Each rib consists of seven thicknesses of deal, firmly and neatly put together with wood screws and by eleven bolts passing through. Each of these ribs weighed about one ton five hundred and was placed firmly in position in about thirty minutes. No scaffolding of any description was necessary in the formation. Six purlins run the whole length of the hall, and between the main ribs, abutting upon the purlins, are smaller laminated ribs upon which is nailed one-inch boarding to form the roof and walls. Over the exterior of the roof is strained calico, painted white, to resist the action of the weather, which is found to be perfecly impervious to water. Its qualities were tested on the 10th of May by a violent storm which lasted several hours but from which not the slighest injury was sustained. The Hall is lit by an unbroken line of roof light, running its entire length, fourteen feet in width and glazed with twenty-one ounce glass. An idea of its size may be better formed when it is stated that it is seven feet longer than the great room of the magnificent structure known as the St. George's Hall in Liverpool. Next to the Great Hall of Westminster it is the largest room in these countries not supported by pillars. The entire extent of the walls of this Hall, to where the ribs of the semi-circular roof spring from the cast-iron pillars, is lined with a beautiful drapery of crimson. This lining is of a rich kind consisting of calico covered with crimson flock, which was designed and adapted by Mr. Jones of this city. The pillars are gilded. In the centre a large fountain was erected by Mr. Langstaff. With the exception of the flooring, the whole body of this building was completed in the remarkably short space of twenty-five days. It may be added that from its peculiar construction it was well adapted for hearing. During its erection a musician tested its capacity with a bugle. Standing at the extreme end of the Southern Hall he blew a few notes which were heard at the farther end of the Northern Hall, 250 feet away, with perfectly unimpaired distinctness." The Corn Exchange room was referred to as the Northern Hall. On either side of the Southern Hall were erected two transepts, each containing an area of 110 feet by 85 feet, and designed to receive the heavier description of goods such as carriages and agricultural implements. "Thus the whole available space of the Exhibition Buildings embraced a superficial area of 42,525 feet." Great care was taken in embellishing the Banquet and Ball Room, which was "ninety feet in length by fifty-three feet in width and forty feet high. It was lighted by ten chandeliers adorned with banners and festoons. The Northern Hall was devoted almost exclusively to textile fabrics, poplins, tabinets, laces, ginghams, crochet, netting. The Western Transept contained furniture and upholstery of every kind. The Eastern Transept held articles of the smaller and lighter kind, glass, stone-ware, cutlery, optical and surgical instruments, ornaments, bookbinding, musical instruments and confectionery. The Southern Hall or Fine Arts Court, was filled with the proudest works of our national sculptors and painters."

It was amid such tasteful settings that the opening Banquet was held on the 9th of June with an address as remarkable for its sentiments as for its speaker. The Lord Lieutenant, Lord Eglington, expressed himself as follows: "It is true we have not here the statues of Italy, the carvings of Austria, the malachites of Russia, the porcelain of Sevres or the velvets of Genoa; but we have what you and I value far more, the products of our own country. We have the marbles of Cork, of Kilkenny and of Connemara. We have our tabinets, we have our lace embroidery, we have the results of the industry of the sons and the handiwork of the fair daughters of Erin. But allow me to ask what is there that the genius of Ireland cannot accomplish, whether it be the highest effort of human ambition or the humblest essay of talent? Does not Irish blood flow in the veins of him whose career of glory not one defeat, not one selfish act has tarnished? Was it not Irish genius that shone in the calm and lustrous eye of Canning, which sparkled in Sheridan, which gave command to Burke, which lent point to the irony of Tierney and which taught Goldsmith to write of Nature, which enabled your own Moore to breathe forth words of beauty, words of fragrance as sweet as your own harp, but nervous as the arm by which it was struck? And to come to your own county and even to your own city, was it not the genius of Cork which made Curran what he was? I would ask you does modern art own a better or a more worthy votary than Maclise?"

So much for the vaulted roof and the high rhetoric— but how did the public respond, what had the press to say and what exactly was on view? Attendance figures were impressive, considering the state of public transport in the city itself and in the surrounding countryside. From the public opening on the 10th of June, 1852, to the final day, the 10th of September, a total of 138,375 visits were made. Of these 54,936 were by season ticket holders while 74,095 were paid for at the door. Those paying at the door were particularised as follows: 6,022 paid two shillings, 1,018 paid one shilling and six pence, 18,937 paid one shilling and 48,118 paid sixpence. Maguire commented that those figures showed that "the humble classes readily availed themselves of the opportunity afforded of witnessing the varied evidence of the genius, skill, labour and capability of their own country." Highest attendance was recorded on Monday, July 26th, when 4,320 came along. Among the more enthusiastic visitors were the parties of school children who were admitted free in the mornings between 9.00 a.m. and 11.00 a.m., "always under the vigilant eye of their sedate and cautious superiors." A thousand children came on the 10th of August; on other days the South Presentation Convent sent 727 girls; the South Presentation Monastery sent 1,167 boys; the Protestant schools of St. Paul's, Christ Church, St. Nicholas, St. Peter's and St. Mary's Shandon sent a total of 434 boys and girls. The North Presentation Convent sent 939 girls on the 17th of August, while two days later the North Monastery sent 293 boys.

The London "Times" followed the unfolding of events with particular attention. On the 8th June, 1852, it reported "that His Excellency and the Countess of Eglington will arrive at the Dublin Railway terminus about 4 o'clock on Wednesday, the 9th of June; will be there received by the Mayor, city authorities, executive committee with the usual military honours and will be accompanied by a procession of the nobility and gentry of the county and city in their carriages through Blackpool to Patrick Street, Grand Parade, South Mall, which will be lined with troops, and along Albert Quay to the Bandon Terminus where their Excellencies will take their departure for Castle Bernard for the night." Again on the 11th of June the "Times" gave a resume of the steps which led to the whole project: Mr. Daniel Corbett, a highly respectable citizens of Cork, accompanied by Mr. John Shea, his son-in-law and ex-mayor of Cork, waited upon Sir Thomas Deane and suggested to him the propriety of taking steps to have an exhibition of the industrial products of the province of Munster. Sir Thomas Deane at first considered that the proposition was not one which would be received by the public with complete satisfaction and general reliance upon the success of the undertaking. He feared that the unrivalled splendour of the Exhibition held in the Crystal Palace would cast an Irish Exhibition into the shade. At the subsequent public meeting Mr. Corbett, Lord Bernard, Sir Robert Kane and Sir Thomas Deane had spoken. Sir Thomas Deane and Sir Robert Kane had waited upon the then Lord Lieutenant,, Lord Clarendon, "who highly approved of the project." On the return of this deputation to Cork it was decided to make the event a national one. A new deputation, consisting of Mr. Corbett and Mr. Shea went to Dublin to co-operate with Mr. John C. Deane, the son of Sir Thomas. The Lord Mayor of Dublin summoned a meeting at the Mansion House "attended by the leading manufacturers and citizens of Dublin." A metropolitan committee was established. Mr. Corbett and Mr. Shea next proceeded to Belfast and had interviews with the Mayor and leading manufacturers;" by whom they were received in a flattering and highly favourable manner." The two gentlemen next proceeded to Drogheda, Limerick, Clonmel and Waterford. This account from the "Times' largely covers the ground already gone over by Maguire, yet it adds some interesting details.

The paper's description of the Exhibition Building deserves quotation in full: "The Exhibition building, filled with the various objects of art and industry, and crowded by all classes and grades, will present a brilliant 'coup d'oeil'. The splendid arch of the dome with its moulded cornice adorned with shields and banners, supported on retiring columns backed with crimson drapery, overshadows a lengthened perspective of beautiful statuary, gems of art, gushing fountains and georgous fabrics, whose converging lines from floor, wall and ceiling meet or concentrate on a magnificent organ. The entrance or Northern Hall, entered from the quays, is 76 feet square and 50 feet high, divided into nave and isles, the nave rising into a species of clerestory with elevated side lights. This fine apartment combines in various glass cases all the fine texture articles, damask, linens, tabinets, crochet and embroidery. From this Hall is a noble arched entrance, 20 feet wide, descending by six steps into one of the finest rooms in Europe. the Fine Arts Hall, 182 feet by 53 feet in the centre and 45 feet high." Not content with this picture of magnificence the "Times" had a look at the kitchen: 'the kitchen department reminds one of the olden time, the roasting grate alone is 12 feet wide with hot hearth, charcoal stoves and platform for kettles." The citizens themselves appeared caught up in a flurry of activity: "Cork is like a bee-hive, full of life, expectation, energy, bustle, business; a great impetus has here been given to trade; human industry is awake and active. It was glorious to witness how the workmen laboured; here were the anxious architects running to and fro to see that their designs and plans were accurately observed, there were seen the members of the Committee occupied in giving their directions. There is not a tradesman in the city unemployed." This last assertion would indicate that the Exhibition had already gone far to fulfil a cherished aim of its organisers.

The "Times" of June 12th carried more comment: "All things considered the affair seems to have been quite successful, and from the number of English and Scottish visitors attracted thither by the cheap fares of the Chester and Holyhead Railway Company, there is but little doubt that not only Cork itself but the whole of the southern counties will feel the substantial benefits of the vastly increased intercourse between the two islands." This statement underlines the comment made earlier that the age of the railway had arrived and was seen in its full potential transporting crowds to great national events. A further comment would seem justified, namely that the large numbers of the general public coming to Cork by rail and sea in 1852 ushered in the Irish tourist trade as we now know it. True, the city had seen quite a big influx of visitors in 1843 for the annual meeting of the British Association for the Advancement of Science, but that was a specialised event. A final piece of reporting from the "Times" deals with the Grand Ball held on June 13th: "Seven o'clock was the hour appointed for assembling and when at that hour the guests began to arrive the whole population· of Cork turned out to receive them. Covers were laid for 600 and at the appointed hour every seat was occupied by a guest. Upwards of 1,200 ladies and gentlemen attended the ball and dancing was kept up with great zest until long after daylight this morning." And so it was that they danced all night down by the riverside. In preparing for this night of gladness the ladies no doubt visited the premises of Messrs. O'Hara in Patrick Street who had adverised a fine selection of feminine adornment in the "Cork Examiner" on 13th February, 1852: "Mr. O'Hara respectfully invites attention to his present magnificent stock of Velvets, Satins, Brocades and Glaced Silks, Lace Dresses, Paris Muslins, Fans, Head Dresses and Fancy Foreign Goods." On the 16th of the same month a firm that was to have a long association with the city announced its opening at 30 Patrick Street, Messrs. Grant and Company; it was offering "Silks, Shawls,

Fancy Dresses, Stuffs, Prints, Linens, Calicoes, Muslims, Stays, Ribbons, Bonnets, Millinery, Flowers, Laces, Gloves, Hosiery, Handkerchiefs and Small Wares." In passing it might be of interest to note that the St. Vincent de Paul Society in its Grand Draw for the same month was offering among its prizes "a three month Free Ticket on the Cork, Blackrock and Passage Railways," a line which doubtless contributed much to the attendance at the Exhibition. Considering the emphasis being laid on Irish manufacture by the organisers it was unfortunate that the official Catalogue was printed in England and this drew letters of protest to the "Examiner" on June 2nd from two printing concerns with long and distinguished association in the commercial life of Cork, Messrs. Guy Brothers and George Purcell. The same newspaper on June 4th carried a notice signed by Francis B. Beamish, chairman, intimating that the Committee were issuing "Season Tickets of Admission from 12 to 3 o'clock each day. Tickets for Grand Banquet cost £1. Tickets for Grand Ball at Exhibition Pavilion on evening of Friday, 11th June:

Ladies 10/-   Gentlemen 12/6
(to include Supper, Wine and Refreshments)

It is requested that Ladies and Gentlemen will appear in Dresses of Irish manufacture." Gradually the Exhibition was making itself felt in the commercial life of the city and in the advertisement columns of the "Examiner." On June 7th the following appeared:

"Royal Oyster Tavern. Market Lane, off Patrick Street. Established 1820. Mrs. Heron respectfully apprises her numerous Patrons that she will supply them during the Exhibition with Breakfasts, Luncheons, Dinners, Suppers at her usual Moderate Charges. Parties visiting the above Establishment can be accommodated with Beds."

However, the good Mrs. Heron had another enterprising competitor in the business of Beds, as the following notice indicated: "Mr. William Quinlan, having taken the Upper Part of House No. 111 Patrick Street, has fitted up the entire of the Spacious Rooms as Bedrooms. They will be let moderately and Servants Attendance provided." In the same issue of June 7th the "Examiner" carried a notice on traffic regulations for the opening next day at 11 o'clock; "On Thursday all Carriages to pass over Parliament Bridge and set down at the Exhibition Buildings, with the horses'

heads towards the East. Anglesea Bridge will be kept exclusively for foot passengers both going to and returning from the Exhibition." The stipulation regarding horses' heads is interesting and must afford some comfort to the harassed modern motorist—in all the devilish refinements of official torture suffered by him or her there is rarely any explicit regulation regarding bonnets. On June 9th the paper carried an indignant statement from Maguire himself on the matter of the Catalogue. He very much regretted that it was printed in England, and had been totally unaware of the sub-committee's decision as he was in London on business. Messrs. Fitzgerald, Confectioners, of No. 1 Bridge Street, catered for the creature comforts of the crowds and the following newspaper notice of tariff showed that it would have been extremely difficult to spend a £1:

"Tea, Coffee and Chocolate per Cup	£0.0.6
Luncheons	0.1.0
Cold Dinner	0.2.0
Jellies per Glass	0.0.4
Sandwiches	0.0.4
Porter and Ale per Bottle	0.0.4
Mineral Waters	0.0.4
Ices per Glass	0.0.6
Brandies and Wines per Glass	0.0.6"

As they sipped their jellies, their mineral water and their brandies what had the patrons seen and what were they chatting about? Maguire gives a detailed account of the exhibits, but it goes beyond a mere bald enumeration as he seeks to put things in the context of the Irish economy of the day. Dealing with Agriculture he pungently remarked that "scratching the soil either with the fork of a tree or with a plough of almost as primitive construction will not enable the Irishman to compete with the growers on the banks of the Danube or the Mississippi." Chief exhibitors in this section were Messrs. Bowman, Carrigan, Fitzsimon, Frazer, O'Byrne and Sheridan of Dublin; Hayden, Hyde, Kennedy, McKenzie, O'Brien, Perrott and Steele of Cork; Graham of Waterford; Robinson of Belfast, Harrison, Lee and Son of Limerick, English, Chapman and Keating of Clonmel, Ritchie of Ardee, Williamson of Mallow, Smith of Tralee, and Doctor Barter and the Rev. Mr. Bury of Cork. A local millwright, John Kennedy, had received several orders for an improved "Furze, Straw and Hay cutter," the invention of Mr. Thomas

Jennings. Thomas and Francis Jennings took a prominent part in the public life of Cork; their mineral water establishment in Brown Street was one of the best known business premises in the city, and it is of interest to note that it was still situated there until just over a year ago. Sadly, this old street which once witnessed the living activity of men and work is now blighted and reduced to the shambles of a car park. As was the case with the Beamish and Crawford families, so too, the Jennings took an active part in the cultural life of the city and the Minute Book of the Royal Cork Institution has frequent references to their activities. A display of Flax in its raw state attracted exhibits from Lady Bandon, Mr. Cummins of Anne Mount, Cork, Messrs. Pim of Youghal, Robinson of Belfast and Russell of Limerick. Flax was being grown plentifully in Ulster but hardly at all elsewhere in Ireland. Meanwhile, as Maguire noted, "the Russian was sending his raw material as well as his manufactured material into this country to the value of millions of pounds annually while our fields are lying waste." Glowing tribute was paid to the great Irish railway contractor, William Dargan, who pioneered flax growing in the South "by the erection of mills and the sowing and purchase of flax at Kildinan." In the company of Professor Shaw of Queen's College, Cork, Maguire had addressed meetings on flax-growing in Limerick, Waterford and Clonmel.

In view of the industry which has been created by a native government in the matter, it is interesting to find him pinpointing pioneer work on obtaining sugar from beet. Professor Sullivan, a Corkman destined to succeed Sir Robert Kane as President of the University, exhibited "nineteen specimens by which the manufacture of Beet-root Sugar is so fully illustrated.' Hitherto they had associated the sugar can "with burning suns and panting Negroes, with slavery and with death, but now we have evidence which upsets all our previous notions." Minerals on display included native copper ores, lead ores, silver, gold, antimony cobalt, malachite and iron pryites, once thought to be useless but latterly sent to England from Bantry for the manufacture of sulphuric acid. There was also a collection of marbles and building stones, with slate, clay and sands, including some discovered by Mr. Deering at Rostellan, useful in the manufacture of glass and porcelain. Reference was made to the Geological Survey then being executed by the Board of Works and to the Ordnance Map showing mineral deposits "under every field in the country." Mr. Egan of Cork showed a "splendid collection of chimney-pieces, tablets and columns for busts, the materials for most of which have been procured from the quarries in the vicinity of Cork." Tribute was paid to "the exquisitely worked altar of Italian marble executed by Samuel Daly of this city," and to the cut-stone baptismal fonts of Mr. Egan and Mr. Scannell. Messrs. R. J. Lecky, the Cork engineering form, designed the complicated machinery used for extracting Valentia slate, so valuabe for use and ornament "as roof ridges for public buildings, table slabs, billiard tables, dairy shelves, cisterns for keeping pure water, garden seats, roofing and flagging." The slate was quarried on Valentia Island, Kerry, from an underground tunnel 100 feet high and 150 feet wide.

Machinery was "the miracle-worker of the age" and the Cork firms exhibiting were Messrs. Harding, Hewitt, Perrott, Paul McSwiney, Lecky, Mangan, O'Connor, Stell, Topp and Wright. Also on view was some "of the beautiful work done at their Inchicore factory" by the Great Southern and Western Railway. This is a significant early tribute to the work of Irish railway engineers, the men whose work was increas-ingly to play so dominant a role in the commercial and social life of nineteenth century Ireland. There were fine door locks by Messrs. Barnwall of Dublin and Burke of Cork, domestic ranges by Messrs. Murphy and Perrott of this city and general hardware by Messrs. Phelan of Water-ford—all the more significant in that "the Irish grocer believed that a respectable tea-canister could not be procured out of Birmingham." Mr. Murphy of Cork had maintained his reputation as a bell-maker and the peal of bells run at the Exhibition had been despatched to Mel-bourne on the orders of its Catholic Bishop, Dr. Goold. Mr. Murphy had been awarded the first-class medal at the Great Exhibition in competition with the bell-founders of Europe. As well as lead pipes by Mr. Hodges of Cork there was also a display of pottery and tiles. Regarding the tiles Maguire stated "that architects of the greatest local eminence, including Sir Thomas Deane, were unaware that those tiles which are used for tessalated pavement in churches and other public buildings were to be had in this country."

Public notice was also focussed for the first time on "three new branches of Irish industry, Fancy Biscuits, Pearl Barley and Confectionery." Hitherto, Carlisle, Liverpool and Reading had supplied Ireland "with crisp and delicate fancy biscuits," Scotland had supplied our cooks with "that nutritious article" known as French or Pearl Barley, while Bristol had the "monopoly of supplying our sweet-mouthed youthful population with delicious indigestibles." To Messrs. George Baker of Cork went the credit of first competing with the biscuit makers of Carlisle and in eight years they had driven their rivals from the local market and were extending their trade from Cork to Belfast. Also exhibiting in this article were Messrs. Jacob of Waterford and Boland of Dublin. Pearl Barley was displayed by Messrs. George Waters and James Daly of Cork, by whom it was first made in Ireland. Dalys had erected a mill at Spring Hill where much youthful employment was given by the manufacture of this commodity which Scotsmen used "in thickening soups and boiling into porridge." Regarding Confectionery Maguire noted that "those tantalising cases of 'lollypops' which have arrested the attention and excited the profound admiration of our juvenile visitors have been contributed entirely by Dublin manufacturers, Graham and Company and Morton and Polson." In the matter of Preserved Provisions the display of Mr. John Gamble of Cork took pride of place and the following testimonial was quoted in their regard:

"Whitegift Hall, Goole, 15th December, 1849
Sir, In reply to your letter I have to acquaint you that the party from H.M.S. Investigator which visited the spot where the Fury's provisions were left, found the vegetables and soups preserved by Messrs. Gamble in excellent condition after having lain on the beach exposed to the action of the sun and all kinds of weather for a period of nearly a quarter of a century; but that there were not any meats found, the whole of these having been taken for our use during the winter we passed at the spot after abandoning the Victory.
Mr. J. H. Gamble.

I am, Sir, Your obedient Servant,
James Ross, Capt., R.N."

Irish Whiskey was exhibited by Messrs. James Daly and George Waters. In 1849 the distilling trade in Ireland had consumed two million barrels of grain, the produce of 200,000 acres of land. Yet there had been a dramatic decrease in the consumption of whiskey due to Father Mathew's Temperance Campaign, a decrease vividly illustrated by the following statistics: in 1839 the make was 12,296,342 gallons, but by 1844 this staggering figure had fallen to just over 5,000,000 gallons. Two other factors were to contribute to the decline, first the high level of taxation and second the Famine. Remarkably, however, though the Famine depressed the whiskey trade, it boosted that of tobacco and snuff. Maguire painted an evocative picture of the place of the pipe in the life of the Irish peasant: "The Arab tightens his shawl around his waist when, amid the desolation of the desert, he feels the gnawings of hunger; the poor Irishman has recourse to his friend and consoler, the short-stemmed, smoke-blacked pipe when he is equally visited amid the beauty and fruitfulness of his own Green Isle. It was the constant companion of his happier hours, the soother of his cares in better days and, perhaps, too often the inducement to a lazy lounge over his gate." Consumption in 1840 was 5,128,850 lbs. of tobacco and by 1847 this had risen to 5,949,691 lbs. Except for a small import of English cigars and snuff, almost all the tobacco consumed was manufactured in Ireland; in fact, Messrs. James Lambkin of Cork and Lundy Foot of Dublin had secured a firm footing in the English market for their snuffs for the "relief of the jaded statesman or overworked lawyer." Cork 'high toast" snuff was also much valued in Belfast. Exhibitors in tobacco and snuff were Messrs. Blackledge, Clarke, England, Hosford and Lambkin of Cork, Arthur Mason of Waterford and Lundy Foot of Dublin.

Book printing and book binding were illustrated by Messrs. Hodges and Smith, McGlashan, Gill and Duffy of Dublin, Nash and Guy of Cork and Redmond and Sutherland of Waterford. In the matter of Linen the Exhibition was indebted 'to the patriotic and liberal spirit of several of our Northern manufacturers for a gratifying display of those beautiful and costly fabrics for which that portion of our island is so celebrated." Messrs. Richardson of Banbridge, Co. Down, exhibited linens, cambrics, diapers, sheeting, towelling and tickens. From Belfast there came specimens from Messrs. Andrews, Coulson and Company, Ewart and Son, Fenton and Company, Messrs. McCay and Robert

Roddy. Among southern exhibitors were Todds of Limerick and Shorten and Howard of Bandon. Maguire hoped that "the manufacture of linen will again be familiar in the South and that the hum of the spinning wheel and the shuttle will be heard issuing from the door of the thatched cottage." But if linen belonged to Ulster then velvet and poplin were the pride of Leinster, with Messrs. Pim and Atkinson of Dublin among the many who excelled. The firm of Messrs. Jones of Cork had made the splendid velvet lining the Exhibition walls, with a pile and colour equal to that of the products of Genoa and Lyons. With regard to elegance and utility few things mattered more to a nineteenth century gentleman than his carriage, and Maguire waxed eloquent over the fine exhibits made in Ireland: "I have witnessed with delight the genuine admiration which the display of Irish carriages elicited from visitors of every class, station and condition, from our own people as well as from strangers." It was necessary to overcome the prejudice of the Irish consumer who was so willing to pay higher prices for London models no better than those made at home. Irish craftsmen excelled in making the whole range of Broughams, Clarences, Barouches, Phaetons, Side-Cars, Gigs and Drags. Cork firms exhibiting were Messrs. Edden, inventors of the "four-wheeled car," and Messrs. Isaac Julien, Thomas Hannan, John Walsh and Anthony Quinn. Two-thirds of Mr. Edden's carriages on display were sold to strangers, some going to Scotland and others to the West Indies. Foremost in Furniture was Mr. John Fletcher of Patrick Street, Cork, whose "gladiatorial table" had won a prize at the Great Exhibition. He showed his "Shamrock Table" comprising thirteen kinds of the rarest Irish timber. Woollen goods and flannels were displayed by Messrs. Cogan of Midleton and Nicholls of Glanmire. In the matter of Hats there was up-to-the-minute news on style: "the old beaver hat is now almost entirely done away with, the silk hat having superseded it and with reason, for the silk hat looks as well, gives about equal wear, weighs less and is cheaper." Happy days when one hoped to get by with silk. Local manufacture was in the hands of Messrs. Graham, Chabrel, Vanesbeck, Wright, Richards, Deveraux and Moffit. A silk hat cried out for a pair of Gloves and a fine display of hand-stitched articles was exhibited by Miss Condon, Mrs. Breakwell and Messrs. Mollard, Francis, Mc-Grath and Dowden of Cork.

The firms of Bradford and Elliot made cutlery, razors, scissors and pen-knives in the city, and Maguire was able to assert that "the two greatest generals of modern times, Napoleon and Wellington, than whom, perhaps, there were no better judges of steel, were more than once indebted to the house of Bradford for the luxury of a clean shave." A variety of Optical, Mathematical and Nautical instruments was displayed by Messrs. Thomas Bennett and Henry Hunt of Cork. Bennett had "dumpy and irrigating levels, ships' binnacles and compasses, barometers, thermometers, vacuum and pressure gauges for steam-engines and an electro-magnetic machine." Hunt exhibited a full mounted five-inch theodolite and a three and a half foot, full-sized acromatic telescope. The best compasses "almost in the world are made in three places, Liverpool, Trieste and Cork, and the compasses of this city are highly prized and largely purchased by masters of foreign vessels." Regarding the "recent extension of the Electric Telegraph system" Maguire referred to the electro-magnetic and medico-galvanic instruments manufactured by Mr. A. Quinne of Queen's College. Other samples in this sphere were a large acromatic telescope by George Newenham and barometers by Giovanni Binda, both of this city. Regarding articles for the Toilet it was no longer necessary to cross the Channel for 'old Brown Windsor" or to go up the Rhine for "Jean Maria Farina." Both were being made in the city by such firms as W. and H. M. Goulding, Donegan Brothers, Coleby and Company and Messrs. Dyas and Harman. Indeed, Donegans were exporting toilet soaps and oils to Gibralter, the West Indies and the Leeward Islands. A whole range of Brushes was being manufactured by Varian Brothers of Cork for the home market as well as for export. Herewith is a catalogue of said brushes: tooth brushes, hair brushes, clothes brushes, shoe brushes, carpet brushes, hat brushes, machine brushes, horse and harness brushes, painters' brushes, paper stainers' brushes and whitewash brushes.

Mr. T. McCarthy of the city exhibited a case of combs of buffalo, ivory and tortoise-shell, besides beautifully-designed dress combs for ladies. Shoe-blacking was displayed by Messrs. Josiah Martin, Goulding and O'Connell of the city, who were among many Irish manufacturers who had "emancipated the public from the monopoly of Day and Martin." For those so denuded as to be unable to make use of Mr. Varian's hair brushes there were the Perukes made by the local firm of John O'Leary and Joseph Piggott. O'Leary displayed a Zephyr wig which would "deceive Cupid," while Piggott had a "consolatory case of ornamental hair." But the ultimate in matters hairy came from Dublin with Mr. Birkbeck offering "transparent wigs to a hairless public." If the bald were catered for, the toothless were not neglected as Mr. Alfred Jones of Cork was at hand with "his valuable case of dental specimens."

Maguire lamented the demise of the Cork Glass industry, but Mr. D. Sheehan displayed and sold some beautiful dinner services made from Rostellan silex. Two local firms exhibited a variety of Feather work, Messrs. C. & J. O'Sullivan and Messrs. Booth and Fox, employing four hundred female workers. The steam machinery for the O'Sullivan plant had been made in the city by Messrs. Paul McSwiney. Booth and Fox had successfully exhibited at the Great Exhibition and had built up a large export trade in eiderdowns, muffs, capes, cuffs, boas and trimmings. The muffs of Booth and Fox were highly esteemed in Paris, and the firm imported more feathers from St. Petersburg, the principal market, than "all the houses in the United Kingdom." They had a large share of the London market and their machinery had likewise been designed by Mr. McSwiney. Music notes light as a feather were to be heard from the range of Irish-made Musical Instruments. Mr. J. Bray of Dublin had a double-action harp, while Mr. Telford of that city and Mr. Murphy of Cork displayed organs. Mr. John Murphy, also of the city, exhibited a double-bass and a violincello made by himself. Another local man, Mr. D. Harrington, showed a set of silver-mounted Union Pipes, with Maguire commenting that 'the pipes of this humble mechanic are as justly celebrated as the pianos of Broadwood or Collard." Certainly a large claim! Music strings were being made for over thirty-five years by Mr. Patrick Connell of Hanover Street, Cork, and had been praised by many "in the belief that their harp, guitar, violin or violincello were indebted to Italian skill for their ravishing sounds." In the line of Leather and Boots and Shoes attention focussed on the local firm of Daniel Murphy and Son who extensively imported bark and valonia from Smyrna and the Mediterranean, and who were the first direct Irish importers of hide from South

America. The makers of the two Prize Boots at the Great Exhibition had been Irishmen, from Dublin and Cork, and local firms on display were Messrs. Blake, Clancy, Deasy, Hyde, Fouhy, J. Murphy, M. Murphy, Mollard, Roche and Smelt. Mr. G. Austin of Dublin showed a wide range of dressing cases, work-boxes, writing desks, despatch boxes and jewel cases.

In relation to Silver Plate and Jewellery, Maguire had to tell of a sad decline in Cork; whereas in 1800 there were about fifty silversmiths and twenty goldsmiths, in 1852 there was not a single manufacturer. The story was scarcely less depressing in regard to Clock-making, despite the earlier traditions of craftsmen like Richard Deeble, William Bagley and Ackens and Son. However, "the genius and mechanical skill of a local tradesman, Mr. James Mangan," was coming to be recogised. His clock in Shandon Steeple was "one of the largest in Europe." Mr. Samuel Haynes of the city exhibited a Turret Clock similar to those he had made for the termini of the Cork and Bandon Railway. The section for Drugs, Chemicals and Mineral Waters included the specimens of Messrs. Jennings of Brown Street with soda water, vichy, magnesia, carbonate and wheat starch in crystals and powder. Lithography, Engraving and Ornamental Penmanship included samples of the work of the local firms of Guy Brothers, with gold and flock business cards from William Jones. The city firms of Messrs. Lane, Harris and Gibbins displayed Chandeliers, Lamps and Gas Fittings, while horse-shoes were shown by Messrs. Ashe and Myles. Mr. W. P. Flynn of Cork exhibited two refrigerators while Mr. Osborn Bergin had a working model of an automatic fire extinguisher. This particular piece of hardware might have been of practical use a few days before the opening of the Exhibition when the "Examiner" of June 7th carried the following snippets of news: "A fire broke out yesterday in Mrs. Fisher's premises, Maylor Street, about half past twelve. Through the exertions of the Mayor, Mr. Peterson, and the Firemen of the Atlas Assurance Company it was speedily extinguished without inflicting any material injury. Mrs. Fisher and her family were at prayers when the accident occurred." Was this to be attributed to the power of prayer or the prowess of the Mayor of Cork in the matter of putting out fires? To return to the Exhibition and the domain of Hosiery and Lace, Mr. William Dowden had a range of hosiery and plain inside waiscoats and drawers, while the firm of Messrs. Lawsons displayed spun silk socks of their own make. The Ursuline Convent, Blackrock, also displayed hosiery while Messrs. Treacy had satin and cloth vests highly embroidered by young females of the city. Various other specimens of lace, crochet and embroidery came from what was termed the "Female Industrial Movement" which included Lady O'Brien's Associations in Clare and Limerick, the Clonakilty Embroidery School, Lady Deane's School at Blackrock, the Sisters of Mercy School at Rutland Street, the South Presentation Poor School and the North Presentation Convent School. Many of these schools were on contract to supply the Queen's Old Castle with the products of their deft fingers.

Amid this multiplicity of goods and gadgets the Fine Arts were not neglected. There were drawings from the Cork School of Design at Emmet Place and from the North Monastery School, as well as from the Schools of Design in Dublin and Belfast. Of particular note were the exhibits of the artistic genius of Irish painters and sculptors. James Barry, a native of the Blackpool district of the city, was represented by one of his lesser works, the portrait of George the Fourth. Samuel Ford, also from the city, had "The Fall of the Angels" on view. Also on display were works by Butt, Brocas, Roe and O'Keeffe. Maguire did not specify what works by the better-known Grogan were on view; he referred to him as one "who brings the spectators almost into the midst of the last century when ladies coquetted in hoops and gentlemen wore bag-wigs and swords." One of the finest pieces on view was the portrait of Lord Monteagle by Sir Martin Arthur Shee, late President of the Royal Academy. Perhaps the greatest work on display was a piece from the hand of the Cork artist who had already won high acclaim in London, Daniel Maclise. It was the original study in oils for the fresco in the House of Lords, "The Spirit of Justice.' Maguire had "gazed at it over a hundred times, and each time with as keen a sense of pleasure as at first." Through the exertions of Sir Thomas Deane there was also on view "The Tempest" by F. Danby, R. A. Samuel West, a native of the city, was represented by his 'Charles the First Receiving Instruction in Drawing from Reubens," while another native artist, William Fisher, had on view his portrait of Robert O'Callaghen Newenham, president of the Cork

Society of Arts, and his portrait of John Craig, executed for the city Savings Bank and still on display there. Another city artist, James B. Brennan, showed his portrait of Sir Thomas Deane and of the grand old man of letters in the city, James Roche. This latter now hangs in the University through the generosity of the late Mr. Downes of the Imperial Hotel. Architectural drawings included a "Design for Town Hall, by Sir Thomas Deane, Son and Woodward," and "Examination Hall of the Queen's College, Cork" by the same partnership. Also displayed was the "Convent of the Sisters of Mercy, Cork, by William Atkins." The art of Sculpture was nobly represented by pieces from John Hogan, whose youth was spent in the city and who had won eminence in Rome. Visitors saw his "Head of Minerva," carved in wood, the "Drunken Faun" and the splendid "Dead Christ" in Italian marble. Among Architectural models were those of the City Courthouse and the Dominican church by Sir Thomas and Kearns Deane, a model for the Cork Town Hall by Mr. John Benson and models of bridges by Professor Lane of the University. The display of Irish Antiquities included an Ogham Stone, St. Patrick's Bell, the Tara Brooch and a twelfth century crozier loaned by the Duke of Devonshire.

This account has set out to show that the National Exhibition at Cork in 1852 was a noteworthy event for the city and for Ireland. It generated a great amount of community effort in the city and it brought to the banks of the Lee the best of contemporary Irish enterprise and craftmanship. It made Cork a meeting-place for many traditions and it must have given hope at a time when Ireland desperately needed it. It can hardly be an exaggeration to claim that it was a milestone on the road to the development of Irish industry. In the following year, 1853, Dublin was to mount its National Exhibition with John Benson again engaged to erect the buildings on the lawn of Leinster House on Merrion Square. The whole enterprise was largely conceived and financed by the great railway engineer, William Dargan, who is reputed to have contributed some £100,000 of his personal means.

Both cities were to have many such events in the years following, so pointing to the significance of the first National Exhibition in Cork in 1852.

Chapter IX

PORTRAIT OF AN ARTIST—DANIEL MACLISE

It was Charles Dickens who spoke the last tribute to his lifelong friend, Daniel Maclise, the shoemaker's son from Cork who had won a foremost place in the world of art. The occasion was a dinner of the Royal Academy of Art held in London on 30th April, 1870, three days after the death of Maclise, and Dickens was deeply moved as he spoke to the assembly of the talented and the titled: "For many years I was one of the two most intimate friends and most constant companions of Mr. Maclise, to whose death the Prince of Wales has made allusion and the President has referred with the eloquence of genuine feeling. Of his genius in his chosen art I will venture to say nothing here; but of his fertility of mind and wealth of intellect I may confidently assert that they would have made him, if he had been so minded, at least as great a writer as he was a painter. The gentlest and most modest of men, the freshest as to his generous appreciation of young aspirants, and the frankest and largest hearted as to his peers, incapable of a sordid or ignoble thought, gallantly sustaining the true dignity of his vocation without one grain of self-ambition, wholesomely natural at the last as at the first, 'in wit a man in simplicity a child,' no artist of whatever denomination, I make bold to say, ever went to his rest leaving a golden memory more pure from dross, or having devoted himself with a truer chivalry to the art-goddess whom he worshipped." This farewell from the great novelist to the great painter was to have an added poignancy; it was the last public speech that Charles Dickens ever made, for in June of that same year he followed his friend to his rest.

Perhaps the most familiar of Maclise's works is his immense oil painting in the National Gallery in Dublin, "The Marriage of Strongbow and Eva," in which he captured a dramatic moment in Irish history. This creation was first exhibited at the Royal Academy in London in 1854. Two other works in the historical narrative style in which he excelled are seen annually by thousands of visitors to the Long Gallery in the House of Lords, the frescoes depicting the "Meeting of Wellington and Blucher at Waterloo" and the "Death of Nelson," completed respectively in 1861 and 1865. Throughout his life he retained an intuitive sympathy

with Ireland's troubled past and with the romantic associations of her ruins and her legends; yet he moved with great simplicity and with high esteem in the sophisticated world of the London artistic and literary set. His friendships were wide and enduring, and apart from the historical paintings in the grand manner, he has left a rich collection of portrait drawings of friends and patrons such as John Constable, Nicolo Paganini, Benjamin Disraeli, William M. Thackeray, Thomas Campbell, Thomas Carlyle, Samuel Taylor Coleridge and Sir Edward Bulwer-Lytton. His portrait of Dickens was chosen as the frontispiece to the memorable biography of the novelist written by John Forster. Among the many literary works which he illustrated were the "Fairy Legends of Ireland" by his fellow-townsman Crofton Croker, the "Reliques of Father Prout," also by a fellow-townsman, Francis O'Mahony, and Moore's "Irish Melodies."

Maclise was born in Cork in 1806, the son of Alexander McLeish, a private in the Elgin Fusiliers, and Rabecca Buchanan who were married in the Old Presbyterian Church, Prince's Street on Christmas Eve, 1797. There were seven children in the family and Daniel was baptised at the Prince's Street Church on 2nd February, 1806, by which time his father was in business as a shoemaker. There has been a good deal of local speculation as to where exactly in the city the family home was situated; however, this hitherto unpublished extract from an Autobiographical Manuscript now preserved in the Library of the Royal Academy of Arts, London, clarifies the matter finally: Maclise states that he "was born in that city surnamed the beautiful, in a house in George's Street, near Grafton's Alley, January 25th 1811." George's Street is now named Oliver Plunkett Street, while the baptismal record shows that the artist was taking some poetic licence in giving 1811 as the year of his birth. He received a good basic education in literature in one of the many small schools which were to be found in private houses in many parts of Cork at that time. Writing about himself in the third person the Manuscript goes on to depict his boyhood years: "He derived a competent knowledge of the French and Italian languages from the very able professor, C. V. A. Marcel, Consul of France, resident in that city. His earliest inclinations were for Art and hours were constantly stolen from time which ought to have been devoted to other studies for the indulgence of this favourite one. The copy book was constantly scratched over by many a rude grotesque, the blank cover of each school book offered tempting space for a frontispiece, the Latin grammar was profusely illustrated, and Murray's Reader assumed the appearance of an illustrated Manuscript."

A great amount of information on Maclise's boyhood days in Cork comes from a friend who shared them and who was to be his biographer. It was in 1871, just one year after the artist's death, that Mr. Justin O'Driscoll, M.R.I.A., a barrister at law, published his "Memoir of Daniel Maclise, R.A." With the information he gives that his friend had been to school with "a gentleman famous for having educated some of the best classical and science scholars of his time," there can be little doubt but that the school was the one on Patrick's Hill conducted by the Rev. T. D. Hincks, Minister of the Old Presbyterian Church and founder of the Royal Cork Institution, to which a chapter of this work has been devoted. O'Driscoll continues the boyhood tale: "When little more than a child he manifested in what direction his talents lay. He excited the delight and astonishment of his schoolfellows by the pen and ink sketches with which he adorned their copy-books, and the wonderful facility with which he could dash off a queer face, or an irreverent caricature of the master. He left school when scarcely fourteen years old and was placed in the banking house of Messrs. Newenham where he remained but a very short time. He was even then far from deficient in classical acquirements. He had read Shakespeare and Milton, Spencer and Chaucer, as well as many of the English poets and dramatists, history and romances, tales of chivalry, and legends of his own land." It is possible to see in his taste for historical reading and in his love for the legends of Ireland the early nurturing of that taste for the heroic and the chivalric which so influenced his choice of subject as a mature painter. But the youth found time for other diversions outside of art, in particular he had an interest in music, walking and swimming as the "Memoir" recalls: "He received lessons on the Spanish guitar from an old Italian named Fabri, and acquired considerable proficiency on that instrument. Fabri conceived a great affection for his pupil and persistently refused to accept any remuneration. He was, however, more than amply rewarded by having his attentuated figure sketched in every conceivable attitude than his vanity suggested. About this period some young associates of Maclise got up a gymnasium in Cork and he practised there. He was then a singularly fine and muscular lad and rather famous for feats of agility and strength. Many moments were passed on board the yacht of his friend, J. L. and as the little craft, wafted by the evening breeze, glided down the river Lee Maclise might be seen sitting in the stern with pencil in hand, transferring to his portfolio sketches of the charming scenery with which the banks of that beautiful river so abound." With the boat moored off Blackrock Castle he often swam over to Little Island. Many Sunday afternoons were spent on long walks out the Lee Fields, almost always yielding some sketches of nature scenes.

The young artist was fortunate in that there were at that time in the city a number of gentlemen of taste and influence who discerned his potential and made it their business to give him every encouragement. Indeed, in those years from 1815 onwards Cork experienced something of a literary and artistic golden age, with writers, poets, painters, sculptors and a number of houses where they gathered in convivial company to admire paintings, to browse through books and to intoxicate themselves with good talk and fine wine. This epoch of taste and talent in Cork was graciously evoked in the Catalogue for the Maclise Exhibition in the National Portrait Gallery, London, in 1972, which was published by the Arts Council of Great Britain. It stated that "Maclise was fortunate to have been born in a city which then had an active cultural life, or he might never have managed to launch himself. His contact with literary and intellectual society stimulated his imagination and gave him a lifelong passion for books. He was well-read in the classics and in contemporary romantic literature. His taste for historical narrative, his love of chivalric and heroic events, and his attraction to the bizarre and macabre, can all be traced back to his adolescence." Among those patrons of the arts were Mr. Richard Sainthill who lived in the picturesque Queen Anne-style town house still standing in Emmet Place, and Mr. Thomas Crofton Croker, the writer and antiquary. The "Memoir" describes the course of events: "His wonderful skill of hand attracted the notice of the late Mr. Sainthill, a lover of the fine arts and a most learned antiquary. He perceived that the drawings of the boy bore the impress of unquestionable genius and in this amiable gentleman Maclise found an ardent and influential friend. He had access to the library of Mr. Sainthill which was filled with antiquarian and legendary literature, and through him Maclise first became acquainted with the late Thomas Crofton Croker, the accomplished author of the 'Fairy Legends of Ireland,' and many other well-known works, and whose warm and unswerving friendship for Maclise exercised a not unimportant influence on the earlier part of his career." The first edition of Croker's book was published in 1825; for the second edition Maclise executed a series of pen and ink drawings which were a prelude to many such creations in the years ahead. He also attended the lectures of Dr. Woodrooffe at the School of Anatomy in what is now Parnell Place; his biographer notes that "this early discipline of his hand and eye in the science of anatomy contributed much to produce that marvellous facility and accuracy in delineating the human figure which imparts such a charm and grace to all his works."

Other sources of intellectual and artistic enrichment came from Mr. Newenham, the banker, who lived at Summerhill; from the old Quaker family of the Penrose's who were so actively involved in the commercial life of Cork, and whose mansion at Tivoli was to give shelter to Sarah Curran after the tragedy and the heartbreak of the execution of Robert Emmet; from the Cork Library which had been established in Pembroke Street in 1792 and whose original entrance door may still be seen in that street, and from the Cork Institution whose premises were still on the South Mall. Maclise himself conjures up this round of events and ideas in his Autobiographical Manuscript: He found in Mr. Newenham's House at Summerhill "a residence entirely congenial to his drawing taste, for Mr. Newenham had a gallery of pictures very well selected, and besides being the resort of all who could at all pretend to taste there was in the home carried on by the daughters and the father the actual experience of the Arts of Painting and Modelling, colours, canvas and the easel. The Model Stand and Clay were familiar objects and it was here with borrowed colours and on an imposing table that his first experience in oil colour occurred, and a portrait was produced of his old lady patron, the Miss Spratt. About this time he copied from the well-known prints all the large heads of Raphael's Transfiguration, as well as the careful outline of Michael Angelo's Last Judgment, as well as the attributed Guide in the Catholic Chapel in Carey's Lane of the Crucifixion and many of Barry's etchings of his pictures in the Adelphi." The old chapel in Carey's Lane has long since given way to the Pugin-designed church of Ss. Peter and Paul; James Barry, the contemporary and rival of Sir Joshua Reynolds, became the first Irishman to become a member of the Royal Society. He was born and reared in a humble cabin at Blackpool in Cork. In a footnote to O'Driscoll's book there is the following anecdote: "It is related of Barry that when a mere boy he performed the journey from Cork to Dublin on foot with his first picture, 'The Conversion of the Pagan Prince by St. Patrick.' It was placed in a remote corner of one of the Exhibition rooms where it was unlikely that any eye would rest upon it. It did not, however, escape the observation of the great Edmund Burke; he inquired of the secretary the name of the painter. 'I don't know, Sir,' said that gentleman, 'but it was brought here by that little boy,' pointing to Barry who was standing modestly near his work. 'Where did you get this picture, my boy?' said Burke, 'who painted it?' 'It is mine,' said the proud boy. 'I painted it.' 'Oh, that is impossible,' said Burke glancing at the poorly-clad youth. Barry burst into tears and rushed from the room. Burke instantly followed him, soothed him with kind and encouraging words and was ever after his friend."

Maclise continues his recollections in the Manuscript as follows: "Perhaps it is not unworthy of mention that he owes deep obligations to Dr. Woodroofe who afforded him every facility in his study of Anatomy. He had for years attended the Doctor's lectures and devoted himself many winters to actual dissection. The Cork Institution afforded him gratuitously admission to their lectures and professors Davy and Taylor, who annually delivered discourses on Chemistry and Natural History, always left a ticket at his disposal. The Institution had a valuable Library to which he had at all times free access; he was also allowed to have any books from the Cork Public Library. He was introduced to the family of the Penrose's whose beautiful seat, Wood Hill, was close to the demesne of his friend Newenham and possessed also a very remarkable picture gallery, one of the chief of the south of Ireland. He studied there for many years and made many copies, one of the well-known Venus Rising from the Sea by his townsman, Barry." He referred to Mr. Richard Sainthill as "a gentleman who confirmed all his inclinations, whose antiquarian knowledge and various literary attainments eminently qualified him for inspiring a youth with a true regard and attachment, even where both did not already exist."

These personal memories of the youth of Maclise, being published here for the first time, are of considerable importance in evoking the atmosphere of Cork in those earlier decades of the last century. They quite clearly show a taste for literary merit and artistic appreciation in a provincial city which did not have the advantage of the great collections of books and paintings to be found in a capital city. The library and lectures of the Cork Institution are also shown to have been of service to the community, and more especially to this sensitive youth who otherwise would have been deprived of the broader horizons he so clearly relished. Not less noteworthy was the patronage afforded him in the private houses of citizens of superior wealth—indeed it is interesting to see how these people had used their money to acquire literary and artistic collections which enriched the cultural life of the city.

That cultural life was to be greatly enhanced in 1822 when Cork came into the possession of a splendid collection of classical casts of some of the finest pieces of sculpture in the Vatican Galleries. When they arrived in Cork they had a highly prestigious pedigree, for no less than a Pope, a Prince and a Lord had been involved in the proceedings. In 1818 Pope Pius VII decided to express his gratitude to the British people for the return to the Vatican Galleries of a great many of the priceless works of art which Napoleon had looted and scattered over Europe. After Waterloo the British Government set about having them returned to the Vatican. To show his appreciation the Pope commissioned Canova to superintend the making of the casts which included the Apollo Belvidere, the Medici Venus, the Dying Gladiator among them. The casts were duly shipped to London to be presented to the British people through the Prince Regent, later George IV, himself a patron of the arts. For some reason His Royal Highness was unappreciative of the Papal gifts and they languished first at the London Custom House and then in the garden of Carlton House, the royal town residence. At this stage Lord Listowel, also an art parton with a fine gallery at his country seat at Convamore near Fermoy, made representations to his friend the Regent with a view to having the casts donated to the citizens of Cork. Lord Listowel was one of those Irish peers who were particularly active in the promotion of the welfare of Ireland not only in art but in manufacture and education. His speeches in Parliament were informed and blunt in analysing the cause of Irish discontent; for Cork city and county he had an especial concern. The Regent readily complied with the request and the casts were despatched to Cork to be given into the custodianship of the Society for the Promotion of the Fine Arts which had been founded in 1815. They remained in the care of the Society until 1822 when it found itself in financial difficulties. At that stage the Royal Cork Institution accepted them and in its Minute Book for the period makes reference to what it calls the Cast Room, though, as will be seen shortly, Maclise was to upbraid the Institution for what he considered to be neglectful storage. When the Government gave the Institution the use of the Old Custom House (now the northern portion of the School of Art) in Emmet Place in 1832 the casts were moved thither, and there they have remained until the present day, still used as models by the aspiring young artists of Cork.

It is now time to let Maclise himself tell the story of this whole episode as he recalled it in his Manuscript: "The Pope had presented George the Fourth with a valuable collection of Casts from the Antique, and the King had presented it at the solicitation of Lord Ennismore, a well-known patron of Art whose collection of pictures at Convamore between Fermoy and Mallow was said to be finest in the south of Ireland, to a number of gentlemen who formed themselves into a Committee for its management. All the neighbouring gentry were enrolled as subscribers; a former Theatre once supported by the Apollo Society of Amateur Actors was fixed upon as the most suitable place for the reception of the valuable collection of Casts. It was situated in a principal street, Patrick Street, and the stage was screened off by a well-painted scene of the interior of a Greek Temple. The Pit was boarded over, the Gallery was partitioned off. The boxes remained nearly as they were, and the Statues were arranged around the Parterre with much taste and movable pedestals under the Superintendence of a London gentleman who was sent over for the purpose, and whose name happened appropriately enough to be Corkaigne. This Collection was subsequently removed to the Cork Institution where it was looked upon more in the light of lumber than anything else, many of the Statues being placed in a damp cellar. The Collection is still, I believe, inappropriately located in the obsolete Old Custom House where there is neither light nor space to view it with effect." In the following passage Maclise movingly recalls the effect of the Casts on his youthful sensibilities: "The effect of the Collection of Casts on his mind was most important; he literally had never seen a plaster Cast. The effect of that mass of excellence—beautiful and actual moulds from those originals that were worshipped by generations—on his young fancy was at first overwhelming then it was inspiring. For years and years by day and night he studied from those perfect forms." Among those who also learned the craftsmanship of his art from the Casts was Maclise's contemporary, John Hogan, later to become probably Ireland's greatest sculptor of the nineteenth century. They were friends together on the South Mall and at the anatomy lectures in Parnell Place.

Another major influence in Maclise's life came in August, 1825, when the distinguished novelist, Sir Walter Scott, visited Cork. The tales of the high chivalry and romances of the Scottish border lands had made the Waverley Novels into popular favourites across the world, and Scott had been the first writer in history to become what is now called a best-seller. Apart from his achievements as a novelist he was to have a marked influence in the way people thought and wrote about history, being one of the seminal forces in creating a more romantic and humane view of the past. Nowhere were his novels more avidly read than in Ireland, while his popularity was further increased by his public support for Catholic Emancipation. Having been rapturously welcomed in Dublin, the great man set off by coach to savour the dreamy beauty of the Lakes of Killarney. Early in August, 1825, he travelled into Cork and stayed at the Imperial Hotel on the South Mall accompanied by his daughter and son-in-law, Mr. and Mrs. J. G. Lockhart, and the lady novelist, Maria Edgeworth. Lockhart was later to write the biography of Scott, regarded as one of the great biographies of the nineteenth century. It was, therefore, a distinguished literary trio which descended on Cork in that late summer with Scott himself, distinguished in achievement and in appearance, creating a stir of welcoming delight. Perhaps a little cameo from that time best captures the atmosphere. Tom Moore had written from Devizes to wish Scott a pleasant Irish visit: "I wish most heartily that I had been in my own green land to welcome you. It deights me, however, to see that the warm hearts of my countrymen have shown that they know how to value you." Scott replied: "In Ireland I have met with everything that was kind and have seen much which is never to be forgotten. What I have seen has, in general, given me great pleasure; for it appears to me that the adverse circumstances which have so long withered the prosperity of this rich and powerful country are losing their force, and that a gradual but steady spirit of progressive improvement is effectually, though tacitly, counteracting their bad effects. The next twenty-five years will probably be the most important in their results that Ireland ever knew. And so to descend from such high matters, I hope you will consider me as having left my card for you by this visit although I have not been happy enough to find you at home. You are bound by the ordinary forms of Society to return the call and come to Scotland. Bring wife and bairns. We have plenty of room and plenty of oatmeal and, entre nous, a bottle or two of good claret. We will talk of poor Byron who was dear to us both."

Lockhart in his "Life" recounts the Cork visit briefly: "Having crossed the hills from Killarney to Cork, where a repetition of the Dublin reception — corporation honours, deputations of the literary and scientific societies and so forth—awaited him, he gave a couple of days to the hospitality of this flourishing town, and to the beautiful scenery of the Lee, not forgetting an excursion to the groves of Blarney among whose shades we had a right mirthful picnic. Sir Walter scrambled up to the top of the castle and kissed, with faith and devotion, the famous Blarney stone." Back in the city from his Blarney frolics Scott went to Bolster's Bookshop situated in Patrick Street where the former premises of Messrs. Guy stood at No. 70. Bolster's was then one of the literary shrines of the city, much frequented by writers and artists, and Scott went there to sample the books and pick up the London papers. Among those who gathered to savour the presence of greatness was young Maclise who made three outline head and shoulder sketches of Scott. His biographer, O'Driscoll, continues the story: "having selected that one which he considered the best he worked at it all night, and next morning brought to Bolster a highly finished pen and ink drawing, handled with all the elaborate minuteness of a line engraving. Bolster placed it in a conspicuous part of his shop, and Sir Walter with his friends having again called during the day, it attracted his attention when he entered. He was struck with the exquisite finish and fidelity of the drawing and at once asked the name of the artist who had executed it. Maclise, who was standing in a remote part of the shop, was brought forward and introduced to Sir Walter. The great author took him kindly by the hand and expressed his astonishment that a mere boy could have achieved such a work and predicted that he would yet distinguish himself. Sir Walter then asked for a pen and wrote with his own hand 'Walter Scott' at the foot of the sketch." This pencil on paper sketch, $10\frac{1}{8}$ x 8 inches, is now preserved at the British Museum, inscribed in pencil as follows: "Sir Walter Scott, Bart. Sketched from the Life at Mr. Bolster's Cork, 9th August, 1825. By Danl. McLise." The Arts Council Catalogue comments that "Scott was one of Maclise's heroes, and his predilection for medieval and chivalric subjects undoubtedly reflects the influence of the Waverley novels. Maclise depicted Scott in his early Irish genre painting, 'Snap Apple Night,' draw a caricature of him for Frazer's Magazine, and showed him in an illustration to F. Mahony's Reliques of Father Prout." On Bolster's advice the Scott sketch was lithographed and five hundred copies were sold as soon as they appeared. It was the first public recognition of a rising star in the world of art, and it was fortuitous that it was inspired by a man who had already won for himself an enduring place in the cabinet of literature.

Pressed by his friends to open a portrait studio, Maclise did so at the corner of Patrick Street and Princes Street, though, as his biographer remarks, "not without great reluctance and diffidence on his part." In an age before photography, portrait painting offered good prospects for making a living; it attracted a fashionable clientele, while in a garrison city like Cork there was much demand for family portraits among army officers. One of those earlier drawings was a pencil on paper sketch of Richard Bettesworth Sheares and his niece, now in the keeping of the Ashmolean Museum, Oxford. Sheares was the son of the 1798 patriot, Henry Sheares. Among some military portraits was a sketch of Colonel John Townshend, at one time ADC to the Duke of Wellington; dated July 1826, it is now in the possession of a descendant of the sitter, Mrs. Salter-Townshend, of Castle Townshend, Co. Cork. Later in the summer of 1826 Maclise and a friend set off from Cork on a sketching tour of county Wicklow, where he was deeply impressed by the natural beauty and the historic associations of that delightful part of Ireland. In his Manuscript Autobiography he relates that he and his friend "slept in Peasant's sheds and cocklofts, dined in cabins on Potatoes and Poteen, were benighted on the mountains in the neighbourhood of Duff and the Sugar Loaf, and slept soundly beneath large stones on its summit on beds of heather they had plucked for shelter, and in short led quite a little adventurous and romantic life for the period." Quite a number of his surviving Irish landscape drawings come from this period: they include the Scalp, Glen of the Downs, Vale of Avoca, Waterfall in the Devil's Glen, Hoar Abbey near Cashel, The Artist Sketching the Rock of Cashel and Lismore Castle. These are all deposited at the Victoria and Albert Museum, London. Their style is at once descriptive and romantic, whether in pencil or water-colour.

By the summer of 1827 Maclise had at last acquired enough money to yield to the frequent requests of his patrons, Sainthill and Crofton Croker, that he should seek entry to the Royal Academy of Art in London where he would have the artistic training and opportunities not available in Cork. Croker was then a clerk in the Admiralty in London and in July, 1827, Sainthill wrote to him from Cork regarding the young artist: "I may say in a word his object is to get employment at his pencil so as to enable him to study at the Royal Academy. The first thing for him to do is to get himself cheap lodgings and to learn how to live on a frugal plan, as his resources are not very strong. Let him see what will be interesting to an artist in London, and while he is doing this he may meet with what he wants."

Maclise arrived in London on 18th July, 1827, took lodgings in Newman Street, off Oxford Street, and entered the Royal Academy. He could have found no better or more influential friend than his fellow-townsman Croker. Standing under five feet in height and described by Walter Scott as "little as a dwarf, keen-eyed as a hawk and of easy, prepossessing manners," Croker had published the 'Fairy Legends of Ireland" in 1825, with its second edition illustrated by Maclise. In London he had a wide circle of friends to whom he introduced the stranger from Ireland, including Tom Moore, Miss Edgeworth, Mr. and Mrs. Hall, Mr. Jerdan, editor of the Literary Gazette, Miss Landon, and that other Cork exile, Francis O'Mahony, the noted "Father Prout." As in the case of the Scott sketch, Maclise was again fortunate in having his pencil and paper ready at the right moment. On the 1st October, 1827, the young actor, Charles Kean, was making his debut at Drury Lane theatre; sitting in the pit was Maclise, and the result was a sketch which Croker had lithographed. It had a large sale at 10/- per copy, bringing the young artist not only needed funds but his first recognition in London. There were many commissions for portraits in pencil and water-colour and his quarters in Newman Street began to be known. There he had a two-roomed flat—a small drawing-room where he received his clients and a bedroom. Meanwhile he had been working diligently at the Royal Academy and in 1829 was awarded the Gold Medal for his historical composition, "The Choice of Hercules." The presentation was made at a grand dinner of the Academy presided over by Sir Martin Archer Shee and attended by such notables as Lord Brougham, the Duke of Sussex, the Bishop of London and a flourish of the nobility and patrons of art. The high point of the gala evening was the announcement of the winner of the coveted Gold Medal and it was a memorable moment for the young Corkman when his name drew rounds of enthusiastic applause. He described his feelings to a young medical friend: "When the decision was known the clapping of hands from the roomful was not unpleasant to my ears, as it displayed a general feeling in my favour. I have since heard on good authority that all the members voted for me. Sir Martin made a most eloquent discourse. After my hand had been well wrung with congratulations I found Donovan, Roche and other friends in the hall. They had already heard of my success, so went and had some champagne. Then it was raining as I came home; I unlatched the door, tumbled upstairs, broke my lamp, and was obliged to go to bed in the dark. On Sunday when I awoke I felt ill, dined out and drank too much wine. On Monday I got very wet and on Tuesday had a severe cold and sore chest. Wednesday an increase of ditto—pitch plaster to my breast, mutton broth and gruel. I took last night two of your pills with good effect. I have written home . . . so I give God thanks not so much that I had succeeded as that I had not failed. Write and tell me how you got on. I heard a distant tinkle of the bell, so good-bye."

Soon after this success he exhibited at the Academy for the first time with a humorous scene from Shakespeare's "Twelfth Night." It was at this time also that he made the first of his many drawings of Benjamin Disraeli and members of his family. In 1831 came a sketch of Nicolo Paganini, while the following year brought a portrait of the novelist William Makepeace Thackeray to whom Maclise had been introduced by yet another Corkman in London, William Maginn, editor of "Frazer's Magazine" which gathered around it quite a dazzling set of literary and artistic personalities. The sketch of the Irish composer, Michael Balfe, to be seen at the National Gallery in Dublin, was made in 1843. One of Maclise's most significant works was his oil painting of Charles Dickens which came in 1839; it marked not only a notable artistic creation but the beginning of a lifelong friendship between the two men, a friendship that brought some of the happiest and most carefree moments in both lives. The Arts Council Catalogue describes the painting, now on view in the National Portrait Gallery, London, as "his masterpiece as a portraitist, a neatly composed cabinet picture that conveys all the energy and imagination and sheer magnetism of the young Dickens."

In 1832 Maclise had come home to Cork for a holiday and was delighted as his biographer notes, "to find himself among his old friends again, and they welcomed him with pleasure and pride." That visit was to result in an endearing evocation of Irish country life, the oil painting entitled "All Hallows Eve." At that time the parish priest of Waterloo near Blarney was the noted antiquary and Irish scholar, Father Matthew Horgan. In company with another Cork scholar, John Windele, and his Quaker friend, Abraham

Abell, he devoted much of his leisure time to locating historical remains all over south Munster. Over a period of many years this lovable trio of antiquarians tramped over the fields and the hills of the countryside locating holy wells, ancient raths, forts and stones, and one tangible fruit of their researches is the fine collection of Ogham Stones at the University in Cork. Windele's diligence is reflected in the Windele Manuscript Papers at the Royal Irish Academy in Dublin. The Maclise painting had its origin in an annual feast given in a barn at Waterloo by Father Horgan, an event described as follows by O'Driscoll: "It was the invariable custom of the good priest to invite a large party on All Hallows Eve; it was a social gathering where persons of superior position in society were to be found unaffectedly mingling with the poorest peasatry of the parish. Crofton Croker and Maclise were invited to this entertainment, and whilst the young artist, charmed with the novelty of the scene, surrendered himself heart and soul to the enjoyment of the night and joined in the harmless hilarity that prevailed, he contrived to sketch every group in the barn. On his return to London in the beginning of November, 1832, he commenced his wonderful picture of All Hallows Eve, and he wrought with such unceasing diligence and rapidity that it was ready for the Exhibition of 1833. As the earliest specimen in oil of his powers on a large scale its appearance produced an almost electrical effect on the public. The principal characters are portraits of Sir Walter Scott, Crofton Croker, the Sisters of the Artist, Perceval Banks who was married to Anne, the younger sister, and the old Clergyman who appears in the background compelling two of his Boys who had been trying their shillelahs on each other's heads, to shake hands and be friends."

Apart from portrait painting, Maclise quickly won a reputation for his caricatures in Frazer's Magazine, already referred to in this chapter. Under the editorship of the former Cork schoolmaster, William Maginn, it became one of the more exciting journals on the London scene, offering pungent social comment and campaigning for the reforms advocated by liberal thinkers. It attracted such writers as Thackeray and Carlyle, while Samuel Taylor Coleridge was closely associated with its promoters. Between 1830 and 1836 Maclise contributed eighty caricatures to the

Magazine and they constitute a catalogue of most of the leading artists, literary and political figures of the age. The collection was published by Chatto and Windus of London in 1874 under the title "A Gallery of Illustrious Literary Characters." Maclise was to specialise in historical narrative works, bringing an almost photographic exactitude to all the detail of costume and accessories. The National Gallery, Dublin, has an example of this genre in the oil painting dating from 1836 entitled "An Interview between Charles I and Oliver Cromwell," in which the artist's sympathy clearly lies with the royal family group. Also in Dublin can be seen the oil painting "Merry Christmas in the Baron's Hall," a romantic evocation of medieval life partly inspired by the hearty view of Christmas that Dickens was to popularise. The work entitled "Caxton's Printing Office," full of costume detail and realistic draughtsmanship, was highly proclaimed when it was exhibited at the Academy in 1851, receiving the approbation of the veteran Turner. The monumental work to be seen in Dublin, "The Marriage of Strongbow and Eva," represents Maclise's role in the realm of epic art based on grand historical themes. It evokes the clash between the old Gaelic order and culture, with its broken crosses, its bards and harps and the mailed brutality of the Norman warriors. The multitudinous detail of the bodies of the dead and the wounded, together with the figures of Strongbow, Dermot and Eva or Aoifa, make it a compelling composition and a vivid portrayal of a dramatic epoch in Irish history.

The theatre was to provide Maclise with many subjects for elegant creation. The Tate Gallery holds his "Scene from Twelfth Night," first exhibited at the Academy in 1840, a work of singular charm with a mastery of such accessories as the botanical details of flowers and leaves. The central figures of Malvolio, Olivia and Maria in the garden are wrought with a remarkable richness of costume detail. The noted actor, Macready, was to say of it, "his picture of Olivia I can look at it forever; is it beauty, moral and physical, personified." The water-colour work, "The Play Scene from Hamlet," now in the Forbes Magazine Collection, New York, was greeted by the "Times" as the "lion of the gallery" in 1842; an oil study of Hamlet's head and shoulders for this work can be viewed in Dublin. In 1843 Queen Victoria commissioned Maclise to execute a scene from the novel "Undine" as a birthday present for Prince Albert. The work entitled "Scene from Undine," now in the Queen's Collection, bears evidence of the artist's skill in the use of fairies, goblins and nymphs, something that was coming into fashion following the publication of Grimm's Fairy Tales and Croker's Fairy Legends. A similar theme is evident in the oil painting, "The Origin of the Harp," completed in 1842 and on view at the City of Manchester Art Gallery.

Yet another sphere of artistic outlet for Maclise was that of book illustrations. His designs for "The Chimes" by Charles Dickens, the Christmas story that was published in 1844, are full of the fantasy of fairies and goblins which appealed as much to the novelist as to the artist. A similar comment would hold for the illustrations in "The Cricket on the Hearth" made in the following year. Perhaps Maclise's best work in this sphere was seen in the 1845 edition of Tom Moore's Irish Melodies. Moore's work was first published in 1807, based largely on Edward Bunting's Collection of Ancient Irish Music, and Maclise had an enormous affection for the sentimental recollections of Ireland's past glories and tragedies. Strongly influenced by the German school, the one hundred and sixty drawings touch on chivalry, revelry, love and death, with a profusion of flowers and leaves. Moore himself stated: "I shall only add that I deem it most fortunate for this new edition that the rich, imaginative powers of Mr. Maclise have been employed in its adornment, and that to complete its national character an Irish pencil has lent its aid to an Irish pen in rendering due honour to our country's ancient harp."

The two great frescoes of Wellington and Nelson in the House of Lords bring the genius of Maclise most vividly before the public. The Arts Council Catalogue writes of them as "Maclise's masterpieces and a summary of all that he stood for as a history painter. His extensive researches into military details and accessories was undertaken in an attempt to reconstruct the past as accurately as possible. Yet Maclise's realism is primarily a matter of detail. The overall conception of the frescoes is highly idealistic and dramatic. His vision of the forces of history is expressed in terms of the suffering and death of individuals. In the final analysis, his frescoes are memorable for the human sympathies and emotions which they arouse."

The engagement to execute these monumental frescoes came about as a result of the rebuilding of the Houses of Parliament, when a Royal Commission under the chairmanship of Prince Albert set about choosing artists and themes to embellish the chief apartments. Between 1845 and 1849 Maclise completed his "Spirit of Chivalry" and "Spirit of Justice" for Westminster. Then from 1858 to 1865 he worked on the two frescoes in the Long Gallery of the House of Lords, each painting measuring 45 feet 8 inches in length. For the "Meeting of Blucher and Wellington at Waterloo" Maclise conducted the most minute research into all the details of army uniforms, such as caps, coats and buttons, as well as armour, to give realism to his evocation of a battle which dominated the folk-memory of Europe throughout the nineteenth century. His anatomical knowledge is clearly evident in the portrayal of men and horses in the various poses of pain and death. The whole composition is a masterly exercise in draughtsmanship as well as a moving human study of a memorable historical event. When looking at it one is moved by its eloquence of expression and by the deep compassion of its comment on the human condition. In working on it Maclise must have known that very many of his fellow townsmen were in Wellington's army, and that it was from Cork that the Duke set out in 1807 for the Peninsular War when he and his army were welcomed by the underground patriots of Portugal as their gallant allies against the French invaders.

Maclise the artist was obviously in the front rank of his peers, but what of Maclise the man? Tall and well-built, he had a commanding presence while all of his contemporaries spoke and wrote of the great charm and simplicity of his personality. John Forster in his Life of Dickens delineates Maclise as follows: "A greater enjoyment than the fellowship of Maclise at this period it would indeed be difficult to imagine. His unquestionable turn for literature, and a varied knowledge of books not always connected with such intense love and such unwearied practice of one special and absorbing art, combined to render him attractive far beyond the common. His fine genius and handsome person, of neither of which at any time he seemed himself to be in the slightest degree conscious, completed the charm." The Arts Council Catalogue comments that "the aura of success surrounding him, combined with great natural charm, assured his popularitly, but did not spoil him. He remained as he had always been, amiable, large-hearted and carefree. Even those who had most cause for envy were won over by the unaffected simplicity of his manner." He never married but his affair with Lady Sykes in 1838 created a passing sensation. He always retained a deep affection for his familly, and his parents and one of his sisters lived with him in London until their death. Nor did he ever forget the city of his youth, as his letters to his friend and biographer, Justin O'Driscoll, indicate over the years. In one such letter written in November, 1861, he was asking his friend to go about buying "a little cottage" in Bray to which he might escape to "inhale such air as might enable me to endure the fogs of the Thames." It was these London fogs and the depression he felt while working for eight years on his frescoes in what he called that "gloomy Hall in Westminster" that resulted in a growing deterioration in his health from 1860 onwards. In particular he seemed to have had a weak chest. There was also noted by his friends a dampening of his spirits and his zest for life. His sister, Isabella, had always been his close companion and housekeeper, and when she died in April, 1865, a deep shadow of grief came over him. He was still contemplating retiring to Ireland but was deterred by an almost morbid fear of seasickness on the crossing. In addition he was keenly hurt by unjust treatment by the Fine Art Commissioners regarding payment for his work in the House of Lords. A high distinction was offered him in 1865 when he was selected as President of the Royal Academy, but he declined to accept the office. His biographer remarks of that decision: "his devotion to art was disinterested and unalloyed by any selfish considerations; he refused to divide his attention or falter in his allegiance to it; he was not impelled in its pursuit by the hope of any worldly distinction."

In 1868 he exhibited one of his last notable works, "The Madeleine after Prayer," a scene inspired by the poem "St. Agnes Eve" by John Keats. It was bought by a Dublin merchant, Mr. John Wardwell, who received a note from Maclise: "I assure you that my satisfaction is complete in thinking that, amid all the agitations of disestablishment and disendowment, Ireland can still give heed to the claims of art." The great political issue of the day was Gladstone's decision to disestablish the Church of Ireland, a decision that owed something to the need to conciliate Ireland after the Fenian Rising. The last picture that came from the hands of the artist had an Irish theme. It was exhibited at the Royal Academy in 1870, entitled "The Earls of Desmond and Ormond." It displays Maclise's continuing devotion to Irish history, with the defeated Earl of Desmond being carried off the battlefield by the soldiers of Ormond.

It was in early April, 1870, that he developed a cough at his home, No. 4 Cheyene Walk, Chelsea. On April 6th he accompanied his niece, Miss Banks, to the Oxford and Cambridge boat race, but he seemed not at all well. Very quickly his doctor diagnosed acute pneumonia, and his biographer describes the end: "Although he felt the inevitable change stealing over him, his thoughts still turned to the art he loved so well. On the day before his death he attempted to retouch a little sketch but the pencil dropped from his fingers. He continued to grow weaker and nature refused to rally. As the congestion increased he appeared to suffer pain, but his fortitude and sweetness of temper lingered with him to the last moment, and he passed away gently and almost imperceptibly on the morning of April 25th, 1870. He was buried in the cemetery at Kensal Green in the same vault which holds the remains of his father, mother, brother and sister."

Such was the life and achievement of the artist from Cork who brought honour to his city and to Ireland. His name is commemorated in a London street out beyond Kensington. This writer had hoped that some day a plaque might be erected at the premises of Messrs. Guy in Patrick Street where the young artist met the great novelist, Sir Walter Scott. But that premises has now been flattened to the ground. It is hoped that this account will revive a more general interest in this lovable human being who came from among us and who used his time and his talents in the pursuit of excellence.

Chapter X

THE PURSUIT OF USEFUL KNOWLEDGE—
THE ROYAL CORK INSTITUTION

Between 1800 and the opening of the University in 1849 the Royal Cork Institution was the home of the cultural life of the city. It was so very literally in that most of the amateur learned societies, such as the Literary and Scientific Society, the Cuvierian Society and a number of debating societies used its premises in Emmet Place, now the Crawford School of Art, for their weekly or monthly meetings. The premises were also used for a wide variety of committee meetings in connection with charitable organisations and with leading matters of public interest. Indeed, that dignified pile of classical design in Emmet Place, with its red brick and limestone surrounds, evokes the memory of a galaxy of eager men who devoted their time and talents to the pursuit of science, art, literature and history, and whose names were honoured in nineteenth century Cork. There was James Roche, diminutive in figure but with a mind that ranged widely over the great issues of his day, a wine merchant, banker, writer, scholar, collector of books; imprisoned in France during the French Revolution, he lived to preside in the Aula Maxima at the inaugural ceremonies for the opening of the University on the 7th November, 1849. There was John Hogan, the greatest Irish sculptor of the century, who had first learned his craft from the collection of classical casts housed in the Institution; associated with him was his great contemporary, Daniel Maclise, who also found in the casts the first inspiration in a career that was to make him one of the greatest historical painters of the age, with a reputation in Ireland, Britain and Europe. There was Sir Thomas Deane, the local architect who gave to the city the Gothic charm of the University building, and who was subsequently to be associated with such notable architectural achievements as the Museum at Trinity College, Dublin, and the University Museum at Oxford. With him in the Institution were the Pain Brothers, his rivals in the upsurge of civic architecture that characterised the first half of the century in Cork.

Then there were Mr. Beamish and Mr. Crawford, brewers of porter and patrons of culture, and Thomas and Francis Jennings, makers of mineral water and amateur scientists. The goodly fellowship included Richard Dowden, wit, botanist, Mayor of Cork, Dissenter in religion but the close friend and generous patron of the genial Apostle of Temperance, Father Mathew. Living in a room upstairs in the building was the eccentric and lovable Quaker, Abraham Abell, manager of the Savings Bank and devoted to antiquarian pursuits. Associated with him were two other friends of the antique, John Windele and Father Matt Horgan, parish priest of Waterloo near Blarney. This intrepid trio tramped around the countryside of south Munster locating, sketching and describing the historic remains of castles, abbeys, forts and holy wells. The fine collection of Ogham Stones in the University is the result of their diligent care. These men and those associated with them from among the clergy, the doctors, the lawyers and the leisured gentlemen created in the city a taste for the things of the mind; they translated that taste into action and gave the citizens opportunities for cultural stimulation which they would otherwise have missed. In providing a convivial atmosphere for these men and these tastes the Royal Cork Institution was giving good service to the city; it was also creating a pattern found in many other cities in the first half of the last century. That pattern was marked by a rapidly growing popular interest in science and by a desire to stimulate that interest through public lectures and demonstrations. It was pre-eminently the age of useful knowledge. All classes came to share the new enthusiasm and while the leisured and middle classes found mental challenge or fashionable satisfaction in the pursuit of the scientific and the useful, the more enterprising of the working classes were anxious to improve their understanding of the new processes by which they were earning their living. If the Royal Cork Institution was mainly middle class in its membership, yet the son of a shoemaker was allowed to use its facilities. Such was Daniel Maclise.

The Institution was founded as a result of a course of lectures given in 1803 by the Rev. Thomas Dix Hincks, minister of the Old Presbyterian Church still standing and in use in Princes Street. As the man who originated this notable enterprise Hincks deserves more recognition than has hitherto been given him in his adopted city. Premises were secured on the South Mall opposite the Imperial Hotel and courses of public lectures were given on science and on the application of scientific principles to industry and agriculture. A Botanic Garden was established out at Bally-phehane, now the site of St. Joseph's Cemetery; at the Institution premises a Library was built up which in time was widely used more particularly by the medical and legal professions. By 1811 the first agricultural journal in Ireland was being published and premiums were being offered to farmers for improved methods of cultivation. In 1829 the Institution became the first public body to formally petition the government to establish what was termed a provincial academical institution in the city. From its foundation until 1831 the Institution was in receipt of an annual grant from Parliament, and it was to compensate for the withdrawal of that grant that the government handed over to it the former Custom House premises in Emmet Place which afforded greater space for various activities. As with all such voluntary societies the Institution had its high peaks of achievement and its low troughs of malaise, depending on the energy of those directing it and the level of public response. An obvious high peak was referred to by Dr. Bullen, the permanent lecturer in Chemistry, when giving evidence before an Education Commission in 1838. He was able to state that "I was attended by about four hundred. I lectured twice a day and there were as many as the room could hold, and many persons in the evening could not get in." Those who crowded in to see demonstrations in Chemistry and Electricity, Botany and Mineralogy were reflecting the current interest in practical science in an age when science still had something of the vibrant appeal of an amateur study and the curiosity of something new.

Before giving a more detailed account of the followers of the useful and the scientific in Cork it might be of interest to sketch the broader canvas of which those activities formed a part. Four companies of natural philosophers, to use the then common description, generated an interest in science in these islands. These were the Royal Society of London, the Lunar Society of Birmingham, the Royal Institution of London and the Royal Dublin Society. Each one has a history of wide general appeal apart from their technical achievements in more specialised fields. The foundation of the Royal Society in London in 1660, with a charter from King Charles two years later, is generally regarded as the beginning of an organised interest in scientific matters. It was founded by a small group of natural philosophers seeking congenial company in which to discuss their interests and display their experiments. Basing their philosophy on that of Bacon they expressed their aim as being that of "enlarging knowledge by observation and experiment." The full significane of that policy can only be appreciated in the context of the times. As regards formal education it was nothing less than a revolutionary principle. For more than a century afterwards the study of science had not yet found its way into the universities or the schools. The classics and philosophy were considered the full and proper studies for gentlemen. What scientific knowledge there was came from the books of Aristotle and Plato and the medieval schoolmen. Knowledge of the universe, of the heavenly bodies and of natural laws could all be found in the books of ancient wisdom. The Royal Society set out to substitute observation and experiment for books, and the significance of the Royal charter was that it gave them respectability in a highly sceptical climate. The early members, most of whom were very remiss in paying their subscription of one shilling per week, included such luminaries as Dryden the poet, Christopher Wren the great architect, and that man of many parts and many words, Samuel Pepys the diarist. The two most famous scientists were Sir Isaac Newton and Robert Boyle from County Cork, the "father of Chemistry." In time the Royal Society achieved a commanding eminence in the world of science and today it is a mark of distinction to be elected a Fellow.

On the 25th June, 1731, a learned body with similar aims was established in Dublin, the Royal Dublin Society, and ever since it has contributed richly to the advancement of science, agriculture and the arts in Ireland. Each member was enjoined to "choose some particular subject either in Natural History or in Husbandry, Agriculture or Gardening, or some species of Manufacture, and make it his business by reading what had been printed on that subject, by conversing with those who made it their profession, or by making his own experiments, to make himself master thereof." A most significant point in regard to both the London and the Dublin bodies was that they introduced the principle of specialisation. The Lunar Society, founded in Birmingham in 1766, met monthly on the night of the full moon in the Unitarian Chapel in Cross Street. Its name derived from its meetings by moonlight, and this in turn was accounted for by the very practical consideration that the night of the full moon was the safest one on which to be out on unlit city streets. Many members were working natural philosophers, owners of mills, iron works, potteries or dye works where they themselves actually worked at the bench or in the yard. They included James Watt whose projects on steam-power were to have such powerful effects in ushering in the Industrial Revolution; Mathew Boulton with his iron foundry; Josiah Wedgwood whose pottery was to be so highly prized, and Richard Lovell Edgeworth, amateur scientist, improving landlord, educationalist and father of the novelist, Maria Edgeworth. Prominent even among such company was Joseph Priestley, Unitarian minister, discoverer of oxygen and a writer with liberal views on religious and political freedom as well as on the need for a new concept for practical education. Many members of the Lunar Society were religious Dissenters and in their writings they challenged the monopoly of the Established Church in Parliament, civic life and higher education. Excluded from the public schools and the universities on religious grounds, as were Catholics, they established Academies for the higher education of their sons, offering a curriculum of practical subjects and modern languages in contrast to what they termed the "elegant imbecility" of the classical studies of Oxford and Cambridge. Priestley taught at two of these academies, at Warrington and Hackney, and the connection with Cork becomes clear from the fact that Thomas Dix Hincks studied under him at Hackney. Differing in creed and class from the establishment of the church and and the landed gentry, Priestly and his associates had welcomed the American Revolution as an assertion of freedom; similarly they gave open support to the principles of the French Revolution and paid for it when a mob pillaged the chapel at Cross Street, burning Priestley's books and apparatus. The natural philosopher fortunately escaped to America. Edgeworth paints a memorable portrait of the members of the Lunar Society in his Memoirs:

"Mr. Keir with his knowledge of the world and good sense; Dr. Small with his benevolence and profound sagacity; Wedgwood with his unceasing industry, experimental variety and calm investigation; Boulton was his mobility, quick perception and bold adventure; Watt with his strong inventive faculty."

Of more immediate interest to Cork was the foundation in 1799 of the Royal Institution in Albemarle Street, London, in premises which it still occupies today. Its inspiration came from Benjamin Thompson who, having fought on the royalist side in the American War, went as a soldier of fortune to Bavaria where he was given the title of Count Rumbold by the Elector because of his efficiency in military matters. He was also something of an amateur scientist, and coming to London in 1799 he took counsel with members of the Royal Society and determined to establish a body for the promotion of scientific interest among the public. He acquired and equipped the premises at Albemarle Street at his own expense and the Royal Institution was formed with the stated aim of "diffusing the knowledge and facilitating the general introduction of useful mechanical inventions." More than any other body it was the Royal Institution which gave science a public platform and a popular following, and this it did more especially through its Friday evening Discourses when crowds of the really earnest and the fashionably curious flocked to its spacious lecture theatre. Indeed, it is in that theatre that many of the great scientific discoveries from 1800 to the present day have first been publicly expounded. The Institution was fortunate in that its first resident Lecturer in chemistry was not only a meticulous researcher but was also gifted with an accomplished platform manner. Known widely for his invention of the miners' safety lamp, Sir Humphrey Davy brought eloquence and lucidity to his lectures and demonstrations. When he came to Dublin to lecture for the Royal Dublin Society great crowds queued to hear him. He was to be succeeded at Albemartle Street by yet another distinguished scientist and speaker, the young bookbinder's apprentice whom he had appointed as his assistant, Michael Faraday. Not the least of Faraday's achievements was the series of Christmas lectures for school children which he inaugurated and which still fill the theatre each year.

Something of this new wisdom of science and utility was brought to Cork in 1790 when the Rev. Thomas Dix Hincks arrived to begin his ministry at the Old Presbyterian Chapel still in use in Princes Street. Born in Dublin in

1767, the son of a Customs official transferred from Chester, he had spent a short spell at Trinity College with the intention of entering the Church of Ireland ministry. Relinquishing that idea he went to Hackney Academy where he came under the influence of Joseph Priestley. Hincks was a man of large vision and generous mind and he brought to his adopted city an abiding affection which neither time nor distance ever dimmed. Many years later when in his ninetieth year and living in retirement in Belfast he sent down to Cork a touching note of thanks in reply to a message of goodwill from the Institution he had founded. Shortly after his arrival in the city he opened a school at his house on Patrick's Hill where he taught classics as well as introducing a broader range of subjects in mathematics and elementary science. His evidence to the 1838 Parliamentary Commission on Education in Ireland contains some interesting insights on the youth of Cork in 1790 as he recalled the early days of his school:

"At Cork many shopkeepers applied and were amongst the most eager to obtain admission for their sons. I instructed them in mathematics, geography, history, and in as many branches of useful knowledge as circumstances would permit."

As Priestley and his associates had shown a keen interest in public welfare, including provision for public hospitals, better sanitation, good civic design in laying out streets and squares, as well as religious and civil rights for those not subscribing to the Established Church, so too, Hincks took an active interest in his fellow citizens. He published a pamphlet advocating Catholic rights; also he began giving in his home a series of lectures and demonstations on science. It was this which led in 1803 to the formal establishment of the Cork Institution when a number of gentlemen each contributed thirty guineas for the purchase of apparatus and for securing of a suitable premises. This was located on Jameson's Row on the South Mall, opposite the Imperial Hotel, until the move in 1832 to what is now the School of Art. The lecture syllabus for 1803 was nothing if not comprehensive, embracing language, literature, logic, elementary mathematics, natural history, matter and its properties, sound, gases, alkalies, acids, electricity, hydrostatics and mechanics. By 1807 the Institution had gained the prestige of a Royal Charter and, more importantly, an annual Parliamentary grant of £2,000. In an age when neither the universities nor what passed for secondary schools were financed by the State this grant is significant of a level of achievement. The constitutions were based on those of the Royal Institution in London, with a general body of Proprietors later to number 400, each paying thirty guineas, and an executive body of thirty Managers meeting weekly. As at London there were specialised committees dealing with finance, the library, agriculture, science and the Botanic Garden. Advertisements were placed for full-time lecturers in the Cork, Dublin, London and Edinburgh newspapers and appointments were made. Law and medical libraries were built up, an exhibition of farm implements was on permanent view at the premises, and Hincks as Secretary edited the first farmers journal in Ireland, "The Munster Farmers Magazine." Premiums for progressive farming, such as the novel method of sowing potatoes in drills to get a better yield, were awarded to farmers in the counties of Cork, Limerick and Waterford. In 1809 a site was acquired at Ballyphehane for a Botanic Garden and Mr. James Drummond was appointed Curator. In the same year "an extensive course of lectures on Chemistry and Mineralogy" had been given on the South Mall with a "respectable attendance." Twenty lectures on Botany were given in 1810 while Mr. Peall of the Royal Dublin Society had lectured on the "veterinary art to many respectable and scientific gentlemen as well as to Farriers and Grooms." Meanwhile, out at the Botanic Garden building was going ahead on a Greenhouse and a Hothouse to receive "rare and exotic plants from friends of the Institution." A total of £402.17.0½ had already been spent on the work, an extensive Shrubbery was planned, and "walks had been laid out and gravelled." The Annual Report of 1811 recorded that Mr. Drummond had spent July and August down in West Cork and Kerry collecting "rare native plants," while a collection of foreign oaks had been acquired. Dr. Fitton had sent "Scotch minerals" from Edinburgh University, together with geographical observations and maps.

A significant indication of the status of the Institution came in 1813 when Edmund Davy accepted an appointment as lecturer in Chemistry, a position he was to hold until 1826 when he left to take up a similar post with the Royal Dublin Society. It was while in Dublin that he did his pioneering work on acetylene. Davy was the cousin of the great man of science of the day, Sir Humphrey Davy, and his assistant at the Royal Institution in London. It was hardly the increase in salary from £75 per annum to £100 which alone induced him to come to Cork. Nor did he allow himself to slumber in what might have been regarded as a provincial backwater, a point borne out by a steady flow of research papers published in learned journals. His first such paper was printed in the prestigious "Philosophical Transactions" of the Royal Society in 1817. Dated "Cork, December 20th, 1816," it carried the title "On a new Fulminating platinium, by Edmund Davy, Esq., Professor of Chemistry and Secretary to the Cork Institution. Communicated by Sir H. Davy, LL.D., F.R.S." Later papers from Cork dealt with experiments to improve the quality of flour consequent on a bad harvest in Munster, with analysis of the air in the Fever Hospital, with the properties of hard water from a local artesian well, with the excretions of the boa constrictor, and with the action of iodine on oils. Davy's papers, therefore, put the name of the Cork Institution in the forefront of scientific publications. His account of his experiments with flour conjures up a picture of natural philosophers in Cork engaged in curious proceedings involving dough and high temperatures.

Davy had succeeded Hincks as Secretary in 1816 when the latter moved to a classical school at Fermoy. Suggestions that there was a certain amount of ruffled feeling in the affair would need further clarification before being set out here. Hincks was later to have a distinguished academic career at Belfast while remaining in close lifelong touch with developments at Cork. It was altogether fitting that one of his sons, all of whom were born in the city, became first professor of Natural History when the University was opened in 1849. Another won distinction as an Egyptologist, while a third played a leading role in Canadian public life, being Prime Minister for a period. The Dictionary of National Biography gives outlines of members of the family. The Institution began to feel the cool breezes of financial hard times in 1826 and it appealed to have its position examined by a Commission on Education in Ireland which was looking into the use being made of public grants in the area of elementary education. The Commission had been established mainly because of a formal petition to the Government by the Catholic Hierarchy who were not satisfied that their schools were being fairly treated. Their claims were largely upheld and the main outcome was that all public grants to voluntary school societies were withdrawn and the money channelled into the creation of the National School system in 1831. In response to the Institution's request a commissioner came to Cork and took oral evidence on its affairs. The result was published as a Blue Book, the Seventh Report of the Commissioners of Education, 1827. The eventual outcome was that the annual parliamentary grant to the Institution was withdrawn, and it was to compensate for this that the Government gave it the former Custom House premises at a rent of £60 per annum. The Report did not make any adverse criticism of the activities associated with the various courses of lectures or the library, but it did recommend that the Botanic Garden be disposed of as being of little useful purpose and as an immediate saving in outgoings. News of the proposed withdrawal of the grant created a deep crisis of confidence among the Managers and Proprietors and there were serious discussions on the advisability of disbanding the Institution. One formal proposal to the Government was that the Library and apparatus should be used for the foundation in Cork of some type of provincial academical Institution— this can be seen as the seed of the later movement, also spearheaded by the Institution, which flourished in the city from 1838 to 1845 as the Munster Provincial College Committee. Through public meetings and private lobbying of members of parliament that Committee was to achieve a wide range of support and to have considerable influence in the decision by Sir Robert Peel to establish a University College, a decision implemented in the Irish Colleges Bill of 1845 giving university institutions to Cork, Belfast and Galway.

The site of the Botanic Garden is still in public use in Cork as St. Joseph's Cemetery, previously and, perhaps, more appropriately known as Father Mathew's cemetery. A few memories from its last days in the possession of the Institution may be recalled. When giving evidence to the Commission on the 27th September, 1826, Mr. Drummond stated that "there are not a great many that resorted to it for the purpose of studying botany scientifically, but there are a great many that resort to it for the purpose of seeing the flowers. The Garden is very badly situated for visitors; there are four months in the year from November to February when the roads are bad and very few go there, but in the months of March, April and the following there are a good many persons who visit it." Unfortunately, however, not everyone coming to the Garden had such innocent intentions as admiring the flowers and the Instiution Minutes for 1st January, 1827, record more dramatic nocturnal happenings. Since the previous May "there have been a series of robberies of roots and plants" that deprived the Curator of that portion of his income deriving from the sale of duplicate specimens. "On the night of November 16th last forty young apple trees were stolen whose value may be estimated from their being raised from grafts which the Horticultural Society of London thought of sufficent importance to present to the Cork Institution for the purpose of disseminating superior fruit trees throughout the country." The Curator may have been caught off guard on the night of November 16th, but on the following night he was alert and agile: "A robber was shot by him accidentally, the gun discharged itself accidentally as he rushed through a quickset hedge in pursuit of the thief. A Coroner's inquest was held which brought in a verdict to this effect. These events drew upon him an expenditure of about £8." Nor did Mr. Drummond's vigilance end with the corpse in the quickset hedge; the Minutes continue the saga. "Having received an intimation where the apple trees from the grafts of the Horticultural Society had been disposed of, on the 18th ult, he proceeded with a constable and a warrant to the spot and succeeded in recovering the recognised trees." The thieves at Ballyphehane had not counted on the talents of this horticultural Sherlock Holmes! It was when the Institution disposed of the Garden that it was bought by Father Mathew for use as a Catholic cemetery, and not even his later fame as the Apostle of Temperance matched the affection which this action won for him from his own flock. The great man is himself buried there in a spot chosen by him. It was as Father Mathew's Cemetery, or as the Gardens, that it was known all through the nineteenth century. It contained some fine examples of the work of the sculptor, John Hogan. Mr. George Measom in his invaluable "Guide to the Great Southern and Western Railway," published in 1866, found it "laid out in the style of the Pere la Chaise in Paris. The graves are distributed over the greater part amid the shrubs, plants and flowers brought hither at con- siderable expense by the original proprietors." Today even that hallowed spot bears obvious signs of the hands of the vandal and the neglect of the community.

The 1827 Report stated that "the delivery of the various courses of lectures appears to be at once the most success- ful and important part of the Institution." Dr. Taylor, lecturer on Natural History reported that "his morning course is usually attended by persons of a higher order and the even- ing lectures by commercial persons or shopkeepers." Mr. Cuthbert, one of the Managers, was of opinion that "the lectures were of great utility in the town, they are very much attended by the ladies particularly, and by scientific men; every man that wishes to improve himself attends either morning or evening." This statement mentions the two concepts so cherished by nineteenth century social reform- ers, utility and self-improvement. It also gives substance to the claim that the Institution pioneered adult education in Cork, a tradition happily maintained in this century by the University. The mention of ladies attending courses on botany, chemistry, electricity and natural history puts a large question mark over the received opinion that members of the fair sex whiled away their days with the innocuous ritual of embroidering lace, or with drawing-room sessions at the square piano, or with practising the elegant refine- ments of dropping a curtsy. Mr. Lecky, also a Manager and uncle of the great Trinity College historian, felt that the lectures "had raised a spirit of inquiry among the middling classes." Dr. Tuckey was of the opinion that they were "of especial benefit to young men, giving them a taste for science and literature in general." As well as the normal courses on chemistry, botany, natural history and agricul- ture, there were occasional series given by guest lecturers. Moving ahead to the records for November, 1838, approval was given for three such courses. Dr. Caesar, who had a recognised Medical School on the South Mall adjacent to the County Club, was to give a six-month course for medical students in the Institution at Emmet Place; permission was given to the Literary and Scientific Society to hold lectures on the premises, while Dr. R. Bryce of Belfast was to give a series on the theory of Education. He was recognised as one of the leading Irish educationists of the day. Four interesting names were given as sponsors of this particular course, those of James Roche, William Crawford, Francis Beamish and Thomas Deane. Commerce and culture forged a partnership.

Further contemporary evidence on the Institution comes from yet another Parliamentary Report on Education in Ireland, the Wyse Report of 1835-'38. It was chaired by Thomas Wyse who had played a leading part in O'Connell's campaign for Catholic Emancipation and had entered Parliament in 1829 as member for Waterford. He had made a specialised study of the whole field of education and was associated with the influential body of opinion in Ireland and Britain which looked to extended education as the lever of social progress. He was especially connected with the early years of London University founded in 1828 to embody many of the principles propounded by Priestley to give a practical, scientific education to the rising commercial middle class. London was seen as a brash educational upstart by the older foundations of Oxford and Cambridge, violating every cherished principle of religion and learning. As it set out to give higher education to all who came without religious distinction, it was by constitution undenominational in contrast to Anglican ethos of the older universities. This, and its situation, earned for it the epithet of the "Godless College of Gower Street. If it was to be damned in the matter of religion it was to be scorned in its pretext to be a place of serious scholarship. Its courses in medicine, engineering and practical science were regarded as altogether unbecoming to the true nature of a university, a charge further sustained by the fact that it was non-residential. Wyse championed London not as an apostle of godlessness and materialism but as a realist who saw its principles as answering the needs of a new age in which religion could no longer be exclusive and the classics alone were no longer adequate for the needs of society. He was closely involved in Ireland with all the delicate and widespread negotiations connected with the setting up of the National Schools in 1831, and as a Catholic who had taken the trouble to inform himself minutely on the principles and practice of the church's education policy in Europe he was in close consultation with the Archbishop of Dublin, Dr. Murray. The frequency and cogency of his educational contribtutions in Parliament made him a recognised authority on the subject, and the Report of his committee issued in 1838 is a most valuable insight into Irish conditions and opinions. It was this Report which formally recommended to the Government that provincial university institutions should be established in Ireland, so making it a key document in the history of the University at Cork, Indeed, it was that Report which led to the establishment in 1838 of the Munster Provincial College Committee, with Wyse as its parliamentary spokesman and with the Institution as its main local centre of support. In view of recent developments it is interesting to recall that from 1838 until the Bill of 1845 establishing the Queen's Colleges, both Cork and Limerick were competing as the site of the proposed Munster College, with William Smith O'Brien, M.P., leading a vigorous Limerick sub-committee. But the final selection of Cork seems to have been generally accepted.

Among those who gave lengthy evidence for the Wyse Report was Dr. D. B. Bullen, lecturer in Chemistry at the Institution since the departure of Davy. His career was to straddle both the Institution and the new University as in 1849 he became the first professor of Surgery and Dean of the Medical Faculty. A portion of his evidence has already been quoted, stating that "I was attended by about four hundred and there were as many as the room could hold." However, Bullen was no champion of bread-and-circus education for the masses and he cast a cold eye on popular taste: "they are pleased as long as they are amused, they get a smattering knowledge of the science but they do not acquire any deep or useful knowledge." He felt that the Institution's greatest benefit to the public came from its library and he painted a picture of a city of diligent readers: "I do not know any city where there is a greater desire for useful knowledge than in Cork. I attribute it very much to the domestic habits of the people of Cork who are fond of staying at home in the evening and reading, and to the existence of the Cork Library and of the Cork Institution Library." The premises of the Cork Library referred to by Bullen may still be seen in Pembroke Street, with its classical doorway and the title and date of foundation, 1792, picked out in raised stone lettering. It was a subscription library well patronised by the gentry and professional classes. Apart from its collection of books it provided a useful service in carrying the newspapers of the day which were dear to buy and were little more than broadsheets giving short accounts of home and foreign news and the movements of ships.

In 1843 the Institution was closely involved in the first ever international conference to be held in Cork, the annual meeting of the British Association for the Advancement of Science. Over a thousand visitors from Ireland, Britain and the Continent assembled in the city in the August of that year, bringing a glittering round of lectures, soirees, conversaziones, excursions and grand balls. The Institution's premises became the venue for many of the lectures while the Imperial Hotel was the social centre. Prominent in organising the affair were James Roche and Sir Thomas Deane; indeed, all the Managers were to some extent involved. On the 14th August, 1843, the "Cork Examiner" caught something of the excitement of the occasion by publishing a list of the dignitaries already in the city. They included the Most Rev. Dr. Crolly, Catholic Archbishop of Armagh; Sir William Rowan Hamilton, perhaps the greatest Irish mathematician of all time; Thomas Crofton Croker, the noted Cork antiquary, wit and writer, author of the "Fairy Legends of Ireland." Croker was on a visit to his native city from his post at the Admiralty in London. His dandified and diminutive appearance had prompted Sir Walter Scott to remark that he was himself the incarnation of an Irish fairy. Present also was the Rev. T. D. Hincks from Belfast, returning to the scene of his early labours and to his Institution. Adding literary distinction to the scene was another guest, Charles Dickens. The "Examiner" reported that among those later expected were Lord Listowel, patron of the arts and forthright commentator on Ireland's grievances in the House of Lords, the Earl of Rosse, especially connected with astronomical observation, Mr. William Smith O'Brien, M.P., Mr. Thomas Wyse, M.P., Dr. Robert Kane, and the celebrated French chemist, M. Dumas. They all duly arrived and so did the earnest nationalist writer from Dublin, Thomas Davis. None enjoyed the proceedings more than Charles Bianconi, the "King of the Roads," who was especially delighted to be invited to give an account of his remarkable transport enterprise. With such an assemblage of those in pursuit of useful knowledge there was much wining and dining, with the following details announced in the local newspapers: "Imperial Clarence Hotel, Cork. Mr.

McDowell has the honour to announce to the Nobility, Gentry and Public generally he will have ready each day from Thursday, 17 inst, an Ordinary in the lounge and Clarence Room of the Hotel at which will preside one of the Distinguished Members of the British Association, which will ensure respect and comfort and make these meetings the Feast of Reason and the Flow of Soul. Dinner on the Table precisely at six. Cost, inclusive of Wine, 4 shillings." In one respect at least the Institution did not cover itself with glory in connection with this important scientific meeting, for the "Examiner" felt compelled to comment rather acidly on the dowdy appearance of its rooms.

In drawing this survey to a close some extracts from the manuscript Minute Book will give the flavour of the times. The Managers Meeting of 3rd April, 1848, was attended by Mr. James Roche, Mr. James Daly, Mr. Abraham Abell, Mr. Francis Jennings, Mr. Thomas Jennings, Dr. D. B. Bullen, Dr. Harvey and Sir Thomas Deane. The latter proposed that "the School of Design obtain the upper floor of the building at a rent of £80 per annum." Thanks were voted to the "British Institution of Science for Catalogue of Stars." The meeting of 6th December, 1849, was concerned with greater facilities for newspaper reading in the Library, with proposals to include the following papers: the Times, the Globe, the Express, the Spectator, the Observer, Saunders Newsletter, and the three Cork papers, the Examiner, the Constitution and the Southern Reporter. The "inner Library to be fitted up in a comfortable manner and the House Committee be empowered to furnish it." A list of proposed new subscribers to the Library laid before the meeting of 4th March, 1850, makes an interesting commentary on gentlemen involved in the public life of the city, including names from the academic staff of the new University and some names still over shop fronts and on brass plates in the city streets: Samuel Beale, Joseph Beale, George Purcell, Richard Guy, T. Dunscombe, T. Bennett, J. Carroll, G. Mason, N. Cummins, N. Peterson, W. Minhear, Rowland Davies, Dr. Tivy, Dr. Corbett, Dr. Cotter, Sir William Lyons, Professor Fleming and Professor Boole. The latter was to acquire a world reputation with his book, "The Laws of Thought," described by Bertrand Russell as the foundation of modern mathematical thinking. The meeting of 7th

October, 1850, granted the request of Richard Dowden to have the fee paid by the Cork Literary and Scientific Society for the use of the Lecture Room reduced from £10 to £5 per annum, while in the following month there was agreement to the request of the first President of the University, Sir Robert Kane, that the scientific apparatus of the Institution be loaned to the University, with the stipulation that "for each article a receipt be given." The devotion of James Roche is especially evident from the Minutes with his spidery signature appearing at the end of each page for almost every meeting from 1st October, 1832 to the 17th March, 1853. The next meeting after that date was to record a warm tribute to the veteran Vice-President of the Institution whose death was mourned widely throughout the city. In a sense Roche and Hincks symbolised the Institution; both were scholars and men with a generous spirit of public service. Not the least significant of their achievements was the fact that in an age often marked by bitterness in religion and politics they succeeded in welding together a public body which drew support from all shades of religious and political allegiance. Hincks was a Dissenting clergyman, Roche was described in a London obituary notice as "the second most learned Catholic layman in the British Empire."

One episode in the life of the Institution has not been treated of in this chapter, the acquisition of the classical casts from Rome. It seems better to deal with that in considering the two foremost artists connected with them, Daniel Maclise and John Hogan. At the moment there is not available to this writer any formal notice of the demise of the Institution; after the death of Roche the Minutes increasingly became reduced to occasional jottings. The final entry is for Tuesday, 14th May, 1861, intimating that Professor England from the University was to give a course of lectures on electricity and magnetism. As most of the active members of the Institution had devoted their energies to the campaign for the establishment of the University it would seem that its opening in the autumn of 1849 was the most important factor that led to the gradual decline which can be traced in the surviving Minute Book.

How is the Institution to be assessed? Quite obviously it did not make any unique mark in the world of science; but then it was not given to every such provincial society to produce a genius or discover a gas or invent a technological marvel. Such, indeed, was not its aim. But it did bring to Cork an active interest in the new knowledge which was becoming popular in the world outside. Through its courses of lectures it pioneered the concept of adult education in the city, in addition to supplementing the work of similar bodies as the Literary and Scientific Society and the Mechanics Institute. Before the provision of public libraries its Library helped in the cultivation of wider interests, apart from its specialised service to doctors and lawyers. As the repository of the classical casts it contributed powerfully to the early artistic training of two of Ireland's foremost painters and sculptors, Daniel Maclise and John Hogan. In an age such as the present, so obsessed with paper qualifications, it must be appreciated that the Institution had to rely solely on the inherent interest of its courses to attract and sustain its audiences, as no certificates or qualifications of any kind were to be obtained. Finally, it created in the city and beyond it the climate of public opinion that was to have an influence on the Government in its decision to give a university institution not only to Cork but to Galway and Belfast. For it was the Munster Provincial College Committee, formed largely out of the Institution, that became the first public body in Ireland to campaign for a university outside of Dublin. The Institution, therefore, in its members and in its achievements reflected much that was best in the mind of Cork in the first half of the nineteenth century.

Chapter XI

A UNIVERSITY CITY

With a student population of over five thousand the influence of the University is felt not only in the city of Cork but throughout the whole province of Munster; indeed, the motto emblazoned on its main gates reads "Where Finbarr taught let Munster learn." It was in the autumn of 1849 that academic life began in what was then called the Queen's College and ever since then young people have come in the pursuit of higher studies in the arts, law, medicine, science, literature, history, engineering, agriculture and dairy science, together with the classical languages of Greek and Latin, the Irish language and modern Continental languages. In offering this wide range of specialised knowledge, together with the speculations of philosophy, and such newer disciplines as music, the University seeks to fulfil the dual role of a community of scholars, to diffuse knowledge for practical use and to promote higher research in the interests of scholarship. To study, to read, to reflect, to discuss, to cast a critical eye over learning and life, to extend the frontiers of human wisdom, such have been the historic and honourable tasks of the universities since they emerged in medieval times. Despite the manifold changes in political, religious and social assumptions, despite the explosion in the knowledge of the physical world which the last two centuries have brought, the ideal of the pursuit of scholarship has remained unaltered, as have the centuries-old degrees of bachelor, master and doctor. Continuity in principle and adaptation in method have ensured the survival of the academic community.

For the citizens of Cork and their visitors the most immediate impact of the University comes from the beauty of the original collegiate building set so superbly on a ledge of rock overlooking the valley below. The choice of site was something of an inspired coincidence not only in regard to scenic delight but in relation to historic associations, for the whole modern University area was part of the lands of the original monastic settlement founded by St. Finbarr and his followers in the seventh century. This was where Cork began and where the original school took its place in that flowering of Christian scholarship which earned for Ireland the honoured title of the "Island of Saints and Scholars." As the University came into being due to an Act of Parliament passed in 1845, and as the whole operation of building, staffing and equipping was financed by the State, it fell to the Board of Works to select the site. Contemporary accounts give no hint of any historical awareness in the final decision but for once officialdom had a moment of inspiration. Indeed, the moment was happily prolonged, for the architect and the design resulted in the charm of the Gothic Quadrangle, one of the finest pieces of public architecture in Ireland. The architect was Sir Thomas Deane, a native of the city, who was responsible for much of the civic embellishment that characterised the first half of the last century. His name has, or will have, appeared often in this book in connection with such buildings as the Imperial Hotel, the Savings Bank and the Dominican Church. Later Deane and his sons, and their partner George Woodward, were to be responsible for some fine work in Dublin, including the Kildare Street Club, the Engineering School at Trinity College, and the National Library. In the 1850s Sir Thomas and Woodward secured the prestigious commission to design and build the University Museum at Oxford. From the outset the soft limestone building at Cork elicited wide approval, with Macaulay's encomium being often quoted, "a Gothic college worthy to stand in the High Street of Oxford." Before considering the deeper educational, political and religious issues which underlay the foundation of the University it might be of interest to recall some of the pomp and circumstance which surrounded the inaugural ceremonies held in the Aula Maxima on Wednesday, the 7th of November, 1849.

By the very nature of things the opening of an university institution is not an everyday occurence so it was understandable that something of an air of euphoria should have surrounded the day's events. The "Freeman's Journal," taking its account from the "Cork Examiner," painted a vivid picture: "This interesting event took place at the appointed hour, the magnificent examination hall being the theatre happily selected for the imposing display. For nearly two hours before the time streams of public and private vehicles might be seen flowing to and from the College, and at eleven o'clock nearly the greater portion of the beautiful hall was crowded with the elite of this city. One would suppose the brilliant assemblage of rank, talent and worth was congregated in some old scholastic hall, for though just rescued from the scaffolding through the untiring energy of the contractor and architect, the hall seemed as if it had been built for centuries so deceptive was the grey colour of the scarcely-finished walls, the dull tint of the lofty windows, and the dark staining of the beautiful woodwork of the elaborate roof." The "Illustrated London News" was no less elated in describing the building "executed in a masterly manner. The style chosen by Sir Thomas Deane, the architect, is that of the Collegiate or Domestic architecture of the fifteenth century. One idea is strikingly obvious in the building. Whether viewed in the whole or in detail its adaptation to a given purpose, its appropriateness and fitness are evident."

How did Cork come to acquire a University in those years of prostration following the Famine? In the first place there had grown up in the city a climate of middle class public opinion favourable to such a development, a climate that had been primarily fostered by the Royal Cork Institution which was the subject of the previous chapter. More particularly a campaign to press for Government action in the matter had been mounted in 1838 with the formation of the Munster Provincial College Committee most of whose members were connected with the Institution. In turn this campaign was to influence the Conservative Prime Minister, Sir Robert Peel, when in 1845 he decided to give a university college to Cork largely to meet what he considered to be the just demands of middle class Catholics in the matter of higher education. Similar colleges were to be establised in Belfast and Galway. But before going into the details of those developments another most important question needs to be asked and answered: what was significant about the Cork college? This question needs some consideration precisely because it is largely overlooked in the admittedly meagre literature on Irish university history. The College was a pioneer in that, like its sisters at Belfast and Galway, it marked the first extension in university education in Ireland outside of the ancient foundation of Trinity College, Dublin. But if it was remarkable as an extension in quantity is was also radical in quality. It brought to Ireland a whole new pattern in the philosophy and practice of higher education, a pattern that was already taking shape in England, Germany and America, and that was to become the norm by the turn of this century. It was in the categories of creed, curriculum and class that the changes were most dramatic and enduring. Until after 1850 Oxford, Cambridge and Trinity College were still semi-ecclesiastical by constitution and ethos; all students and academics were officially to subscribe to the 39 Articles, while academics were in Anglican Holy Orders. In effect the institutions were religiously exclusive, debarring all Protestant Dissenters as well as Catholics and Jews. Trinity College made the first honourable breach in this pattern when, following the 1793 Catholic Relief Act, Catholics and Presbyterians were admitted to primary degrees. The curriculum was based on the traditional cluster of theology, philosophy and the classics, so excluding professional studies and the new cult of scientific utility. Because of the high fees consequent on residential colleges the universities in effect catered almost exclusively for the sons of the landed and leisured classes. When the Cork College opened in 1849 it offered a radically different kind of university pattern; being undenominational its courses were available to young people of all creeds, its curriculum brought scientific and professional studies in addition to the traditional disciplines of Latin and Greek, while as a non-residential College its moderate fees were specifically designed to accommodate middle class students. Not less significant was the fact that it was directly founded by the State. It was, therefore, not only a new university college but a new kind of university college.

What considerations shaped the evolution of this pattern of university life, a pattern that was then thought to be so radical and is today taken to be so normal? To a degree that is altogether unique the changes in nineteenth century university theory and practice reflected ideas and demands that came from society at large rather than from within the academic world. In particular they derived from two complementary sources, the view of life propounded by late eighteenth century philosophers and the practical demands made by the increasingly industrial society of the nineteenth century. The new education was a response to new theories of liberty and the new demands of the market-place. Among the great philosophic issues which exercised the mind of Europe for most of the nineteenth century was the conflict between the claims of liberalism and science on the one hand and on the other the traditional Chrisitan view of society based on dogma. The clash seemed to crystallise as one between Faith and Reason. Drawing their inspiration from the writers of the Enlightenment and from the principles of the American and French Revolutions, the liberal radicals campaigned in pamphlet and platform to break what they saw as the stranglehold of oligarchic privilege in the church, in parliament, in public office, in the influence of inherited wealth, in the assumption that the privileged few had a divine right to organise society for the multitude. In Ireland and Britain the liberal cause championed religious and civil liberty, an extension of the right to vote, at first to the rising commercial middle class and later to the working classes, the right to the secret ballot, the abolition of religious qualifications for admission to Parliament, to the legal profession and to membership of local municipal government, as well as the abolition of child labour and the slave trade. It was a formidable programme in the pursuit of human freedom and dignity and it was one of the glories of the nineteenth century that it was largely accomplished. O'Connell's campaign for Catholic Emancipation was in that liberal tradition and in Britain he received welcome support from public figures who were very far from giving personal allegiance to the confessional tenets of Catholicism.

Yet, the Christian church, both the Anglican in Britain and the Catholic in Europe, viewed the liberal creed with undisguised misgivings. The tradition of the centuries was that public order and morality rested on a harmony between Church and State, that men in public office should in their person and policy exemplify the principles of religion as propounded by that form of Christianity recognised by the state. The liberal ethic seemed a prescription for a fatal indifference to religion and a false notion of individual freedom; it would push the norms of orthodox religion from a central place in public life into the realms of private belief. Therein lay the seeds of a profound conflict of ideas which resulted in high passion and prolonged debate, with one of the protagonists being a man who was to play a leading role in Irish higher education, Dr. Newman, Oxford don, Catholic convert, Rector of the Catholic University in Dublin, set up to offset the influence of the undenominational Queen's Colleges. By the end of the century the liberal cause had won, for good or ill, and a pluralistic society had emerged wherein under the law persons were free to practise their religion as they wished but public office and opportunity no longer depended on religious beliefs.

If the demands of liberalism were largely inspired by the insistence of the rising commercial middle class to seek a place in public life commensurate with their wealth and influence, the claims of science reflected the intellectual excitement of the age of utility. The new wealth, the new conveniences, the manifold changes for the better flowing from the Industrial Revolution such as the steam-engine in the factory, the railway lines radiating over the countryside, the steamships bringing such a dramatic change to age-old ways, the post office, gas lighting, the telephone and electricity, all of this depended on scientific experiment and observation. But science was not content merely with the provision of material gadgets; it sought to erect itself into a way of life, a philosophy to explain the life of man and the constitution of the universe. Geologists seemed to cast doubt on the literal interpretation of the Bible, German philologists and historians added their doubting speculations and, particularly shattering, there came Darwin's "Origin of Species," casting doubt on the traditional Chrisitan story of the creation of man. Here again, as with liberalism, there was conflict between Faith and Science, between dogma and experiment. The Christian churches felt besieged and the stage seemed set for a confrontation between the tradition of the centuries and the clamour of the new learning. Yet by the end of the century both sides had become less strident and there was a feeling for a synthesis which would embrace a more rational interpretation of traditional beliefs. But one thing had become firmly established, namely the right of secular subjects to an accepted place in the field of learning. Theology, philosophy and the classics could no longer expect to dominate the world of scholarship.

It was from these twin influences of liberal thought and scientific experiment that the new university mould was fashioned. And it was first given corporate shape in the Anglo-Irish context with the foundation of London University in 1828. Most of its supporters were both middle class and Dissenters, resentful of their exclusion from Oxford and Cambridge on religious grounds and openly critical of what they regarded as the "elegant imbecility" of the curriculum. They were fully in the liberal and scientific camp, seeking inspiration from Joseph Priestley and the Dissenting Academies, a subject referred to in the previous chapter, as well as from Thomas Jefferson's University of Virginia and the new German universities at Berlin and Bonn at which Catholics and Protestants followed a more utilitarian course of studies. If Jeremy Bentham was the high priest of the gospel of utilitarianism its chief propagandist was James Mill whose writings eloquently called for a system of higher education suited to the needs of the enterprising middle class who, as he stated in his journal "The Westminster Review," contributed "everything of value to our nation; it contains the greatest proportion of the intelligence, industry and wealth of the state; in it are the heads that invent, the hands that execute, the capital by which projects are carried out. The proper education of this portion of the people is of the greatest importance to the well-being of the state." To Mill and such of his associates as Henry Brougham, a man agog with a thousand schemes for practical improvement, the ancient universities were manifestly incompetent. Indeed, the question of university reform had been brought to public notice in the influential "Edinburgh Review" as far back as 1808 in a series of scathing articles by the Rev. Sydney Smith, who castigated the futility of what he termed "the needless perfection in producing Latin verse." The Church, he alleged, contributed to the stagnation by "averting from the students the searching eye of reason." But while directing the withering firepower of their invective against the ancient foundations, the middle class radicals also set about establishing an alternative in their own image and likeness. Such was London University. It was the poet, Thomas Campbell, who first outlined the proposals in detail in a lengthy article in the New Monthly Magazine in 1825. The article referred only obliquely to discontent with Oxford but based its appeal on the need for a university in such a great metropolis and on the benefits to flow from a diffusion of knowledge; "in this metropolis, from its enlightened bishop down to its intelligent mechanic there is a general persuasion that man is elevated by knowledge and degraded by ignorance." London would benefit as did such Scottish university cities as Glasgow from having professors "lecturing daily and regularly, with the influence which their lectures are likely to have on public spirit and information."

The new University was financed by a joint-stock company, with support from Dissenters, Jews and such a Roman Catholic luminary as the Duke of Norfolk. It was undenominational, not as an affront to Christian belief but as a pragmatic necessity arising from the policy of admitting students from diverse faiths. The religious formation of the young people was to be left to their parents and pastors, a process all the more natural and easy as the institution was to be non-residential in a conscious effort to cater for what Campbell called the "middling rich," those with an income of from £400 to £1,000 per annum. In a further effort to reduce costs the method of teaching was to be the professorial lecture rather than the tutorial which held sway in the old universities. The curriculum gave recognition to the new studies in science, professional courses, modern languages. So there emerged a new pattern in university theory and practice, a pattern which was to be adopted at Cork and in the new civic universities which were to be founded in Britain in the second half of the nineteenth century and in the present century. If Oxford and Cambridge and the Anglican Church felt little inhibition in heaping coals of fire on what was termed "the Godless College of Gower Street," a name derived from its physical site, they had the weight of tradition to support their sense of outrage. The universities had been one of the glories of the medieval church, and from their beginnings they were semi-ecclesiastical institutions; true, most of the critical thought which often made life uncomfortable for the establishment had come from them, but in their personnel, their constitution and their daily practice they reflected the ethos of the Church. The Reformation did not affect that position, leaving Oxford, Cambridge and Trinity College as Anglican institutions just as their sister Colleges on the Continent were Catholic. The concept of a secular university was a manifestation of that separation of religion from life which the Churches saw as the malign effect of liberalism. London University posed a threat to an honourable tradition as much as to the Christian formation of its prospective students. Moreover, in excluding theology from its curriculum it was deemed to forfeit any right to call itself a university; a place concerned with universal knowledge could not ignore what had previously been considered the queen of the sciences. Added to that defect there was the questionable nature of its secular studies; high fun was poked at its presumption in elevating such subjects as medicine, botany, zoology and engineering to the status of university subjects; a collection of glass jars and stuffed birds belonged more fittingly to a Mechanics Institute! However, despite the outrage and the fun, the heresy of 1828 was in the course of time to become the orthodoxy of higher education.

It was in this climate of the clash between old wisdom and new science that the university at Cork came into being. Indeed, one of its chief proponents, Thomas Wyse, who had entered Parliament as a Catholic member for Waterford in 1829, was publicly associated with the campaign to force a reluctant British Government to give London the right to grant degrees, the basic right that constitutes a university. Because of the cogency and frequency of his speeches on a wide range of educational matters affecting both Ireland and Britain, Wyse came to be respected as an expert on the subject. Consequently, in 1835 he was appointed by the Government as chairman of a Parliamentary Commission to report and recommend on Irish education. The Wyse Report of 1838 advocated the establishment of what were termed provincial academical colleges to meet the needs of the middle class, a matter that could then be attended to as the needs of the mass of the poor had been catered for with the establishment of the National Schools in 1831, a development with which Wyse had been closely associated. Arising out of the Report a public meeting in Cork led to the establishment of the Munster Provincial College Committee formed largely from membership of the Royal Cork Institution and with James Roche as chairman. For the next seven years the Committee received a wide measure of support from across the dividing lines of religion and politics, while a sub-committee in Limerick under the leadership of William Smith O'Brien pressed the claims of that city as the ultimate site. Another public meeting in Cork in 1844 advanced the climate of public support and this influenced the Conservative Prime Minister, Sir Robert Peel, in including an Irish Colleges Bill in the legislative programme for 1845. His decision was warmly welcomed not only on a local basis in Cork but at national level.

Peel has received a pretty bad press in Ireland, chiefly because he happened to be Prime Minister at the onset of the disastrous Famine, but a study of his Private Papers at the British Museum explodes much of the simplistic nonsense that has been weaved around his name. During his premiership from 1841 to 1846 he had to deal with O'Connell's Repeal Campaign and his papers reveal the very considerable extent to which O'Connell impinged on government thinking. In responding to these pressures Peel's Irish policy was guided by two firm principles, first, the need to preserve the political union of Ireland and Britain as essential to the safety and prosperity of both, and second, to treat the Catholic majority in Ireland with absolute justice before the law and with as much magnan·imity as government policy would allow. As a realistic politician he naturally hoped that his policies would wean at least middle class Catholics from supporting what he saw as the reckless demagoguery of O'Connell. But in a mass of his letters on Irish affairs the political issue is not mentioned at all; what does emerge is an insistence on just dealing and a workmanlike urge to improve conditions within the limits of government policy and action. Though a devout Anglican he steadfastly refused government finan·cial support to the Church of Ireland when it established its Church Education Society rather than work within the National School system with their Catholic fellow-country·men; equally he often refers with distaste to Orange intran·sigence. His confidential letter to a new Lord Lieutenant in July, 1844, at once exemplifies his understanding and his hopes for Ireland:

"The old party distinctions engendered, and necessar·ily engendered, by monopoly and exclusion are fast wither·ing away, and there is a great mass of public opinion, Protestant and Roman Catholic, wearied out by agitation and acrimonious controversy that will gravitate towards a Lord Lieutenant in whose judgment and equity and cour·ageous resolution full confidence can be placed." This letter, being published here for the first time, was a recipe for a policy of conciliation. The Colleges Bill was a practical example of the policy in action. So, too, was an allied measure in higher education, his unilateral decision to increase the State grant to Maynooth. Though he envisaged

some opposition to this proposal, he could not have anticipated the torrent of Protestant bigotry which was poured
on his head. Throughout Britain there arose a virulent press
and platform campaign against the decision to vote increased
public money to support Popery in its very citadel in Ireland.
But Peel stood firm and Maynooth got its grant. Queen
Victoria was not amused by the Protestant backlash and in
a private note to Peel she expressed her sense of shock.
Peel's Maynooth victory was, however, bought at a high
price. The Tory Party backwoodsmen sharpened their
knives; this was Peel's second betrayal on a religious issue
relating to Ireland, the first having been his approval as
Home Secretary in Wellington's government of the Catholic
Emancipation Act in 1829. They disapproved of his origins
as coming only from a commercial family rather than from
the landed gentry; they furiously resented his attempts to
drag them screaming into the real world of the mid-nine-
teenth century. When the unfolding tragedy of Famine in
Ireland finally moved Peel to abolish the Corn Laws and so
allow cheap food to be imported into the United Kingdom,
the landed vested interests in the Tory Party felt that this
was more than flesh and blood could stand. They revolted
and, aided by the Whigs, drove Peel from office in 1846.

The Cabinet Papers of late 1844/'45 show the evolution
of the government plan for the Irish Colleges, with evidence
that among those consulted were Thomas Wyse and Dr.
Murray, Catholic Archbishop of Dublin, the Irish prelate
most versed in educational matters due to his close involvement since 1831 with the National Schools system, a system
based on the undenominational principle. Its broad acceptance by the Catholic Church in Ireland, with the noted
exception of Archbishop McHale of Tuam, inclined Peel
to assume that the same principles would best respond to
the acute religious differences in the country. Furthermore,
he drew a sharp distinction between Catholic clerical and
lay education; having provided for a more generous treatment of Maynooth he argued that the proposed New Colleges, as they were originally called in the Minutes, would
cater exclusively for the secular education of the laity,
with due provision for Catholic supervision and instruction
such as giving a seat on the Governing Body to the bishop
of the diocese, providing denominational Deans of Resid-

ence, and allowing College premises to be used for separate religious instruction. But the Colleges were to be undenominational in character and this was to be the central issue in the ensuing controversy. It was a controversy which neither Peel nor Murray nor the Munster Provincial College Committee could have foreseen, but with the passage of the Bill through Parliament in May, 1845, there came a public split among Irish politicians and prelates, with one section demanding that the Colleges be denominationally Catholic and the other willing to accept the government proposals in principle. In their hearts one thing must have been clear to them all, namely that the reaction to the Maynooth grant made it impossible for any Prime Minister to secure Parliamentary approval for state aid for a denominational Catholic university in Ireland. To be blind to this fact of life, as the clerical and lay opponents of the Bill seemed to be, was to indulge in a tragi-comedy of shadow-boxing. The first shots of opposition came not from the bishops but from O'Connell, then coming to the end of a lifetime of service to Ireland. At a Repeal Committee meeting in May, 1845, he startled the members by denouncing the Bill and castigating the proposed Colleges as "Godless Colleges." The shade of London had come to Ireland. Speaking for the Young Irelanders Thomas Davis begged the Liberator to desist; the Colleges were to be welcomed as affording young men of different creeds to meet in harmony in the pursuit of scholarship, so helping to heal the wounds of religious division. When the bishops spoke shortly afterwards their stance was more temperate; they sought amendments to make the institutions more amenable to Catholic thinking but there was no outright rejection. For the next five years the issue simmered, with Murray valiantly seeking a working compromise between Rome, the Government and divided Irish opinion. The appointment of Dr. Paul Cullen as Archbishop of Armagh led to a more firm demand for nothing less than denominational Catholic colleges at government expense, a demand formally adopted at the Synod of Thurles in 1850 when the Colleges were condemned as dangerous to faith and morals, with all Catholic clerics being forbidden to participate in them and parents being admonished, though not under canonical penalty, to forbid their sons from attending. It was in this heated atmosphere of religious controversy that the Queen's Colleges at Cork, Belfast and Galway took shape as constituents of the Queen's University of Ireland.

The reaction to the Colleges presented the quizzical situation whereby the more advanced nationalist opinion, represented by Thomas Davis, Gavan Duffy and the "Nation" newspaper, accepted the British Tory educational initiative whereas the more conservative elements such as O'Connell and Cullen rejected it. Not that Cullen's reaction was inspired by any political disloyalty to the State; he condemned the Young Irelanders as he later did the Fenians. His opposition to the Colleges is understandable as an expression of a doctrinaire suspicion of liberalism, but the contemporary evidence suggests that his fears were not shared by the majority of middle class Catholic opinion which had originally pressed for such institutions. Furthermore, it can be cogently argued that he seriously misread the basic situation in failing to take account of the fact that in so predominantly Catholic a city as Cork the College would by sheer numbers and local atmosphere provide an acceptable ethos for his flock in the same manner as the Belfast College was to do for Presbyterians. Another strand in Cullen''s policy was also fundamental to the issue; his determination to assert the full rights and dignity of the Catholic Church in the public life of Ireland to counterbalance the period of official eclipse from which it was progressively emerging since Emancipation. As did Anglicans and Dissenters he saw Church control of education as pivotal not only to the welding of the Catholic body politic but to establishing a position of strength and leverage in view of the emerging pattern of State participation in public education. But in making full allowance for these considerations it is the opinion of this writer that the stance adopted by the Synod of Thurles was excessively alarmist and based on false presumptions. Whatever about opinions, it is only a matter of fact that it seriously crippled the Colleges in playing their full part in developing those talents of skill and leadership which Ireland so desperately needed in building up its economic life after the Famine. However, Cullen had a positive alternative with the foundation of the Catholic University at 86 Stephen's Green, Dublin, and it must have seemed providential that there was at hand as first Rector someone to lend the prestige of his great name to the enterprise. In 1852 Dr. Newman came to Dublin trailing clouds of Oxford glory. His fame as leader of the Tractarian Movement, his distinction as a writer on some of the major philosophic issues of church and state, and the dramatic impact of his conversion to the Catholic Church, all of this invested Newman with something of a charismatic appeal. The public delivery of his University Discourses in Dublin seemed to confirm the greatness that was to come; but by 1858 he was to leave Ireland disillusioned by what he termed the frustrations and lack of understanding he encountered from Cullen and some of the other bishops. He described the archbishop as having "the intellectual equipment of a sacristan" and of wanting the University to be nothing more than a glorified seminary.

Meanwhile, in the wider university context profound changes were afoot which were to bring Oxford, Cambridge and Trinity into line with the basic provisions of London and the Queen's Colleges. The radical liberals continued to press for university reform as part of their programme of social change in the direction of a more pluralistic and utilitarian society. When in 1852 their pressure led to a parliamentary Universities Commission they had already won a major victory. By 1873 Parliament had passed legislation which secularised all three ancient institutions, so bringing about an unprecedented change in the traditions of the centuries. Staff and students were free to attend the religious services in the collegiate chapels, but religious allegiance of any kind was no longer obligatory. The move was not inspired by any irreligious ideology but as a measure of civic freedom, and while some viewed it as the herald of agnosticism others saw it as a challenge to genuine Christian commitment. The last decades of the century also saw moves for a friendly compromise between the Catholic Church in Ireland and the Government on the university issue, a compromise that was amicably reached with the establishment of the National University in 1908. The bishops formally abandoned Cullen's demand for State finance for a denominationally Catholic system while the Government was willing to meet legitimate demands for the safeguarding of the faith and morals of Catholic students as specified by the bishops. In this happier climate the Colleges at Cork, Galway and University College, Dublin, the lineal descendant of Newman's University, joined to constitute the National University of Ireland which was and is undenominational. So ended a half century of bitterness and frustration. Was it necessary to waste so much time?

Having engaged in a mammoth digression round about the university world it is time to return to the academic life of Cork. The appointment of Sir Robert Kane as first President brought the prestige of a distinguished name to the College as he was widely regarded as one of the out-standing Irishmen of his time. He was born in the Pro-Cathedral parish in Dublin on 24th September, 1809, the son of John Kane who owned a chemical establishment, and of Ellen Troy who was a relative of the Catholic Arch-bishop, Dr. Troy. Because of his sympathies with the United Irish rebels in 1798 the elder Kane had been compelled to seek safety in Paris for some years where he studied chemistry before returning to Dublin. Young Robert entered Trinity College with the intention of becoming a doctor; as a Catholic he was enabled to do so consequent on the relaxations which followed on the Catholic Relief Bill of 1793. In 1830 he was appointed clinical clerk to the Meath Hospital while the following year found him installed as professor of chemistry at the Apothecaries Hall. This ended his brief medical career, for henceforth he devoted his enormous capacity for hard work to chemical research and to the publication of his findings. In 1832 he founded the Dublin Journal of Medical Science which later became the Irish Journal of Medical Science. In 1834 he was elected lecturer in natural philosophy to the Royal Dublin Society, his duties requiring him to give courses of public lectures in Dublin and the provinces on a wide range of scientific topics, as well as to report to the Society on the mechanical inventions submitted to it. As the crowds flocked to hear Davy and Faraday at the Royal Institution in London so, too, they came to the R.D.S. to hear Kane who had develop-ed into an accomplished public speaker and a brilliant experimentalist. During his course in 1842 the Society had the service of policemen to marshal those seeking admis-sion. Meanwhile the publication of his research papers in scientific journals had won him a European reputation, in recognition of which the Royal Irish Academy awarded him the Cunningham Medal in 1843. In making the presentation the distinguished mathematician, Sir William Rowan Hamilton, spoke of that "combination of genius and industry which has already caused the researches of Kane to influence in no slight degree the progress of chemical science and has won for him a European reputation." In 1840 the Royal Society in London had awarded him a medal and his election as a Fellow in 1849 brought him the highest distinction in the world of science.

Though busy with his public lectures and his research he yet found time to publish his book, "The Elements of Chemistry," in 1841; it was introduced by Faraday into the Woolwich Academy, while an American edition in 1843 was adopted widely for advanced courses. Nor did his scientific preoccupations preclude him from affairs of the heart. In 1838 he had married Katherine Baily who had already showed her interest in botany by publishing a catalogue of Irish plants entitled, "The Irish Flora." Samples of her work can still be seen in the Botany Department at the University in Cork. In addition to their mutual interest in science both parties were linguists and there is a tradition that some of their courtship was conducted in Greek verses! It was in 1844 that Kane reached one of the pinnacles of his career with the publication of his monumental book, "The Industrial Resources of Ireland," described by Dr. T. S. Wheeler as "the first and most important attempt to apply scientific methods to the evaluation and use of our industrial resources." With exhaustive authority it dealt with the variety of Ireland's natural assets and with suggestions for their use in securing the welfare of her people. Coal, turf, water, minerals, qualities of soil, drainage, crop rotation, canals and railways—all receive careful consideration. All the field work and the laboratory experiments were personally carried out by Kane and involved an enormous amount of personal observation in many parts of the country at a time when travel was so tedious. The book concludes with a theme that was always near his heart, the urgent need for industrial education and for creating a climate of opinion that would shed an obsession with academic education as the only prestigious course for young people. Ireland needed skilled craftsmen and enlightened farmers as much as professional people. Kane was in the new tradition of useful knowledge. With such interests he eagerly took up a new post in 1845 when the government appointed him Director of the Museum of Irish Industry in St. Stephen's Green,

Dublin, designed to focus public attention on the possibilities of the country's natural resources. In collaboration with his assistant, Dr. W. K. Sullivan, Kane experimented with the possibility of growing sugar beet in Ireland, arguing against the then current wisdom which held the climate to be totally unsuitable. It remained for a native government to vindicate his belief.

He was to be enormously involved in seeking to alleviate the disastrous effects of the Famine, the searing memory of which remained with him throughout his long life. Gravely concerned over the ominous news of the potato blight in the autumn of 1845 the Prime Minister, Sir Robert Peel, acted swiftly in appointing a high-powered scientific commission to diagnose the cause and recommend a remedy. The three members were Professor Lyon Playfair of the School of Mines, Professor Lindley of London University and Robert Kane. But the existing state of scientific knowledge foiled the efforts of the commission. It was not until the 1880s that a French botanist was led to apply the modern method of spraying against blight. In 1846 Kane was appointed by the government as one of the eight Relief Commissioners charged with the daunting task of distributing public relief to a starving nation. The following year he became a member of the Central Board of Health which sought to deal with the widespread outbreak of typhus fever which accompanied the great hunger.

When in 1845 Peel responded to demands for extended university education in Ireland, demands mainly voiced by the Catholic middle class, it was not surprising that he should have offered the Presidency of the Cork foundation to the recently-knighted Sir Robert Kane. Not only was he a Catholic, an important consideration in gaining acceptance for the undenominational character of the proposed institutions, but he had shown conspicuous talent and rare dedication in the pursuit of scientific scholarship and in the promotion of the welfare of Ireland. He remained in Cork until his retirement in 1873, and if his tenure of office was marked in its earlier years by public bickering between him and some members of the academic staff, he did achieve the monumental task of creating a university from the blueprint of an Act of Parliament. His successor was his former assistant in Dublin, Dr. William Kirby Sullivan, who had received his early education at the North Monastery in Cork.

A fluent Irish speaker, he had been associated with the Young Irelanders and had held an appointment in Newman's Catholic University. His appointment by the government was significant in view of his more advanced nationalist opinions. Like Kane, he maintained a close link with local civic interests and was foremost in promoting native industry. The beautifully-bound Report of the Cork Industrial and Fine Art Exhibition of 1883 contains a lengthy survey by him of the country's potential. The book was produced by Messrs. Purcell of Patrick Street, its cover resplendent in gold leaf with the letterings in Irish language characters, and with the names of the four provinces in the Irish originals. One sentence from Dr. Sullivan's pen might have relevance for today: "To judge by the present provision for intermediate and higher education in Ireland it would seem as if all the youth of the country were destined to be clergymen, physicians, lawyers or civil servants; industry certainly has no place in it, and is not a factor in the discussions on education which perpetually go on, I regret to say, without much fruit." This noted scholar died as President in 1890, leaving a wide reputation which a British periodical described as that of a man "of great intellectual power and most multifarious and varied accomplishments, scientific, literary, archaeological, and above all philological." His deep commitment to Irish language studies had led him to encourage Eugene O'Curry and to collaborate with the Royal Irish Academy in the study of ancient texts. Such public bodies as the Royal Commission on Technical Instruction, 1883, and the Parliamentary Committee on Irish Industries, 1885, drew fully on his expertise. In unveiling the Celtic Cross over his grave in St. Finbarr's Cemetery, Cork, in June, 1894, his friend, Denny Lane, said of him: "there was not an Irish town he did not know, there was not an Irish shire through which he had not walked. The history, the geography, the geology, the botany, the agriculture, the industries of Ireland were familiar to him."

All academic staff were appointed by the Government, and at the opening of the College in the autumn of 1849 it was interesting that the Dean of the Medical Faculty was Dr. Bullen who featured in the previous chapter giving evidence as a lecturer in chemistry at the Royal Cork Institution; incidentally his son's name was the first to be entered on the College rolls. It was also fitting that the first professor of Natural History was the Rev. William Hincks, son of the founder of the Institution. From its inception the College had a Chair of Celtic Languages. The first 115 students were equally divided between Catholic and Protestant, and despite the Synod of Thurles this proportion was maintained throughout the century. It was chiefly after his death that George Boole, first professor of Mathematics, was to achieve eminence as a mathematical thinker. His grave may be seen at St. Michael's Church of Ireland, Blackrock. Early regulations for the conduct of students would be considered positively draconian in an age so exclusively dominated by the regimentation of blue jeans; in the board-houses licensed by the President students had to be indoors "by nine of the clock in the Winter and Spring terms and ten of the clock in Summer term." The playing "at games of Chance, Cards or Dice" was forbidden, as was "the introduction of spiritous liquors into the houses." Equally forbidden was the "frequenting of Smoking-rooms, Taverns or Public-houses."

Nor did the internal fitments at once match the external splendour; in May, 1850, with academic life eight months in session the Registrar, Francis Albani, sent off a list of complaints to the Board of Works, of which item number eleven was: "the President's Office, still remaining totally unfurnished, it is required that it be provided with carpet, fire irons, office table with desk and drawers, a press, six black chairs and some shelves." There was also a plea that the Bursar's Office should have a "door and lock." The needs of academics were disarmingly simple! Nor was there much consolation in knowing that the muse of knowledge was being pursued in Gothic splendour when the firegrates were billowing smoke and the Stone Corridor was flooded when the wind was south, all of which matters featured in a letter to the Board of Works on the 26th of March, 1850, which "disclaimed making any serious charges against Sir Thomas Deane as an architect."

Among those present in the Aula Maxima for the inaugural ceremonies was Mr. Denny Lane who had graduated from Trinity College and the Temple, London, as a bachelor of Arts and Law. Apart from his business interests he came to hold a foremost place in the cultural life of the city, and in a lecture to the Literary and Scientific Society in 1885 he delivered some thoughtful recollections and judgments

which seem a fitting conclusion to this chapter. His closing remarks may have been coloured by that expression so often used in every age, "the good old days," but
they may equally record the passing of an earlier concept
of the educated gentleman as someone with wide tastes
in reading and with a broad and lively interest in all that
was finest in life and conversation. For it was in the closing
decades of the century that the gifted amateur was beginning to lose ground, to be succeeded today by the certifi-
cated specialist knowing more and more about less and
less. Here is what Denny Lane had to say: "With respect to
our literary status in Cork in 1885 I see no evidence of
progress. With far greater aids to learning I see less learning. We have now what we had not then, a provincial College, a School of Art, penny papers instead of sixpenny
ones. We have telegraphs, telephones, railways, swift steam-
ers, penny postage and many reforms in other matters. But
with all these aids do we find in the middle class a mark
of improvement? I regret to say I do not see it. Of the men
who have emigrated from us within the last decade I can
only name one who has made his mark in literature, Mr.
Justin McCarthy. Our great schools exist no longer, partly
from the fashion of sending away boys to English and
foreign schools to get a thin varnish of French or an electro-
plated English accent. I have met a good many of them
and none have come up to the standard of the home-keep-
ing youth of my boyhood, furnished with homely wit and
homespun knowledge. So far as literary matters are concerned I am repelled by the baldness of conversation, which
for the most part is confined to a repetition without varia-
tion of what I have read in the papers of today or yesterday.
I find young men thinking of entering a university at the age
when my companions left it, and yet I hear complaints of
overwork which I never heard in my youth. I see few
young men who are enthusiastic on any subject except
cricket, lawn tennis, yachting or cycling. Cricket, a stupid
game introduced from England, to the prejudice of honest
hurley, seems to me one of the great agencies employed
to deprive our youth of intellect; and I noticed some time
ago when moving about England that the talk of nine men
out of ten was of cricket or horse-racing. Nothing can
contribute more to keeping a sound mind in a sound body
than healthy exercise, but the body is not everything. In

these remarks I address myself to the middle and upper classes of society. In the humbler classes I see a marked advance, especially noticeable since the Intermediate Education was applied."

This consideration of the earlier history of the University at Cork has tried to demonstrate the wide issues involving not only for the academic community but for the structure and values of society as a whole. If the nineteenth century created new university patterns, and if Cork fully reflected them, it was largely because much of the pattern of religious, political and economic life was undergoing profound and enduring change. Perhaps the most fundamental feature of that change was the creation of the secular society in western civilisation, so replacing the theocratic order on which Christendom had been built. For the university that was a decisive break with tradition, all the more so as it was itself in its origins one of the glories of the medieval church. But the academic community adapted to the new philosophy of public life, and continued to serve society as the custodian of universal culture, as a centre of excellence and as an institution where the right to independent thought is safeguarded. In this tradition the University of Cork takes its place.

Chapter XII

THE LOOK OF CORK, 1800-1900

It was in the nineteenth century that the people of Cork put forth their enterprise and their exuberance to give to the city a new shape and an enduring beauty. In doing so they made an imaginative use of their geographical assets, laying out the new streets and quays along the two arms of the river Lee, and using the steep hills to achieve quite startling panoramic views. By 1800 the very considerable task of arching over the many channels and waterways to the east of the Grand Parade had been largely accomplished, and this whole area of reclaimed land was to be used to create the modern city centre. Patrick Street was shaped and curved along a channel which had seen ships berthed only a generation previously. It became a dignified main street, long and wide, with a profusion of architectural styles exhibited in fine shops. The Grand Parade was certainly grand at least in its width, while the South Mall acquired a graciousness and an opulence of building style which still please the citizens and impresses their visitors. This extension beyond the former confined space of the ancient medieval city was to highlight the usefulness and the visual appeal of the two channels of the river, bringing ships up into the heart of the city and providing the citizens with the immemorial fascination of the movement of water and the pleasure of seeing swans gliding past their doorsteps, their shops and their warehouses. But it was possibly in the use of stone that Cork came to acquire a distinctiveness that is rare in the cities of these islands. The two natural local stones, the red sandstone of the northern hills and the soft white limestone of the southern quarries, were used to provide dramatic contrast not only in the formal public buildings but in a wide variety of quayside warehouses, granaries and rows of private dwellings. This splash of red and white has had the good fortune not to suffer the begriming of greater industrial cities, so today it offers colour, relief and a visual excitement to a walk about the city. The old stonemasons used it superbly in making the banks and insurance offices on the South Mall and in lining the quay from St. Patrick's Bridge to the North Mall.

Not content with all of this making of new streets and broad avenues in the city centre in the valley, there took place something of an exuberance of public and private building on the sloping hills to the north and the south. The century saw the erection of two cathedrals, each exemplifying the glory of the local stone, St. Mary's rising with its mellow red on the northern hill and St. Finbarr's on the southern with its soft whiteness and the grace of its three spires. To the two cathedrals was added the Gothic charm of the University whose limestone Quadrangle moved Macaulay to pronounce it worthy of the High Street at Oxford. Then there came the villas of the merchant princes and the professional classes who were following the nineteenth century cult of respectability and were moving out from the narrow streets and lanes of the old city. They built for themselves some finely proportioned residences along the sloping parklands of Sunday's Well, Montenotte and Tivoli, many with long gardens reaching down to private moorings at the waterside. On the southern side they favoured Ballintemple and Blackrock, so providing the city, and in particular the river entrance to it, with an air of good taste and solid achievement that befitted the growing commercial importance of Cork. One of the major political developments in nineteenth century Irish history was to lead to an upsurge on public building in Cork as in other cities and towns throughout the country. When the Catholic Emancipation Act of 1829 brought success to Daniel O'Connell's liberal campaign, it resulted in a sustained programme of ecclesiastical architecture. The city was to be enriched by some very handsome structures in both Gothic and classical styles with the Capuchin Church of Holy Trinity commissioned by Father Mathew, the Dominican Church on Pope's Quay, St. Patrick's Parish Church, St. Vincent's at Sunday's Well, and Ss. Peter and Paul's built to a Pugin design off Patrick Street. These, together with the rebuilt St. Luke's and Trinity Presbyterian, added richly to civic adornment.

The nineteenth century brought to the cities of Ireland, Britain and Europe one altogether distinctive type of public building, the railway station, the symbol of the new age of mass travel. Railway architecture was invariably dignified with the aim of presenting this vast enterprise in accordance with high standards of public taste. The cities so gained a variety of florid Gothic, or classical elegance, or neat structures in red brick. Cork acquired the very pleasing Great Southern Railway terminus in red brick, with its detailed ornamentation in its many chimneys; the Bandon Railway terminus near the City Hall brought classical proportions and gleaming limestone to the quayside. Other corporate bodies made a significant contribution to the visual aspect of the city; the Harbour Commissioners, a most important body in a community that made so much of its living from ships and the affairs of the river, built the new Custom House further downstream from the former premises in Emmet Place; the Steam Packet Company erected a neat little piece of classical frontage on Penrose Quay; while the prestigious Committee of Merchants who directed the thriving business of the Butter Market with noted finesse, were the first to invest the new South Mall with their imposing Commercial Rooms, later to become incorporated into the Imperial Hotel. The Butter Market itself, up on the northern hill at the foot of Shandon, added its heavy classical portico to the busy scenes made by great crowds of farmers bringing in their firkins of butter to be weighed, graded and packed in oak casks fashioned by the craftsmanship of the coopers. As the greatest export outlet for agricultural produce in Ireland, the city quays were lined with the tall masts of sailing ships waiting to be victualled for the long weeks at sea or taking aboard the salted buttter, the tallow for candles and the meat offal to be shipped to Liverpool, Hamburg, Rotterdam and Carolina.

The century saw yet further additions to the varied styles of bridges that spanned the two channels of the Lee. Wooden bridges, metal bridges, limestone bridges, sandstone bridges, bridges that opened upwards and bridges that opened outwards, and bridges that fell down— the city had a profusion of river crossings. The bridge that fell down was replaced by the present elegant structure of St. Patrick's Bridge, resplendent in its three arches and its colonnaded balustrade. But apart from the buildings there were other pieces of street furnishings that belonged exclusively to the nineteenth century. There were the gas lamps; each one throwing its mellow light on the cobbled streets, each one serviced by that nostalgic figure, the lamp-lighter with his long pole. Even he brought another piece of machinery to the street scene; whereas in mid century he did his rounds on foot, by the close of the age he was balancing his pole on a bicycle. This modest conveyance was, with the steam-engine, probably the most generally useful of all the inventions of that age of men and their machines. Yet another wonder in a century of wonders was symbolised by another item of street furniture, the pillar box on the corner into which citizens dropped their mail to have it conveyed at incredible speed to faraway places at a fraction of the cost they had to pay only a generation previously. To the elegant cast-iron lamp standards and the sturdy pillar boxes there was added at the close of the century all the paraphernalia of the trams— the lines, the loop-lines, the overhead cables. Against this backcloth of new streets, new buildings and new appurtenances there were various public servants to be seen, the Royal Irish Constabulary, the postmen, the sanitary inspectors, the Corporation workers. To these were added the great variety of street traders and hawkers of fish, fruit, vegetables, flowers, matches, buttons and thread and shoe laces, brooms and firewood, many with their own distinctive cries, as well as chimney sweeps and men who sharpened knives. To these traditional city cries there came another towards the end of the century when the "Echo" boys spilled onto the streets in the late afternoon.

Before doing a walking tour of some of the more significant areas of the city it seems desirable to survey some of the talking-points, the issues of the day, which featured in the minds and hearts of the citizens of Cork throughout the century. Here it must be realised that for the first fifty years a great proportion of the mass of the people were barely literate, that even for the middle classes newspapers were very dear, that they were mainly devoted to short snippets of foreign news and internal events, that even until the end of the century they did not carry photographs. Neither was there the general climate of mass concern with outside happenings which has become a feature of the modern age of political democracy and of global coverage of personalities and events brought to our breakfast tables and our firesides by the popular press and by radio and television. This constraint on public participation is well illustrated in regard to that one battle which coloured the mind of Europe throughout the whole century, the Battle of Waterloo; in some instances it was only many months after the event that the ringing of the church bell announced the victory in remote villages in the far north of England.

The century was born amid the tumult of dramatic happenings abroad and at home; abroad the French Revolution and the rise of Napoleon were to change the map of Europe and profoundly influence all subsequent political thought. At home there was the United Irish rebellion, bringing a new revolutionary and separatist stream into the current of Irish nationalism. Then there followed the Act of Union and the passing of the Parliament in College Green. Corkmen were involved in these climactic events and in the gallant and gentlemanly episode of Robert Emmet; there was the Capuchin, Father O'Donovan, who had been dragged to the guillotine in Paris and yet lived to carry on his ministry in Blackamoor Lane; there was the young wine merchant, James Roche, imprisoned by the republicans at Bordeaux; he, too, survived to become the "father" of learning in the city in the middle decades of the century. The Sheares brothers were to be executed as United Irishmen, while Sarah Curran was to nurse her grief with the Penroses at their residence in Tivoli. The rise of Daniel O'Connell was to be a phenomenon not only in Irish but in European terms; he showed for the first time how a great mass movement could be welded together in a constitutional struggle based on the liberal principles of religious and civil liberty, so his victory was saluted not only by the Catholics of Ireland but by the champions of human freedom in Britain and throughout Europe. He frequently addressed vast meetings in Cork, while the last public dinner given to him in Ireland was held at the Imperial Hotel in June, 1845. The impact of the Famine has already been alluded to in the chapter on Father Mathew. The Fenians, Parnell and the great upsurge in literary and cultural life associated with the Gaelic League were to enter significantly into the public life of the city. By 1900 the face of life in Ireland had been changed out of all recognition from that of 1800; the Catholic majority had achieved the social and political representation due to their numbers; the bulk of the land was being transferred to the tenant farmers through a succession of Land Acts; Gladstone has disestablished the Church of Ireland, so leaving it free to continue its ministry at a purely spiritual level while at the same time removing a longstanding grievance and a source of religious discord. Basic to public life was the change in Britain and Ireland from oligarchic government to democracy with the progressive extension to the man in the street of the right to vote. The age of the common had dawned. One silent revolution had contributed to it, the extension of universal elementary education. It was in 1892 that attendance at National school was made compulsory in Ireland.

It was against this background of events and ideas that nineteenth century Cork grew into a thriving commercial city. A ramble through the streets of today is probably the best way to invest them with the recollections of yesterday, so bringing a new awareness to the everyday pleasure of being out and about. The South Mall is a suitable starting point, as much for its past as its present. Until the turn of the eighteenth century it was still marsh land outside the eastern city walls; indeed when in 1690 the Duke of Marlborough led his charge on the walls from the tower of the Red Abbey, he and his men waded through a boggy surface on which grew rape seed, then used to make oil for lamps. The area was in fact known as the Rape Marsh. The episode in which one of his staff officers, the Duke of Grafton, was mortally wounded by a ball reputedly fired from a breach in the walls by a Cork blacksmith is still recalled by the narrow little lane named Grafton's Alley, lately dignified into a street. By the mid eighteenth century the area had acquired a new name, Dunscombe's Marsh, in view of the fact that the Corporation had leased it to a prominent merchant of that name. From about 1750 to 1800 a great deal of development took place on both sides of the present main thoroughfare which still had an open channel of water running its full length. Merchants built their houses with flights of stone steps leading up to the front doors, while at the water level there were basements into which goods could be loaded from barges. Some of the stone steps still remaining recall the days when the Mall looked something like a canal in Amsterdam. By 1801 the channel was arched over and as the century advanced the street came to acquire a gracious dignity that would do credit to any city. It became long and wide, while its rows of public buildings preserved a human scale as they met the skyline. By 1900 it looked substantially as it does today, with its long vista framed in the west by the slender triple spires of St. Finbarr's Cathedral and in the east by the masts of ships at the quayside. Between the spires and the masts, both so evocative of the history and the commerce of Cork, there is to be seen an opulence of architectural grandeur that typified so many of the nineteenth century cities. The banks predominate with the massive assurance of their classical architecture, full of the detailed craftsmanship of the stone mason's art and resplendent in soft white limestone. The Savings Bank, with its fluted classical pillars and fine proportions, begins the string of pearls. Its corner site also reflects a typically nineteenth century preoccupation with status. On the nearby corner stands another celebration of the stonemason's craft, the former Provincial Bank. Very much worth noticing are the top panels in which are carved some delightful representations of industry, commerce, agriculture and navigation.

Walking up westwards the pleasing classical frontage of the former County Club comes into view, happily preserved and restored by its new occupants. Just around the corner in Pembroke Street is the elegant little doorway of the old Cork Library, with its wise old owls looking out from the pediments on either side and the date, 1792, in raised stone lettering. Next comes the elaborate frontage of the Imperial Hotel, which as the original Commercial Rooms of the Committee of Merchants, was the first notable public building to appear on the Mall. Next to it are two of the old premises with outside stone steps. The texture of the brickwork in them, in contrast to the red brick so profusely found elsewhere on the street, has traditionally led to the belief that the contractor used Dutch brick which had been unloaded on the quays having been used as ballast on the voyage to Cork. The frontage of the former Cork Gas Company premises offers a complete contrast to the more formal classical style so far noticed. It is a highly decorated piece of Victorian town building with the fancy and contrasts of the romantic style so beloved of John Ruskin and so well exemplified in many of the creations of the noted Cork architect, Sir Thomas Deane. The use of natural foliage and of gargoyle heads typified the exuberance of the romantic revival which gathered force from the middle decades of the last century. Passing the auction rooms of Messrs. Marsh, which also date from that era, the impressive proportions of the former Munster and Leinster Bank come into view, with formal classical style and a feast of cut limestone. From that point to the Grand Parade junction there are a variety of lesser premises, mostly built in harmony with the character of the street and each one recalling something of the legal, commercial or medical life of the nineteenth century city.

If the north side of the Mall displays the lightness of limestone and the formal dignity of classical styles, the south side has the warmth of red brick and the elegance of Georgian doorways. While not by any means matching the superb grace of the Dublin squares, the Mall does offer a notable example of the simple dignity of large windows and of the carving and intricacy that went into making the doorway the centrepiece of aesthetic interest. Many citizens have regretted that one of the banks saw fit to interpose an erection of insipid glass into this sweep of traditional elegance. This comment has been more frequently and more pungently expressed regarding the colossus of concrete and glass which now replaces the former red brick premises at the south eastern end of the street. If the Mall offers the visual variety of red and white stonework and of classical and Georgian styles, it particularly demonstrates the work of two architectural firms which between them were responsible for a great deal of the civic embellishment of nineteenth century Cork.

Sir Thomas Deane and the brothers John and George Pain have left their handprint on a range of buildings stretching from Blackrock Castle to the University, and including the Savings Bank, Holy Trinity Church, the Courthouse, St. Mary's Church, the Catholic Cathedral, St. Patrick's Church and the surviving facade of the old Gaol. Thomas Deane won his first major commission when in 1811 he was selected at the age of nineteen as the architect of the Commercial Rooms on the Mall. The Committee of Merchants who directed the Butter Market up at Shandon with remarkable enterprise and finesse, as well as being responsible for much of the general commerce of the city, desired a commodious building in which they could meet to transact their affairs, to consult the national and foreign newsheets, to study navigation charts and to drink claret in convivial company. Their selection of the Mall as the site of their new premises not only underlined the shift away from the old city but set the new street as a prestigious centre for public affairs. The fine proportions of young Deane's Commercial Rooms still remain as they first looked when the butter merchants and their clerks first went inside in 1813 to calculate their business in the currencies of Europe. It is to be assumed that these wealthy and rather cosmopolitan gentlemen were careful to follow the best in high fashion; if so they were dressed in either of two outfits. Powdered wigs had gone out of fashion since 1800 to be replaced by beaver hats in beige, black or grey. Gentlemen following the simple elegance of the Beau Brummel style usually wore a blue jacket with brass buttons, a buff coloured waistcoat, a stiff white cravat and pantaloon breeches with silk stockings. The other style involved a double-breasted knee-length redingote coat, stiff collar reaching up to side whiskers, top boots and a top hat. Most gentlemen carried fob watches, gold or silver snuff boxes and gold-mounted walking canes.

Thomas Deane in association with his younger brother, Kearns, was again the architect for the Savings Bank in 1842. Perhaps his finest work was to be the Gothic charm of the University Quadrangle which won the acclaim of the citizens at its opening in the autumn of 1849. This is more fully covered in the chapter on that subject, though Macaulay's tribute is worth recalling, "a Gothic college worthy to stand in the High Street of Oxford." Apparently it was Kearns who was chiefly responsible for the elegance of the classical St. Mary's Dominican Church by the quayside. After 1850 Sir Thomas, his son of the same name and their gifted partner, George Woodward, moved to Dublin where in time the firm was responsible for some of the most significant work to grace that city in the second half of the last century. This included the Kildare Street Club, the National Library, the Science and Art Museum and the distinctive Engineering School at Trinity College. This latter building is of Byzantine style with Venetian influence and its beauty moved John Ruskin to tears. Its intricate ornamentation in exterior doors and windows and the use of coloured marble in the interior make it worthy of a visit. The Deane firm won the prestigious commission to design and build the University Museum at Oxford which was completed in 1860 in the neo-Gothic style. One of the Oxford Fellows, W. Tuckwell, in his "Reminiscences" recalled the advent of Sir Thomas Deane, his son Thomas, and Woodward. The latter he described as "a grave and curiously silent man; of his partners, men greatly his inferior, the elder, Sir Thomas, was a ceaseless chatterbox; the younger, son to Sir Thomas, stammered. Speaking in Congregation one of the Fellows hit off the trio after his manner: one wouldn't talk, one can't talk, one never stops talking." Whatever about the chatter, Sir Thomas Deane was a versatile architect capable of working in a variety of styles. Not the least of his contributions to his native city was his early recognition of the genius of John Hogan when the future great sculptor was still only a boy earning a few shillings as an apprentice clerk. Deane took him into his own drawing-office and so fostered the developing talent of the gifted boy.

It was in 1816 that the Committee of Merchants again sought the services of Deane to build a hotel and coach-yard extending along Pembroke Street behind their Commercial Rooms. With the rapid growth in stage and mail coach traffic there was a greatly increased demand for overnight accommodation in the city. This aspect of commercial life is more fully treated in the chapter on coaches and horses. The Imperial's guest list down through the century is a roll-call of the leading figures of Irish public life and of distinguished foreign visitors to Cork. The chapter on Daniel Maclise recalls the visit in 1825 of the leading novelist of the day, Sir Walter Scott, accompanied by the noted lady writer, Maria Edgeworth. Thackeray's estimate of Father Mathew with whom he took tea on the morning after a banquet when the champagne flowed free is sketched in the chapter on the Apostle of Temperance. The Hotel was host to the first major international conference to be held in the city when in August, 1843, the British Association for the Advancement of Science brought a galaxy of talent and a glittering round of soirees, conversaziones, banquets and grand balls to Cork. Reporting on that event in its issue of 14th August, 1843, the "Cork Examiner" announced that the dignitaries already in the city included the Most Rev. Dr. Crolly, Catholic Primate of Armagh, the distinguished mathematician, Sir William Rowan Hamilton, the Rev. Dr. Hincks from Belfast, returning to the city which he had enriched as founder of the Royal Cork Institution, Mr. Thomas Crofton Croker, the noted Cork antiquary and writer, home from his post at the Admiralty in London, and the man who so captured London life for the world and the century, Charles Dickens. Expected were Lord Listowel, patron of the arts, the Earl of Rosse, the astronomer, William Smith O'Brien, M.P., the nationalist landlord, Thomas Wyse, M.P., the noted educationalist, Dr. Robert Kane, author of the masterly "Industrial Resources of Ireland" and destined to be first President of the city's University, and the celebrated French chemist, M. Dumas. They all came; so did Thomas Davis, the inspiration of Young Ireland; so did Charles Bianconi, the "King of the Roads." Deeply involved in organising this celebration of the useful and the scientific was the hotel's architect, Sir Thomas Deane. The manager, Mr. McDowell, advertised his premises as affording "a Feast of Reason and a Flow of Soul." And for a mere pittance one could eat amid such rarefied company: "Dinner on the Table precisely at six. Cost, inclusive of Wine, 4s. It is requested no fee be given to the Waiters on these occasions, attendance being included in the charge for Dinner." The men of science and their ladies took time off for fun and frolics at the Grand Ball and Supper at the Corn Exchange, later to become the old City Hall, on the 24th of August when "supper was laid for twelve hundred persons." The "Examiner" worked itself up into a frenzy of excitement in depicting the scene; "never were there before assembled in a Cork ballroom so many lovely and attractive women. The walls were lined with 3,500 yards of pure white calico which reflected back the dazzling light of 500 Wax-lights and innumerable jets of gas. The dancing commenced at 11.00 o'clock and was kept up with unabated zest until 2.00. when the company retired to the Supper Saloon." They could have danced all night, while their gaiety by the riverside puts a more human face on the more solemn stereotypes that look out from many history books.

The limestone facade of the former County Club is an elegant piece of classical design that recalls the work of the brothers John and George Pain who came to Ireland from London to execute some commissions for John Nash, the creator of so much of Regency London. The example of their work which has entered most fully into the hearts of the citizens is Blackrock Castle which was completed in 1828, a picturesque landmark splendidly sited by the waterside below the Marina. Generations of excited children have been taken down to see it and to capture the excitement of a castle, while adults have always held that it was only by going as far as Blackrock that one got a real change of air. They went down by the Green boats which put in at the pier in the village, as well as by the Cork, Passage and Blackrock Railway, and finally they had the convenience of being whisked from Patrick Street by the trams. On the quayside a few paces off the South Mall can be seen another specimen of the work of the Pain brothers, the very attractive church of the Holy Trinity which they designed in the Gothic style for Father Mathew. Because of lack of funds the lantern-style frontage and spire were not added until much later. This building is best admired from across the river in George's Quay where it is set off by the charming arch and balustrade of Parliament Bridge and by a group of elegant bow-fronted houses. The Pains also designed the new County and City Courthouse which was erected in what is now Washington Street in 1835; but only the existing fine classical portico and front wall of the original building now remain, the rest having been destroyed in a fire in 1891. The interior of the present building makes good use of Irish marble, black from Kilkenny, green from Connemara, and red from Little Island a few miles downstream from Cork. Yet another example of their work is the facade of the old Goal modelled on the Temple of Bacchus, a heavy and formidable structure which the University happily has preserved in its adaptation of the site.

Apart from the work of architects and stonemasons, the South Mall and its environs reflect much of the cultural history of the nineteenth century city. The Cork Library at the corner of Pembroke Street was an important centre which drew together the lovers of books among the professional classes and the gentry, many of them marked by an individuality which bordered on the eccentric and not a few of them capable of putting on a fine show of cantankerousness.

The Library was originally in Cook Street, with the move to Pembroke Street taking place in 1816. Its foundation as a subscription library in 1792 reflected a trend found in other cities in Ireland and Britain at a time when books were dear and circulation was slow. One can imagine the early patrons passing through the earlier premises in 1792, depositing their mounted canes in the hallstand and proceeding to the reading-room where they doffed their wigs and settled down to read in the broadsheets the disturbing news from France and the debates in Grattan's

Parliament. Among the periodicals most in demand was the "Edinburgh Review" which was in time to bring a whiff of the intellectual excitement of the new radical liberalism that was to shape middle class attitudes in Britain and Ireland in the first half of the century. Writing in the Cork Historical and Archaeological Journal in 1905 its then secretary, Mr. James Coleman, stated that it was "probably the oldest and the only institution of its kind in Ireland. There can be little doubt that all that was brightest and best in the intellect of Cork has been closely associated with the Cork Library ever since its inception; and even a cursory account of its leading members in bygone days would furnish an interesting and informing chapter on the genius, talent, and love of literature for which Cork has always been so remarkable." Directly across the Mall, on Jameson's Row, the Royal Cork Institution had its premises from 1806 to 1832 when it moved to the present School of Art in Emmet Place. The chapter on the Institution gives a fuller account of the activities of those citizens who gave themselves to the growing cult of scientific inquiry which involved the Royal Society and the Royal Institution of London as well as the Royal Dublin Society, and had among its devotees such local personages as Messrs. Beamish and Crawford, the Jennings Brothers, Richard Caulfield, Richard Dowden, James Roche, Dr. Bullen and Abraham Abell. In Queen Street, now Father Mathew Street, off the Mall was one of the more noted classical schools of the century kept by Dr. Porter and Mr. Hamblin.

One of its best-known scholars was Denny Lane who as secretary to the Gas Company lived in the South Mall premises. Gaslight first came to the city streets in 1825 as a result of a contract given by the Wide Street Commissioners to the United General Gas-Lighting Company of London. The original gas-works were sited as they still are today. However, there was growing dissatisfaction at what was considered the exorbitant price charged by the London company and in 1856 the Cork Gas Company was formed under the Joint Stock Companies Act. In the same year it was awarded the contract by the Corporation to supply the city with an alternative gas supply. The Company took a site alongside that of the United General and by June, 1857 its workmen were laying new gas pipes in the South Mall. Foremost in the whole enterprise was the Company's secretary, Denny Lane, whose well-dressed figure became a familiar one on the Mall. Lane had gone to Trinity College after school and then proceeded to the Inner Temple in London, being called to the Bar in 1842. He was an early contributor to the nationalist newspaper, "The Nation," while he was briefly imprisoned following the Young Ireland episode in 1848. His interests in the industrial and cultural advancement of Cork were wide and lifelong, so justifying the tribute paid to him by Richard Caulfield, himself a dedicated antiquary and local historian: "Every line in our annals, every tradition that floated vaguely or clearly in the memories of our people, every relic of our ancient edifaces, every gravestone that bore a record of the men of the past, was of interest to him."

If the South Mall evokes rich recollections of the arts in nineteenth century Cork, its daily routine revolved around the business world of banks, insurance offices, legal chambers, stockbrokers' premises and medical consulting rooms. By 1820 some thirteen of the forty-one physicians in the city were in practice on the Mall; there also in premises now incorporated in the Norwich Union building was the Medical School of Dr. Caesar which had its licentiate recognised by the professional bodies in Dublin, London and Edinburgh. In the same year thirty-four of the seventy-seven solicitors in the city had their offices on the Mall, a circumstance which drew from John Boyle, editor of the "Cork Freeholder" the caustic remark that "they have spread themselves on the South Mall like crocodiles on the banks of the Nile." Throughout the century the Mall saw great public occasions when religious or national leaders were greeted with public processions. On Friday, August 3rd, 1849, it witnessed the passage of the lady who gave her name to a whole era and way of life, Queen Victoria. To boost morale after the depression of the Famine she came to Ireland accompanied by Prince Albert, landing at what was then Cove. On that Friday the royal yacht, "The Fairy," berthed at Lapp's Quay where the Queen was greeted by the dignitaries of the city and county, receiving addresses of welcome from the Church of Ireland Bishop and from Dr. Delany, the Catholic Bishop. A procession of carriages, each drawn by four grey horses, then proceeded through the city via the South Mall, Grand Parade, Washington Street, returning by the Mardyke and Patrick Street.

The "Cork Constitution" described the event: "The cortege wound its way along Lapp's Quay, the South Mall and the Grand Parade. At Lapp's Quay there were several pavilions erected by Mr. Edward Martin, Mr. A. Farmer and others. Outside the Country Club were two balconies erected by Mr. Fletcher which attracted very general attention, being covered with crimson and royal purple cloth, decorated with golden shamrocks, roses and thistles. The galleries and balconies were filled with ladies: The Royal Exchange Insurance Office had a very tasteful gallery erected in front which was occupied by ladies." When the procession turned into what was then Great George's Street, now Washington Street, it was greeted by a large streamer with the words "Cead Mile Failte."

The Grand Parade exemplifies the old and the new quite clearly; its western side follows the line of the ancient medieval city walls while its thoroughfare and eastern side mark the expansion of the modern city centre. It is best admired at night from across the river at Sullivan's Quay, when the river, the lights and the broad sweep of the street create a feeling of spaciousness and grace. Before it was arched over by about 1780 it had on its eastern side a tree-lined walk called the Mall which was reached by Tuckey's Bridge on the site of the present Berwick Fountain. The Mall had some coffee-houses and was a fashionable place for a stroll on Sunday mornings. With the exception of the former Daly's Clubhouse by the waterside and the English Market, to use the former common name, it acquired little architectural distinction. But the Market has entered largely and with a flourish of banter and wit into the lives of generations of Cork housewives. The stallholders were always a racy lot, sharp, shrewd and yet lovable in their enjoyment of their work and their intimate knowledge of minor scandals and coming events. The Grand Parade facade has its own neat dignity, while the Prince's Street frontage has an unexpected charm drawn from a Venetian style in red brick. The interior vaulted roof is very pleasing, while the fountain with its ornate figures is worth admiring as a fine piece of cast-iron. If Napoleon's army marched on its stomach so, too, a city lives on its stomach and over the generations people have sat down at tables in tenements and grand houses to eat what came out of the Market — pigs' feet, pigs' heads, tripe, drisheen, black puddings, herrings, geese, rabbits, turkeys, salt meat and fresh meat, and meat for stewing and meat for boiling, and chickens to make broth for sick children and old people, and skirts and kidneys, and cabbage, potatoes, onions and turnips all fresh in from the market gardens. The Market is governed by Corporation regulations and in 1823 that body was making the following charges on the following delightful range of women: tripe women were to pay one English Shilling per week in season and 6d otherwise; butter women were charged likewise; pudding women paid 1d per day; lemon women the same, so did roasting-pig women. 'Twas hard to make a living!

Near the National Monument with its record in stone of some highlights in national history is a group of late eighteenth century bow-fronted houses, two still clad in the blue slate weathering that was so marked a feature of building between 1750 and 1850. Standing at the end of Old Post Office Lane these houses bring a quaint and endearing variety to the streetscape. But it is worth noting that bow-fronted styles were not universally approved even in their heyday. In its collection of documentary material, entitled "Problems of a Growing City, Belfast," the Public Record Office of Northern Ireland (1973) quotes the following from an act of 1800; "And for the better preventing nuisances, encroachments, and obstructions within said Streets, Lanes and Places be it therefore enacted that no bow-window, or other projection into any of the said streets, shall be built with or added to any house or other building so as to extend beyond the general line of the fronts of the houses in such Streets, or other places in which such bow-windows or other projection is made, except such projections as may be necessary for copings, cornices, faces, door and window dressings." Whether such a municipal regulation ever applied to Cork has not been ascertained but in addition to the examples on the Grand Parade, and those already mentioned on George's Quay, other specimens may be seen in Patrick Street, Camden Quay, the North Mall and Grenville Place. Not the least interesting feature of the western side of the Grand Parade are the remains of the many old lanes which were so much a feature of the ancient city, Old Post Office Lane, Kift's Lane, Tuckey's Lane, Christ Church Lane and Tobin's Lane.

The Augustinian chapel in Brunswick Street was cherished by many generations with its flickering night lights, its tall candles and the odour of sanctity evoked not only by the lingering scent of incense but by the muttered prayers of the poor and the old. Such venerable and ancient ceremonies as High Mass and Solemn Benediction brought spiritual comfort and liturgical pageantry into lives that were often no more than "the short and simple annals of the poor," with long hours of labour, meagre wages and scanty food eaten in the tenements of the Marsh. It always had a numerous retinue of altar boys whose Latin responses were given with a zest and a lilt that almost became a chant. The Latin Mass was not in the language of the people, but the people knew that it was in the universal language of the Church, while their sense of community arose from reading their prayer books or fingering their beads in reverent quietness. However, the matter of attending to one's devotions in Brunswick Street Chapel did have certain hazards, at least for women with shawls. The shawl was commonly said to cover a multitude but all was revealed in a report in the "Cork Constitution" on the 31st of March, 1829, regarding an incident in the Chapel which involved a decent, God-fearing country woman, Mary Callaghan, her married daughter, Mary Fitzgibbon, a certain Joanna Quain who seemed to have had acquisitive tendencies, and Mr. Slattery who kept a Pawn Office. Joanna Quain was brought before the magistrate accused of stealing a blue cloak, the property of Mary Fitzgerald. Mary Callaghan deposed that she came into Cork and went to Brunswick Street Chapel and had the cloak on her which belonged to her married daughter. While reading her prayer book she took off the cloak and put it on the railing near her. In less than four minutes the cloak was taken away and witness saw it afterwards in the Pawn Office of Mr. Slattery. The accused was imprisoned for a fortnight. The moral would seem to be that however desirable it was to be wrapt to the seventh heaven in Brunswick Street it was also advisable to keep one eye on the things of this world. The Augustinians had resumed community life in 1725 in Fishamble Lane, in the Liberty Street area, and in 1780 had leased a site in Brunswick Street where their Chapel was built in 1781. From 1783 to 1787 they had a Boarding Academy with the Capuchin from Blackamoor Lane, Father

O'Leary, as Professor of Rhetoric, and a curriculum which was comprehensive before the concept was invented— Greek, Latin, Spanish, French, Italian, English, History and Geography. This syllabus reflected a city in which, as a Dublin writer of the time remarked, almost every young man had been on the Continent on business.

The Queen's Old Castle stands on the site of one of the two tower-houses which guarded the entrance to the medieval waterway that has become the present Castle Street; the other building stood at the corner of Cornmarket Street. In fact the names of the original structures have been interposed, as the Queen's Castle was the one standing to the north. The building on the site of the present business premises passed to the ownership of the old Roche family and in the seventeenth century the lower part served as the county prison while the upper portion was converted into a courthouse which served the city until the erection of the existing building in Washington Street. In the highly informative book to which reference has already been made, "The Illustrated Guide to the Great Southern and Western Railway," written by Mr. George Measom in 1866, the author states that "of all the monster warehouses in Ireland, always excepting that of Messrs. Pim in Dublin, there are none to be compared with that under notice. Here the most luxurious tastes can be gratified at a very moderate expenditure and all articles of domestic comfort can be had in every variety of form and manufacture. Part of the premises were the old Court House, the present front being the actual front of the old building. The other portions were erected in 1848 by Mr. Fitzgibbon, the father of the present proprietor. There are fifty persons engaged chiefly upon shirt-making. The boot department is on the first floor and employs about fifty hands. The hands employed by the Queen's Old Castle Company number over 200 and the entire premises cover better than one acre and a half of ground." It was while the old courthouse was still on this site that Daniel O'Connell galloped up to it from Derrynane to make his successful defence in the Doneraile conspiracy trial.

In almost every city there is some one street, square, avenue or boulevard that distils the essence of the place and the spirit of the people. It was in the nineteenth century that Patrick Street became the open-air front parlour of the people of Cork; the place to go to see and be seen; the rendezvous for old friends and young lovers; the grand promenade for the fashionable; the place to linger amid the crowds and conviviality of a Saturday afternoon. It witnessed all the vagaries of Victorian fashion, crinolines and bustles and high button boots, and parasols and picture hats, and frock coats, top hats, expansive watch chains and gold-mounted walking sticks. Weaving through the crowds were the messenger boys from the leading stores bringing their cane baskets filled with parcels to the railway stations and the livery yards, while flower sellers and apple women with coloured shawls and starched white aprons added their chorus to the thud of the horses and the rumble of the trams. As the decades advanced, its shops proclaimed the steady advance in the variety and comfort of everyday living which was so marked a feature of the century in all the cities in these islands. The mass production of the Industrial Revolution combined with the speed and the cheapness of railway transport to put into the shops, and so into the homes of the people, more goods, a greater variety of goods and cheaper goods. By 1900 the great mass of the people enjoyed a higher standard of living than perhaps at any other time in history, despite the problems of poverty, bad housing and epidemics which still had to be overcome.

Patrick Street had been created by arching over a channel of water which was still open well after 1750, but because the thrust of commerce was towards the east to take advantage of the deeper stretches of the Lee, it soon supplanted the old South and North Main Streets as the prestige thoroughfare for shops and services. By the end of the century it had acquired such well-known premises as the Victoria Hotel, Newsom's tea merchants dating from 1816, Woodford Bourne's founded in 1824, Guy's the printers and stationers, Grant's the furnishing and fashion shop, the book shops of Massi and Purcell, the latter founded in 1797, Day's the saddlers, Perry's the ironmongers, Murray's the gunsmiths, Egan's the jewellers, founded in 1825, the Central Furniture Warehouse at number 72, owned by Mr. Caffelle who supplied all furnishings and effects for the Opera House. The Munster Arcade, opened in 1866 by Messrs. Robertson, Ledlie and Ferguson who had previously established premises in Waterford and Belfast, was featured in Stratten's Review of 1892 as having departments for "ladies dress goods, bonnets, furs, calicoes, blankets, flannels, Irish linens, napery and sheetings, curtains, carpets, Manchester goods, laces, ribbons, flowers, feathers, fancy drapery, trimmings, underclothing, boots and shoes, woollen goods, Irish tweeds, readymade gents clothing and bespoke tailoring." The establishment employed "upwards of 200 assistants for whose welfare and comfort the proprietors display the utmost solicitude, a fine library of over 1,000 books and billiard and smoking-rooms being provided by the liberality of the firm in order to supply the means of recreation to their numerous employees." Other prominent premises were the London House, Gilbert's the picture saloon, Oakenhead's the seedsmen founded in 1810, Lester's and Blair's the chemists, and Mangan's, clockmakers and jewellers, whose standard clock outside their premises is part of the landscape of the street. Indeed, Mr. James Mangan became something of a public timekeeper in the city; reference to him has already been made in the chapter on the National Exhibition, while his work in installing the four-faced clock in Shandon Steeple ensured a local immortality for his name. The clock in the University tower carried it into the groves of academe. Miss Foley kept a stationery and bookselling shop at No. 101 which, according to Stratten was "visited by all strangers and tourists for those cabinet-sized photos illustrative of several of the most beautiful types of Irish scenery." It is worth noting that in Patrick Street, as in all other areas of the city centre, a great proportion of the business and professional people lived over their premises throughout most of the century; it was only with the coming of the suburban railways and later the trams that the craze for middle class gentility resulted in an exodus to the heights of Montenotte and Sunday's Well and the riverside pleasures of Ballintemple and Blackrock.

The burning of Patrick Street during the Troubles of 1920 destroyed much of the nineteenth century streetscape on the eastern side, but good taste and largeness of vision gave back to the street some splendid new frontages such as those of Egan's, the Munster Arcade and Cash's. One feature of the street today shows a regrettable deterioration in standards of craftsmanship and public ornamentation—the tawdry rash of plastic signs over shop fronts, the symbols of what the poet John Betjeman so aptly called "international nothingness." Nineteenth century Cork, like other Irish cities and country towns, had a rich tradition of woodcarving and handpainted sign lettering which brought a distinctiveness and a grace to shops and public houses. In a pathetic attempt to look as modern as Manhatten much of that tradition has been thoughtlessly cast aside by the battalions of big business. This leads to the situation where, as the Americans put it, having seen one chain store you have seen them all. It is in the lesser, everyday buildings as much as in the great set pieces of public architecture that a city retains for its citizens and their visitors its distinctive character. So far Cork has managed to escape the commercial blight that has ravaged so much of the beauty of Dublin; care must be taken that in Patrick Street good business must not imply a shoddy appearance.

When they came to rebuild St. Patrick's Bridge in 1853 after the previous structure had been demolished by a particularly severe flood there was no question of shoddiness in design or material. With the low curve of its three elliptical arches and the elegance of its colonnaded balustrade, it brings dignity to the principal street of a leading Irish city. The architect was Sir John Benson (1812-1874) who even in his youth in his native Sligo had a natural interest in architecture. He was responsible for the construction of some mills and churches in that county before joining the Board of Works in East Cork as an engineer. During the Famine relief works he directed the building of many new roads, while as engineer to the Cork Harbour Commissioners he was involved in rebuilding the city quays. The chapter on the National Exhibition details his work in designing the massive timber structure that stood behind the present City Hall. Benson was also responsible for what was originally the Athenaeum but which was to win its place in the hearts of the citizens as the old Opera House in Emmet Place, formerly Nelson Place. Yet another of his creations was the delightful Vincentian Church at Sunday's Well, built in the decorated Gothic style, which is seen at its best from the Mardyke as it sits on the hillside like a French chateau. As a twin to Shandon Steeple the tower of St. Mary's Cathedral looms on the northern hills; this, too, is Benson's work, carried out during the episcopacy of Dr. Delany. By an interesting coincidence all of these nine-

teenth century creations can be viewed from their design-
er's best-known work, St. Patrick's Bridge itself.

The offices of the "Cork Examiner" present a neat
piece of classical frontage to the street; behind them in
Faulkner's Lane was the former theatre which first housed
the Classical Casts from which Maclise and Hogan modelled, a subject which is treated more fully in the chapter on
the former artist. The foundation of the "Examiner" newspaper in 1841 by John Francis Maguire was an important
event not only in the dissemination of news but in the
formation of public opinion on the larger issues of Irish
public life. Originally it came out thrice weekly as an evening paper and from the outset it set out to create an
informed opinion that was sensitive to the needs and opportunities of life in Ireland. It adopted a liberal, national
stance not far removed from that of the "Nation," while
the lifelong commitment of Maguire to the promotion of
Irish industry and native talent is strikingly evident in the
editorials of its earlier years. His practical zeal in those
fields, as well as his support for Father Mathew, have
been covered in the chapters on the Industrial Exhibition
and the life of the priest. His name still stands on the plinth
of the Statue; as Mayor and member of Parliament for the
city he brought a full dedication to the many diverse issues
of his times. Directly opposite the newspaper offices the
former Victoria Hotel played host to the citizens and their
guests from the mid 1820s to within a few weeks of the
writing of this chapter. Its first outside visitors came by
Mail coach; then from the 1850s onwards it was a favoured
rendezvous for railway passengers, with its own horse-
drawn omnibus meeting the main trains. When Cobh became a port of call for the great transatlantic liners the
Victoria specialised in an American clientele. As early as
1842 an American in Cork found himself comfortably en-
sconced therein, the Rev. Dr. Pise, and he stated that "I
bent my way to the Victoria Hotel which was recommended
to me by a country parish priest who was on board the
steamer. The system and arrangement of the hotel is more
French than American; you engage a room for one shilling
and sixpence per day and are charged only for the meals
you take in the house." He found much to admire outside:
"Patrick Street which is wide and lined with good-looking
buildings, struck me favourably. The Grand Parade is also

an excellent and pleasant street. The Dyke is beautiful."
But he was not all that impressed with the singing at two
High Masses at St. Augustine's and the South Chapel; at
the former the sermon was preached by a Father Rupel,
at the latter by the Rev. Mr. O'Shea, "both are eloquent
men, the one excels in pathos and the other in ardour and
fancy. The music in both churches was plain and not well
executed. We far surpass the Corkonians in church music."

In the final decades of the century the Victoria was
associated with conventions of the Gaelic Athletic Association and with the man who towered so powerfully over the
Irish political scene, Charles Stewart Parnell. Both as
leader of the Irish Party and as member of Parliament for
the city he would come to Cork by train, alighting at Blackpool. Then a ceremonial procession would form up with
the Chief seated in a horse-drawn landau and accompanied
often by a guard of honour of six hundred horsemen, each
rider carrying a flaming torch. As the procession wound
down Shandon Street and the North Main Street the people
would come out in crowds from the narrow lanes and the
little courtyards to savour the excitement of seeing the
"Uncrowned King of Ireland" go by. Then when Parnell
reached the Victoria Hotel and stood at an open first floor
window, a great sea of faces would look up at him as he
stood there looking so tall, so distinguished, so aloof. And
when he spoke of Home Rule and of the better Ireland it
would bring the vast throng would be silent with expectation and pride. But the wine was to turn sour with the
O'Shea divorce case and the Parnell Split; there followed
that feverish period when Parnell desperately tried to rally
support, making the exhausting train and boat journey
from Brighton to Dublin almost every week. He was to be
seen in the lounge of the Victoria stretched out on two
chairs, his eyes closed with fatigue, his boots drying by
the open fire. So it was that Patrick Street was touched by
the triumph and the tragedy of those tumultuous times.

For over a century Newsom's sold their tea, coffee,
currants and raisins in the nearby premises now occupied
by an international chain store. This old Quaker family
was an integral part of the commercial life of the city, and
when the farmers had brought their pigs and their butter
up to the markets at Shandon it was to Newsom's that
many of their wives came to buy canisters of tea and coffee.

It was at Prince's Street corner that young Daniel Maclise opened his studio in 1825, so beginning a career that was to bring him European recognition as a painter. Also at that corner, in premises now occupied by a large tailoring establishment, was the office for the Bianconi long cars. Passengers assembled there from 1830 onwards at 6.00 a.m. to face the hazards of a journey to Dublin via Kilkenny sitting back-to-back in the open car and all muffled up against wind and rain. A hip-flask of whiskey supplied the only means of internal combustion. Two narrow streets opposite carry their own footnotes to history, French Church Street and Carey's Lane. The former derives its name from the fact that a colony of Protestant Huguenots settled there when forced to flee from France on the Revocation of the Edict of Nantes. They brought to Cork, as to other cities in Ireland and England, their skills as craftsmen and their reputation for hard work. Their church was later used by the Methodist community before the building of the present Wesley Chapel, but the site of the old Huguenot cemetery still exists extending back to Carey's Lane. It must be hoped that the big business appetite for obliteration will spare this quiet patch of the city's heritage.

Before the building and opening of the present gracious church of Ss. Peter and Paul's in 1868, the old Carey's Lane Chapel was hallowed by the prayers and the love of generations of worshippers from the then populous Middle Parish. Until the Catholic Emancipation Act of 1829 both Catholics and Dissenters were not at liberty to build their places of worship on main streets, so the Carey's Lane Chapel was built seemingly in 1786. It was a modest affair, in appearance and fitments, but it became an extremely active centre of community organisation; the Poor School Committee met in its hall and so did the emerging trade unions. The first chapter recalled that a local schoolmaster noted in his diary that he attended a requiem Mass there for Louis XVI of France. In 1848 it acquired as administrator a priest whose past was as dramatic as his future was to be distinguished, Father John Murphy. Born in Shandon Street in 1796, the son of a prosperous merchant and shipowner, young Murphy joined the East India Company as a midshipman. He was back in Cork in 1815 for the consecration of his uncle as Bishop of the diocese, returning soon afterwards to Canada in the service of the Hudson Bay

Fur Trading Company. Back in London at the age of forty-four he decided to study for the priesthood and was ordained in Rome in 1846. From 1847 until his retirement to St. Vincent's, Sunday's Well, in 1877 he spent his days caring for the poor in Carey's Lane and dreaming of building a great new chapel. He was responsible for turning the old Mansion House first into a school taught by the Vincentians, and then into a hospital under the care of the Sisters of Mercy. Soon after his appointment to Carey's Lane Father Murphy commissioned E. W. Pugin of London, a name so prominently associated with the Gothic revival in ecclesiastical and civic architecture in the middle decades of the century, to design the new church; it was almost ten years later that the extra land was finally acquired while the actual building took eight years in the hands of Messrs. Barry McMullen. Lack of money was mainly responsible for the delay and the projected tower and spire were never added. The appeal of the exterior in red sandstone and limestone dressing is matched by the interior embellishments in marble and wood carving; there is black marble from Churchtown near Mallow, red marble from Little Island, green from Galway and white from Sicily. The high altar was designed by Messrs. Ashlin of Dublin and executed by Samuel Daly's of Cook Street, Cork. The richly carved pulpit is of Russian oak, while there is a tradition that in the public houses of the North Main Street men discussed the merits of the carpenters who worked on the ornate confession boxes. The church was opened for public service on the feast of St. Peter and Paul, 1868. In recalling the history of French Church Street and Carey's Lane it is pleasing to pay tribute to Messrs. Arthur Guinness whose premises stands between them; reconstructed in the bow-fronted style of the former premises of Messrs. Oakenhead it adds a note of distinction to Patrick Street and demonstrates that good business and good taste need not be strangers.

Emerging from Ss. Peter and Paul's onto Patrick Street one passes the former premises of Messrs. Guy's on the right hand corner. It is only as this chapter is being written that the dignified shop frontage is being demolished, so taking from the street a landmark that has stood for a century and a half. As printers and bookbinders Guy's were foremost in the commercial life of the second half of the past century; their annual street directories are still of considerable interest to anyone studying the location of business premises or private residences. Previous to its acquisition by Guy's, the shop figured largely in the cultural life of the city as Bolster's Bookshop, selling the novels of Walter Scott, editions of Moore's Melodies and the Dublin and London newspapers. Bolster's Magazine carried the literary effusions of local writers from the 1820s onwards. Though the episode is covered more fully in the chapter on the artist, Daniel Maclise, it is worth recalling that it was in this shop that he had the good fortune to meet Sir Walter Scott on the 9th of August, 1825, when a crowd had assembled to see the great man of letters enter to make some purchases. His Waverley Novels, with their stirring tales of chivalry and romance on the Scottish borders, had made Scott the first mass best-seller in the English language; nowhere was he more avidly read than in Ireland and during his Irish tour of 1825, accompanied by the lady novelist, Maria Edgeworth, and his son-in-law and biographer, J. G. Lockhart, he received a rapturous welcome in Dublin, Killarney and Cork. In the shop the nineteen year old Maclise presented Scott with his pencil sketch of the writer's head and shoulders. Scott's generous approval led Maclise to open the studio already mentioned, while his entry to the Royal Academy at London a year later was the formal beginning of a great career as a painter. This shop, therefore, marks the first meeting of two distinguished personages, the shoe-maker's son of Cork full of youthful promise and the man of letters whose name was a household one across the world. It had been this writer's hope that a plaque might be erected to signify that event but the building has been treated by the bulldozer.

A few steps away the ornate bow-fronted premises of Woodford Bourne's give way to the three-sided Daunt's Square where, according to local lore, the family of the Aikenhead's lived in the shop now occupied by the old-established bakery premises of Messrs. McCarthy; Mary Aikenhead, foundress of the Irish Sisters of Charity, came from this family. Her work is continued by her Sisters at their school near St. Mary's Cathedral, the North Chapel to be more colloquially precise. Yet another religious figure made a fleeting appearance on the Square; when one of the Wesley brothers attempted to preach there he was promptly chased away by a mob organised by a Church of Ireland parson, and escaped with his life only when a Catholic widow allowed him to run into her cabin at the end of the North Main Street. It all had something to do with the church militant, the church suffering and the church triumphant — but which was which? At Castle Street one is back on the site of the old medieval city, but the broad street to the right built over yet another river channel was in the nineteenth century what it still is— part of the folk-culture of Cork. The first thing to do here is to refuse to believe the evidence of one's own eyes; the street sign proclaims that the place is Corn Market Street; no Corkman in his right senses believes this for one moment. It is a fabrication conceived in ignorance and proclaimed with futility! True, there was a corn market built there in 1744 before it was removed to the site of the present City Hall; true, another street sign proclaims that the Coal Quay lies parallel to the nearby riverside. But all of that is a matter of mere logic and tidy sign-posting; the truth is that Corn Market Street was always the Coal Quay and that the Coal Quay was never the Coal Quay — it was the Coal Kay, deriving its pronounciation from standard Elizabethan English usage. What is the Coal Kay? It happens to be an outdoor market but to the citizens it symbolises their city with all the nostalgic warmth of Shandon or the Lee Fields. It means laughter and the assumption of misery, the colourful phrase and the sharp retort, and barefaced robbery and delightful deceit, all spiced with a grand humanity and a local flavour. In its golden age the Coal Kay was filled with women with shawls and if there was poverty there was also gaiety. The reproduced photograph from the Lawrence Collection paints a scene filled with the animation of people and the profusion of bargains. The variety of coloured shawls contrasts with the elegance of two-piece costumes with flowing skirts. Men with black bowler hats lounge in doorways, while the ground is littered with all the paraphernalia of the outdoor market of the 1890s—the wickerwork moses baskets, the brass beds, the vegetables and the crockery.

A short walk down Paul Street leads to one of the most picturesque pieces of streetscape in the city, Emmet Place. Paul Street itself was a fashionable residential quarter at the close of the eighteenth century, having its church of St. Paul's built in 1756 and in 1768 becoming the site of

Tonson's Bank. Directly opposite Ss. Peter and Paul's Church is Browne Street where throughout the nineteenth century, and until two years ago, was situated the mineral water establishment of Messrs. Jennings. The street is now reduced to the wasteland of a car park, but in the 1830s it had a distinguished resident in the house still standing at No. 11, the ebullient Richard Dowden, alderman of the Corporation, Mayor of Cork, wit, scholar, philanthropist, author of a book on botany, treasurer of the Old Presbyterian Church in Prince's Street, devoted friend of Father Mathew and treasurer of the fund to erect the Statue in Patrick Street. He became a partner in the Jennings firm and later went to live at Sunday's Well where he built "Rath Lia" which still stands. When he died at his home on 4th August, 1861, an obituary notice paid tribute to his public career: "In politics, in art, in education, in harmless and innocent amusements, in the promotion of the great cause of temperance, in fact, in all movements which had for their object the elevation of the country, Richard Dowden was sure to be found. Whether as a Poor Law Guardian, a Governor of the Lunatic Asylum, a prominent officer of the Blind Asylum, or in any other activity that called his active benevolence into activity, Richard Dowden was one of the most valuable of our citizens. Cultivated in mind, with refined and scholarly tastes, loving books and pictures, and statues and flowers and plants, and the varied beauty of nature, he was courteous and kindly in his manner to poor as well as rich." He was also the uncle of Professor Edward Dowden, the Shakespearean scholar of Trinity College, Dublin. As well as being a member of the Royal Cork Institution he was particularly devoted to the promotion of the Cork Literary and Scientific Society.

Moving into Emmet Place the pretty facade of the Queen Anne style house catches the attention. In the earlier part of the last century it was the home of Richard Sainthill, numismatist and man of books. He was an early admirer of the talent of Daniel Maclise and it was in the library of this house that the youthful artist was first to acquire that passion for historical reading which was to last a lifetime and to influence the choice of subjects for so many of his paintings. Next door is the establishment begun by Mr. Johnson in 1810 and which continued until the end of the century as a Patent Carriage Works. The chapter entitled

"In and Out of Cork, A Coach and Four," gives interesting eye-witness accounts from the 1860s and 1890s of the varied skills that went into the craftsmanship of making a coach. It details the work of the smiths, the carpenters, the body-builders and the painters who combined to make a coach. In the bedraggled space now standing empty near the quayside there stood the premises of Messrs. Booth and Fox, specialising in the manufacture of quilts and mattres-ses and all the finery of bedroom comforts; as the chapter on the Industrial Exhibition indicates, they imported their furs and feathers from St. Petersburgh in Russia and had a depot in London. It is from the elegant proportions of the School of Art that Emmet Place makes its visual appeal most interestingly. The classical frontage in red brick, dressed with limestone in the window surrounds, creates a delightful cameo of town architecture. The origins of the building belong to the commercial life of eighteenth century Cork and to the river flowing nearby. It was built in 1724 as the Custom House, when the present thorough-fare was the chief dock of the busy little port which was so soon to expand into a European export centre for the butter trade. The tall masts of sailing ships rose up from where cars are now parked, while customs and excise clerks within the building dipped their quill pens in ink-horns and committed to their ledgers all the vital statistics of hogsheads of claret and casks of rum and firkins of butter.

It was precisely because of the very considerable expansion in the shipping trade that the present Custom House came to be built further down river, with Wiliam Hargreaves as the architect. This left the old premises idle but it was to take on a new and most fruitful lease of life in 1832 when the Government handed it over for a nominal rent to the Royal Cork Institution. From being the receipt of customs it then became the home of culture. In a unique way the Institution gathered to itself a remarkable following from across the divisions of creed and politics, generating a lively interest in the new cult of scientific lectures and demonstrations as well as in the broader spheres of litera-ture and art. A full account of this phase in the scientific and artistic life of the city will be found in the chapter devoted to the Institution, while an extended study of the subject is made in an article by this writer in the Journal of the Cork Historical and Archaeological Society, 1976. The School of Art building was the nucleus of the University as it was from it that the Munster Provincial College Committee operated from its foundation in 1838, with the object of persuading the Government to establish a University College in the city. When the College opened its gates in the autumn of 1849 the campaign had succeeded; but even then the President, Sir Robert Kane, requested the scientific apparatus of the Institution for the new seat of learning and, for good measure, the porter at Emmet Place found himself translated in a similar capacity to the Queen's College. Indeed, it was the establishment of the University that was partly responsible for the gradual demise of the Institution throughout the 1850s; the pursuit of natural philosophy passed from the amateurs to the professionals.

But there is one most significant link still connecting 1832 with today, namely the set of Classical Casts which the Institution brought into the building at the date mentioned and which have been used there ever since. The story of the Casts, passing from the Pope to the Prince Regent to Cork, will be found in the chapter on Daniel Maclise. Suffice to recall that their arrival in the city gave rise to something of a local artistic renaissance which produced the distinguished sculptor, John Hogan, and the noted painter just mentioned. The School of Art saw within its portals all of those concerned with the public and cultural life of Cork in the middle decades of the last century, such personalities as James Roche, banker, man of books and something of a cultural impressario, Sir Thomas Deane, the architect of much of the civic embellishment of the expanding city, including the University building, the businessmen who patronised the arts such as the brewers, Mr. Beamish and Mr. Crawford, Denny Lane, patriot, poet and promoter of industrial expansion, James and Geoge Pain, rivals to the Deane family as architects, whose works include Blackrock Castle, the County Club and the Capuchin Church, the painter George Brennan who was closely associated with it when it became the School of Design in 1850. As a meeting place for committees and specialised groups it continues that valuable service down to the present day. Yet despite its long tradition the citizens are not generally aware not only of the elegance of the interior but of the rich treasury of painting and sculpture that awaits them in the Gallery. It was due to the munificence of a member of the brewing family of Crawfords that the harmonious extension to the earlier building was added in 1884. The work was executed by Samuel Hill, building contractor, whose firm was responsible for a wide range of building in the city and county until well into the present century. The donor was William Horatio Crawford who played an active part in public life as a member of the Corporation and Chairman of the Harbour Board. He devoted much of his great wealth to the cultural and architectural embellishment of the city, contributing to the erection of the spires of St. Finbarre's Cathedral and to the cost of the splendid carvings of its West Front. He took a special interest in the promotion of science and art, being largely responsible for the Observatory at the University and for the laying out of the surrounding grounds in harmony with the dignity of the collegiate buildings. He defrayed the entire expense of £20,000 to build the School of Art extension, donating some of his own pictures to the Picture Gallery and purchasing some of Hogan's plaster casts for the Sculpture Gallery. It is fitting that Hogan's fine sculpture of William Crawford, father of the gentleman now being discussed, is now to be admired in the School of Art. William was the co-founder of the noted brewing establishment in 1792 and was distinguished as a man of great compassion for the poor as well as having an active concern for the cultural life of the city. William Horatio Crawford never married; his first love was his valuable collection of books. Aged seventy-six he was found dead by his servants one morning in 1888 sitting in his favourite chair at his home at Lakelands, Blackrock, with a book on his lap. It was a tragedy for the city that his rare collection of books was disposed of by public auction. His memory is honoured by the official title of the institution, the Crawford Municipal School of Art. A third generation of the family, in the person of Sharman Crawford who died in 1943, was to continue the patronage of art and science. His name is remembered in the Sharman Crawford Technical Institute for which he donated the site.

For many generations the elegant little square between the river and Patrick Street was known and loved as the site of the old Opera House. Here the citizens spent nights of gladness enchanted by the magic of the theatre. The fare was rich and varied, Victorian melodrama, Italian grand opera, the productions of touring companies from Dublin and London, the offerings of local talent. They sang and clapped and cried, enlivened by that most stirring musical sound, the vibrant playing of a theatre orchestra. The Opera House was a place for all seasons, it captured the interest of all classes, it brought the universal emotions of drama, the power of words, the beauty of the human voice, the contrived artifice of comedy, the elegance of costume and scenery, to gentle and simple alike. Messenger boys whistled snatches of arias as they made their deliveries on their bicycles, while in the public houses of Shandon Street and North Main Street voices thick with stout gave their rendering of Italian masterpieces. No apples tasted sweeter than those bought from women with white aprons and munched in the "gods" of the Opera House. When the venerable old pile was burned down in December, 1955, many in the hushed crowd of onlookers wept openly. It was a night when nostalgia was the deepest truth. A candle of memories was forever quenched.

The old building was originally erected as the Athenaeum following the first National Exhibition in Cork in 1852. Designed by Sir John Benson, it was intended as a hall for exhibitions of art and as a display centre for industrial and agricultural products. Apparently this line of development did not work out too well, so in 1886 the building began its life as a theatre, possibly helped by the fact that the old Theatre Royal on the site of the present General Post Office had closed down. Emmet Place meets the river at an interesting vantage point; across to the right is the elegant row of redbrick Georgian houses on Camden Quay, to the left is the dignity of the classical portico of the Dominican Church, while rising over the roof tops is Shandon Steeple sending out its peal of bells that "sound so grand on the pleasant waters of the river Lee."

Chapter XIII

OUT AND ABOUT IN OLD CORK

This final chapter is meant as a guide for a walking tour of the old city, starting at Gillabbey Rock where the original monastic site was to be found, and ending at Shandon which has come to symbolise the spirit of the city. The greater proportion of the chapter was serialised in the "Cork Examiner" in March, 1976, but the material on the Shandon area has been newly added.

If Cork is big enough to be a city it is yet small enough to be easily manageable as regards seeing it, and anybody reasonably sound in wind and limb should be able to follow this trail which sets out to retrace the history of the old city along the footsteps of time. The obvious starting point is Gillabbey Rock, not only because it affords a panoramic view of the city of today but because it was to this spot that the founder of Cork, St. Finbarr, came some time between the years 600 and 620. He had left the austere splendour of his lakeside retreat at Gougane Barra and had followed the course of the Lee until he came to this rocky eminence looking out over the marsh below, Corcach Mor na Mumhan, the Great Marsh of Munster. Interesting to recall that after all the centuries part of the area in the foreground is still locally called the Marsh.

A few hundred yards eastwards the Gothic pile of St. Finbarr's Cathedral rises into view, resplendent in local white limestone and with its triple spires reaching to the sky. Designed by William Burges of London, it was opened in 1870 and is a notable celebration of faith and craftsmanship. Of particular interest are the scriptural carvings in the recessed West door and the use of Irish marbles inside. It was here that Finbarr established his monastic settlement, with its rude church, its huts and its farm and the young men who came from many parts of Ireland, Britain and Europe to pray and to study. So this spot took its place in that flowering of Christian scholarship which in the eight and ninth centuries won for Ireland the title of "Island of Saints and Scholars," Insula Sanctorum et Doctorum. Three languages were in use, the native Irish of Finbarr and his succesors and the Latin and Greek of the Church. It was from here that St. Colman left to found his school at Cloyne, a neglected little town which would well repay a visit with its medieval cathedral, very fine Round Tower and its associations with the distinguished eighteenth century bishop and philosopher, Dr. George Berkeley. The Vikings came to plunder the Cork foundation and the Normans came to hear Mass, while Gaelic and Anglo-Irish chiefs requested the honour to be buried here. The Reformation brought the new Divine Service and Bishop Lyons appointed by Queen Elizabeth. Curiously enough none of the previous churches on this site had any architectural pretensions; there was nothing of the style of St. Patrick's, Dublin, or of St. Canice's, Kilkenny, or of the medieval splendour of Bath, York or Florence. Perhaps the most noteworthy feature of this whole spot is the sense of place; for over twelve centuries the people of Cork have come here, natives and planters, Catholics and Protestants, to say their prayers and to bury their dead. The varied strands of history are here gathered together.

Moving out of the main gate and turning left, and left again, there is Dean Street, which contains some interesting examples of late eighteenth century town houses. This street was once a fashionable one, while Vicar Street, off right, has a quaint row of tiny cottages with roofs at eye level—a not inconsiderable advantage on the morning after a night of the Big Wind. This juxtaposition of houses catering for people at opposite ends of the social scale was characteristic of cities generally until the middle of the last century when the railways led to the growth of middle class suburbs— a process accelerated by the coming of the trams in later decades and by the motor car in this century. As Dean Street joins Barrack Street there rises up the fortification of Elizabeth Fort, built at the close of Elizabeth's reign to secure the city amid the alarm of Hugh O'Neill's rebellion and the prospect of Spanish landings in the Cork region. It was from here that a young officer set off for the Peninsular War in 1807, to find a place in history as the Duke of Wellington.

A short walk westwards from Dean Street is rewarded by a view of the original University buildings, designed by the local architect, Sir Thomas Deane, and acknowledged as one of the most charming public buildings in Ireland. Its opening ceremonial in the Aula Maxima on Wednesday, November 7th., 1849, was an affair of pomp and circumstance, with the collegiate buildings in the style of domestic Gothic capturing the admiration of all who saw them. The tribute of Macaulay, the noted historian and writer, can still be sustained regarding what stands on the Quad., despite mixed opinions on what has since appeared in the environs thereof: "a Gothic college worthy to take its place in the High Street of Oxford." Deane had been responsible for much of the upsurge of civic architecture in the city in the first half of the nineteenth century; with his son and their gifted partner, Woodward, he was later responsible for the Engineering School at Trinity College, Dublin, the beauty of which made Ruskin weep. The trio were also the architects for the University Museum at Oxford. If the College was fortunate in an architect who had the wit to combine utility with elegance, it was equally fortunate in its first President, Sir Robert Kane. Educated by the Jesuits at Stonyhurst and later at Trinity College, he became one of the most distinguished Irish scientists of his century, with a European reputation as a chemist. His greatest work was the "Industrial Resources of Ireland," published in 1843, and still a standard work of reference. It was an extensive one-man survey of the soil, minerals and waters of Ireland with a view to exploiting their potential to give employment to the great mass of the poor. It foreshadowed such later significant developments as the use of water-power by the Electricity Supply Board and the work of Bord na Mona. The first professor of Mathematics was George Boole, presently attracting international interest for his pioneer work in mathematical thought. His grave may be seen at St. Michael's Church of Ireland, Blackrock. The College owed its foundation to the exertions of the Munster Provincial College Committee established in Cork in 1838; responding to this pressure, as well as hoping to wean middle class Catholics from supporting O'Connell, in 1845 the Tory Prime Minister, Sir Robert Peel, piloted the Queen's College Bill through parliament. Three Colleges under the original title were founded—one here in Cork, the others at Galway and Belfast. Because they were unde-nominational, they incurred the official disapproval of the Catholic Church, but with their incorporation into the National University of Ireland in 1908 the Colleges at Cork and Galway resolved that issue. By a happy coincidence the scholars of Munster now come to learn at the very spot where Finbarr taught so many centuries ago.

Leaving the saints and scholars to their devices, attention must now turn to the little medieval city which grew up in the valley below, bringing the influence of Norse and Norman settlers to that of the Irish monastery. Directly below the Cathedral is the convent of St. Marie's of the Isle, built for the Sisters of Mercy in 1848. This stands on the site of the old medieval foundation of the Dominicans who came here in 1229 and whose convent bore the same name as that used today. One of the consequences of the coming of the Normans to Ireland from 1169 onwards was that they introduced the new town-based religious orders such as the Dominicans and Franciscans; these orders followed their vocation among the people of the growing cities rather than out in the wilderness of the countryside, and they earned their living not by farming but by the alms of the faithful, hence they were known as mendicant or begging friars. The present building beautifully illustrates the quality of the local red sandstone and is best seen in its vivid colour from the back garden behind Heaslip's Mill; the old wall still standing there is reputed to date from the original foundation. Sharman Crawford Street recalls the name of one of the brewing family whose members contributed so munificently to the cultural life of the nineteenth century city, being associated with building the Cathedral, the Crawford School of Art in Emmet Place, the Observatory at the University and the Technical Institute in this street, a building with pleasing proportions in red brick and limestone surrounds. Walking to the riverside is rewarded by the charm of old stone and the flowing Lee. Here is one of those quiet spots which recall the atmosphere of other days, at once mellow and beautiful. For over two and a half centuries Clarke's Bridge has witnessed the passage of the citizens on foot, in carts, in stage coaches and today in their horseless carriages. From the eighteenth century until the opening of the Western Road early in the last century, this bridge was a busy main entrance to the city from the southwest countryside. Directly over the bridge Hanover Street runs left and right; in the closing decades of the eighteenth century and for the first half of the last century this little street witnessed something of a minor industrial revolution. The Hive Iron Works on the western end, owned by Messrs. Perrott, had its foundry, forge and millwright shops by the water's edge and manufactured waterwheels, turbines, machinery for mills, factories and breweries as well as a wide range of agricultural machinery, some of it for export to Australia. The remains of the warehouse can still be seen in Washington Street where the products of the foundry were for sale — kitchen stoves and ranges, gates, iron bedsteads, safes, chimney pieces, garden seats. The eastern portion of Hanover Street was the centre of the Cork Glass industry, with the foundation there in 1784 of the Cork Glass House Company by Messrs. Hayes, Burnett and Rowe. In due course their warehouse was selling a wide range of fine pieces of claret, wine and whiskey glasses, decanters, salad bowls, goblets, scent bottles and lustre lamps. The conical smokeshaft of the old glasshouse firehouse stood across the river until its demolition in 1915. Still on Wandesford Quay is the site of the second glasshouse in the area, the Waterloo Glass House Company established in 1816 by Mr. Daniel Foley. Messrs. Harte's timber-yards stand where one hundred workmen pursued their skills. A fuller account of this industry can be found in the chapter, "The Commerce of Cork."

Following the bend of the river the older portions of Beamish and Crawford's brewery, founded in 1792, retain something of the outlines of an older industrial archaeology. Dominating the forward skyline is the mass of the early seventeenth century Elizabeth Fort built to overawe the citizens should they feel tempted to flirt with the Spanish enemy who had come too close for comfort at Kinsale in 1601. Crossing over the tiny Proby's Bridge leads to Frenche's Quay. Directly opposite the bridge is Kayser's Lane, possibly the oldest named street surviving in Cork, a consideration largely overlooked in previous writings on local history. This little passageway that climbs up the hillside, with its steps and its small houses, recalls the second strand that went into the making of Cork eleven centuries ago. Some time between 820 and 860 the Norse pirates sailed their longboats up the Lee to plunder the monastery on the hill; they were the best seamen in the Europe of their day, capable of building boats that took them on raids along the coasts of France, Britain and Ireland. They came in search of silver and slaves, spurred on by a love of adventure and the lack of livelihood among the fjords of Norway. Some settled down as traders, with Dublin, Waterford, Limerick and Wexford having their origins as Norse settlements. The pattern was repeated in Cork where they are reputed to have settled at the foot of the present Shandon Street. Interestingly, in many of their settlements there is a Kayser's Lane, as in Wexford, meaning the passage leading to the waterway. This one here beneath the original monastic foundation would indicate that the Norse had become traders and craftsmen side by side with the native Irish, just as in time they were to become Christians. This passageway bearing this name most probably dates from the early tenth century. It signposts the gradual emergence of Cork as a small trading settlement in addition to being a monastic site. A few paces from the lane the limestone arches of the South Gate Bridge bring to mind the third strand in the patchwork of early Cork.

It was the coming of the Normans from 1169 onwards that finally led to the making of Cork into a city and the development of a European lifestyle. The first chapter discusses that matter more fully. The Normans came as knights in armour, as international warriors seeking advenure and conquest. Having captured England so dramatically at the Battle of Hastings it was only a matter of time before they would turn to Ireland, even without the invitation of the maligned Diarmuid McMurrough. They are still in the city, the Fitzgeralds, the Roches, the Barrys, the Burkes, the Cogans, having become "more Irish than the Irish themselves." They made medieval Cork; they procured Charters from the Anglo-Norman Kings of England giving the city legal status; they established municipal government and courts of justice; loyal to the Pope they introduced the new town-based religious orders of friars, the Franciscans, Dominicans and Augustinians; they laid out the South and North Main Streets and the profusion of narrow lanes where merchants and craftsmen lived and laboured; they established guilds to regulate hours and prices for work; they regulated markets; they built parish churches. They gave Cork the lifestyle of a European city such as was to be found in Italy or Germany or Holland, or London or Bristol or York. Above all they gave it the most important visual sign of any such city, namely its fortified walls complete with guard turrets and gates, Nothing mattered more to the citizens than the walls and the gates; they gave protection from the enemy in time of war, while in peace they secured the merchants from competition from travelling hawkers;

they symbolised the common identity of the citizens and their demarcation from the rustic life of the peasants and warriors without the walls. The South Gate Bridge is a reminder of Norman Cork, of the emergence of the city in a sense that all succeeding centuries down to the present were to think of it. It was from here northwards to the North Gate Bridge, with the western walls stretching from Hanover Street to the northern branch of the Lee and the eastern walls stretching thither from the Grand Parade, that the little medieval city grew and prospered, secure by day and night within its walls and gates, with priest and friar and magistrate, with merchant and craftsman and citizen following their alloted pattern of life and labour. And the little ships from Bristol and Brittany came up the river with their caskets of wine and sailed on the tide with cargoes of skin and cloth.

Before leaving the South Gate Bridge walk along Sullivan's Quay on which is situated one of the best-known city schools, dated 1828, where generations of boys have done their sums and learned their letters and memorised their catechism. In the first little street on the right there stood Hennessy's forge where the blacksmith would draw an excited audience of schoolboys to sniff the incense of brown smoke that rose up when hot shoe met horse hoof. The lane off left, Blackamoor Lane, is quite historic. The building on the right contained the schoolroom of the then Cupuchin Chapel and it was there that one of Cork's most beloved citizens, Father Mathew, set his hand to found the Temperance Movement on the 10th of April, 1838. Behind in Cove Street his house stood until demolished a few years ago by the Corporation. At No. 11 in this same street there lived the distinguished nineteenth century sculptor, John Hogan. He was to take over Canova's studio in Rome and his fine statues of Daniel O'Connell and Thomas Davis grace the entrance to the City Hall, Dublin. Two streets from here, in St. Finbarr's South Chapel, his sensitive Dead Christ may be seen beneath the high altar. Having made this detour it is as well to make a feast of it and see the Red Abbey and the South Presentation Convent. The square tower of the Red Abbey is the finest if not the only piece of late medieval architecture in the city. It marks the site of the Augustinian foundation which, in the fifteenth century, was in fields and marshland outside the eastern city walls.

Nearby is the South Presentation Convent which is this year celebrating the bicentenary of its foundation by Nano Nagle, whose grave may be visited in the grounds. She devoted her life and fortune to teaching, feeding and clothing the throngs of poor girls who came from the hovels around to her school in Cove Lane, now Douglas Street. Her Presentation Sisters have since brought her spirit to many parts of the world. Nano Nagle came from comfortable farming stock at Ballygriffin, outside Mallow, and was related by family marriage to Edmund Burke, statesman, orator and writer, best known as author of "Reflections on the French Revolution."

After this diversion, with notice taken of St. Nicholas Church of Ireland rising unexpectedly between the convent and Cove Street, return to the South Gate Bridge. The old city stretching down northwards was small, as were all cities for many centuries later; Elizabethan London was scarcely the size of the Cork of today. It was easy to walk the length and breadth of it as it extended to the North Gate Bridge lengthwise, while it was no wider than Christ Church lane eastwards and Hanover Street westwards. The west wall continued past where the fine classical portico of the Courthouse now stands, down Grattan Street, which was an open channel as late as the eighteenth century, and on to the north arm of the river. The east wall continued from Dun Mhuire on the Grand Parade, along Cornmarket Street, also once an open channel, until it met the river. Everywhere outside this egg-shaped piece of civilised living was water, marsh and sandbank, the whole modern city from the Grand Parade to the City Hall in the east, and from Liberty Street to the Mardyke in the west. Inside there was the multifarious life of goldsmiths, silversmiths, tinsmiths, blacksmiths, farriers, saddlers, pewterers, glovers, glaziers, paper-stainers, coopers, carpenters, wheelwrights, butchers, bakers, chandlers, button-makers, sail-makers, shoemakers, hide merchants and wine merchants and barber-surgeons— all with regulated hours of trading, fixed prices and approved standards of workmanship supervised by the guilds. Houses were mostly of timber, sanitation was primitive, disease hovered closely and average life expectation was well below fifty years. These crafts, these conditions and this size continued substantially unaltered until the beginning of the last century. Socially, the Middle Ages ended only yesterday.

Moving down South Main Street the narrow Old Post Office Lane is on the right. Tradition has it that it was from a breach in the walls where this lane abuts onto the Grand Parade that a blasksmith fired the musket-ball that mortally wounded the Duke of Grafton in the Siege of Cork in 1690. Grafton alley or street off the South Mall recalls the connection. The city was caught up in the Irish/English/French entanglements of the wars of William of Orange and King James II. Seeking support from the Catholic Irish, James had landed in Kinsale in 1688 and was escorted down the South Main Street and over to the Franciscan Abbey on the North Mall where he heard Mass before setting off to fight and lose the Battle of the Boyne. Among those bowing to the haughty Stuart was the Mayor of Cork, Dominick Sarsfield, and his dashing young nephew, Patrick. Hot on the heels of royalty on the South Main Street came the formidable Duke of Marlborough to the Red Abbey to besiege and take Cork for William II. It is asserted that the victims of this bloody interlude were buried in a mass grave on the site in Christ Church lane now being excavated by the Archaeology Department of the University. Whatever the politics, the Siege of 1690 was to have a topographical sequel, for the eastern wall was so badly battered that in the first half of the next century the enterprising citizens began to take their city out into the areas now forming the Grand Parade, the South Mall and Patrick Street. The draining and arching was a remarkable piece of civil engineering.

Back on the South Main Street the Tudor-style facade of Messrs. Beamish and Crawford adds a note of distinction; they have been making stout there for almost two centuries. Along on the right is the architecturally plain Christ Church, one of the most historic spots in the old city. There has been a church on this site since about 1050, and during the middle ages it was one of the two parish churches within the walls. Here the Mayor and magistrates attended Mass at the Assizes and other solemn occasions. It is believed that the poet Edmund Spenser married his Irish bride here as he worked on the "Fairie Queene" out at Kilcolman Castle. That foremost of republicans, Oliver Cromwell, was here having beheaded King Charles and put the key of Parliament in his pocket. He spent the Christmas of 1649 in Cork and he stalked into Christ Church proscribing alike Catholic Irish and Anglican English. The cemetery behind has Irish, Norman, Elizabethan, Catholic and Protestant all one in their common resting-place. Christ Church lane is one of the most ancient passage ways in the city; it looks especially evocative at night when dim lights create their mystery. Noteworthy are the excavations of the Archaeology Department of University College, including the site of the fifteenth century College of the Holy Trinity. On South Main Street and passing the early nineteenth century intersection of Washington Street, there is what was once Brunswick Street on the right. It was here that the Augustinian community resumed life with a small chapel and a classical school in 1784. One of the most important streets of old Cork is just a few steps away, Castle Street. Today it is often choked with frustrated motorists; for many centuries as a waterway it saw the masts of little ships from Bristol, Bordeaux and Oporto, bringing in wine and sailing away with hides. This channel into the heart of the old city was guarded by two stone turrets, the King's and Queen's castles. The latter was to evolve into the courthouse before the erection of the present building, and the old name survives in a business concern which proclaimed itself as the first "monster warehouse" in Ireland away back in the 1840s. It is accepted that the channel of Castle Street guarded by its turrets, gave rise to the arms of Cork. Where the Catholic Young Men's Hall now stands was the site of the medieval castle of the Roche family, and when the street was arched over by the eighteenth century this same site housed the prestigious Exchange, a handsome civic centre with an arcade at street level and a copper cupola overhead. Merchants transacted their business here ; at night there were soirees and grand balls where high society with powdered wigs danced the gavot and the minuet. All of this called for maintenance and the Corporation Minutes of 12th July, 1758, read as follows: "The Exchange to be new painted and whitewashed; the lead over the Council Chamber to be soldered, the leaks stopped and the cupola to be new painted." In the second half of the eighteenth century Castle Street became a busy shopping centre; the Exchange had shops in its arcade, and in particular the street had a number of printers and bookbinders. By 1800 elegant ladies with fans stepped out of sedan chairs to shop there by day, while these same sedan chairs were most serviceable for carrying home inebriated gentlemen at night.

A few yards down on the right is Portney's Lane, old and historic. In 1601 it figured in the Irish/English/Spanish entanglement when Don Juan del Aquilla, leader of the ill-fated Spanish expedition sent by Philip II of Spain to help Hugh O'Neill, shrewdly surrendered his sword to the English commander, Lord Mountjoy, at Kinsale. The Spanish grandee was brought to stay at a merchant's house in this lane to be wined and dined and danced. Returning to Spain he was promptly imprisoned for his treachery. As he languished behind bars did he wistfully recall those nights of gladness in Portney's lane? Directly opposite is where the old Franciscan Chapel stood in Broad lane. Cherished by many generations it was full of atmosphere and of little nooks dimly lit by flickering nightlights, where women in shawls muttered their prayers in decent seclusion and old men sat at ease betwixt heaven and earth. All of these humble haunts have been swept away, to be replaced by Byzantine splendour and glittering mosaics. Old maps of the city show the profusion of lanes in this area; some remain such as Picadilly lane, St. Peter's lane and Cockpit lane, the name explaining its origin; others have somehow been appropriated as private hallways or entrances to business premises. They all deserve to be conserved and put to use in a city which has allowed so much of its past to be foolishly destroyed.

The shell of the old St. Peter's Church of Ireland marks the site of the second medieval parish church within the walls. It is, therefore, of considerable historic interest as it entered intimately into the religious and social life of the city for over six centuries. It can only be deplored that it is now relegated to the lowly status of a storehouse. The lane adjoining was until early in the last century a place where merchants and bankers lived before the craze for suburban respectability got under way. This lane leads to Grattan Street through which the medieval wall ran as it stretched down to the river. This street was an open channel until the eighteenth century with a wooden bridge where the old Quaker building now stands. Contemporary accounts make many references to drunks falling off the rickety structure. The Quaker building, with its classical frontage, is of interest. It was here that William Penn saw the Light and went off to carry it to Pennsylvania. From here, too, was organised much of the enormous charitable work of the

Quakers when the dark shadow of the Famine fell over the city in 1846 and 1847. Grattan street was a fashionable residential area around 1800, later in the century it specialised in cabinet-makers. Off westwards is Henry Street, giving a picturesque view of the river, the swans, the old Maltings, now finely conserved by University College, and Wise's elegant Distillery House. This whole area is full of old stone and rich memories. Henry Street still has one of the first pieces of civic architecture of modern Cork, the main building of the Mercy Hospital with its classical frontage and portico and its Italianate windows. It was built by the Corporation in 1767 as the Mansion or Mayoralty House and witnessed much pomp and circumstance in its heyday. The architect was a Sicilian, Davis Ducart, who also designed Lota at Glanmire. The splendid ceiling plasterwork was executed by the Waterford stuccadore, William Osborne, whose work may also be seen in the Waterford Chamber of Commerce. John Wesley preached in the open air in this street, and the Methodist community in Cork originated in a chapel opposite the Mercy Hospital. A strong plea must be made, indeed, must be shouted to beseech the Corporation to breathe new life into this historic old part of Cork. It could be a pleasant and convenient residential area once again, offering a fulness of life denied to the concrete wastelands where so many of its former citizens now find themselves.

Returning via Adelaide Street attention should be paid to the excavations being carried out by the Archaeology Department of the University. Pieces of pottery found there bear evidence to the medieval and later trade with Bristol and Cornwall. Approaching the North Gate Bridge on the left is the site of Skiddy's Castle, built in 1445, recalling one of the powerful old families of the city. Their name is preserved by Skiddy's Almshouse up at Shandon, presently being refurbished by the Cork Preservation Society. All that was said of the South Gate Bridge is equally true of this second main entrance to the old city; a wooden bridge, a stone bridge, a gate-house, a prison—it has been all of these. It was especially busy in the last century as it led to Mallow lane, now Shandon Street, and to the Butter Exchange where business was such that it remained open twenty-four hours a day, seven days a week. The country people crowded in here from counties Cork, Kerry and Waterford, with their firkins of butter on their ass and cart. And they spent their money at the stalls and shops of Shandon Street and the North Main Street, often complaining of being fleeced as they bought boots, bonnets, flour, tea, sugar and a length of cloth to make a suit. Often the ass was left to find its own way home as its master slept on Cork porter! Across the bridge on the left is the North Mall, whose elegant town houses were sought after by the gentry in the late eighteenth century; it was then a fashionable place for a promenade on a Sunday morning, with dandies and their dames on display. More significantly it was here that the Franciscan Abbey was founded early in the thirteenth century, and this was still in being when James II heard Mass here on his visit already described.

Crossing the North Gate Bridge and moving up Shandon Street leads to a part of old Cork which retained its distinctive way of life and manner of speech longer than any other part of the city. In this respect it had an exuberant flavour and colourfulness of street life that link it to the Coombe in Dublin and the Cockney world of London. Part of the price of modern standardisation of speech and education and of the respectability of the affluent society is the disappearance of such pockets of local variety. No one will lament the demolition of the slums and the passing of poverty and the eradication of fever; but the break-up of a strong community life must cause misgivings, as must its transfer to vast concrete wastelands where an abundance of fresh air and running water cannot create the old neighbourliness and the sense of place. The old atmosphere of Shandon Street, Church Street, Dominick Street, Blarney Street and the multitudes of lanes and alleys that led off them was well painted by the best-known nineteenth century writer on Cork, John Windele, who was born in the city in 1801 and died at his home on Blair's Hill in August, 1865, being buried at Father Mathew's Cemetery. His life was given to books and to antiquarian pursuits, he walked the countryside reverently unearthing and recording the remains of historic forts, abbeys, wells and crosses; in this labour of love he was joined by two other antiquaries, Father Horgan, parish priest of Waterloo, and the Quaker, Abraham Abell. Windele encourged Irish language scholars while himself asembling well over one hundred and fifty volumes of manuscripts, now preserved at the Royal Irish Academy.

In 1839 he published his history of Cork, "Historical and Descriptive Notes of the City of Cork and its Vicinity," and his distillation of the spirit of the north side is worth quoting: "As to population they are a hardy, hardworking, improvident and vivacious race; attached to old usages and habits of thinking and acting. Here have ever been found the readiest and gayest actors in the mummeries of the 'May-day mummers.' None ever equalled them in the hearty ceremony of whipping out the Herring on Easter Saturday, or throwing Bran on the new Mayor. What other part of the city has ever furnished so jolly or so uproarious a train of males or females to sustain the humours of the Irish Carnival, the 'going to Skellig'? The groups of 'Wren Boys' here muster strongest on St. Stephen's morning; and the mimic warfare of a 'batter' between the clans of rival streets is nowhere else waged with more spirit or earnestness. But the march of intellect is even here visible; the mummeries and battering and bran throwing are of recent years becoming more infrequent, and the day may not be far distant when the very memory of these things shall pass away." That day has, indeed, come and the racy life of the streets has given way to a television culture where people know more about the Bronx than about the people and places from which their community was moulded. It is good to extend horizons but it is not wise to be a stranger in one's own place.

From 1750 onwards Cork was rather dramatically winning a place in the economy of Ireland and of Europe as a major centre of the butter trade; farmers were bringing in their butter from the rich pasture lands of south Munster, while down at the quays ships were being loaded with firkins to be exported to Liverpool, Hamburg, Rotterdam and to Jamaica, Barbadoes, Carolina and Georgia. Under its old name, Mallow Lane, Shandon Street would be crowded with farmers and their carts on their way to journey's end at the Butter Market after three or four days on the road. Leading in to Mallow Lane was Blarney Lane, now Blarney Street, the great "butter trail" in from the west. A few paces to the right beyond that intersection is Dominick Street, the cradle of the commerce and prosperity on which the modern city was built. With the Butter Market open twenty-four hours a day, seven days a week at the height of the season, this narrow street would present an animated scene with farmers, brokers, merchants and clerks attending to the business of butter and hides and offal. The street was full of stores and lodging houses and taverns, and in between the horses and the carts there weaved the hardy, barefooted urchins eager to make a penny holding a nag's head while the farmer was busy at the Market, or buying brogues at the stalls in Mallow Lane, or drinking strong black porter in a nearby tavern. Even at the turn of this century the place was full of apple-women, such as the well-known "Apple Annie," and full of women who took in lodgers and made hearty breakfasts for hungry countrymen at three o'clock in the morning. A walk down Dominick Street, so called because the Dominicans resumed community life there in the eighteenth century, leads to the centre of all that bustle and butter, the Butter Market which was so meticulously directed by the pioneers of commercial Cork, the Committee of Merchants. Here the salted butter was graded, weighed, packed into the oak firkins made by the coopers, the kings of the craftsmen, and branded with the mark "Cork C. M.," a mark which carried a unique prestige in Europe and the West Indies. The chapter on the "Commerce of Cork" gives a more extended picture of this whole enterprise. But if the old Market belongs to the commerce of Cork there is something here, also, that belongs to its heart and to its imagination. For Shandon Steeple with its bells and its clocks has endeared itself to the citizens for over two centuries, evoking an affectionate smile from people going about their business in the city beneath and something of a nostalgic tear in the eyes of Cork people abroad. Architecturally it is more of a curiosity than a masterpiece, with its pepper-pot top, its four great clocks and its intriguing mixture of the two natural local stones, white limestone on its west and south faces and red sandstone north and east. It is a reflection of the everyday neighbourliness that exists among the religious denominations that a predominantly Catholic city should have taken the steeple of the Church of Ireland, St. Anne's as the popular symbol of the community.

In this respect it is pleasant to recall that the mystique of Shandon was memorably put into words by a Catholic priest, Father Francis Sylvester Mahony, whose "Bells of Shandon" is the anthem of Cork. He was born in Blackpool in a house where the rebel, Lord Edward Fitzgerald, had found refuge in 1804 and into a family that was to become prominent in the wool industry at Blarney. As was often the case he was sent abroad as a lad to be educated, going to the Jesuit school at Amiens in France. Deciding to enter the Society of Jesus he studied at Paris and Rome, where he was ordained deacon. Indifferent health led to his return to the Jesuit College at Clongowes Wood, County Kildare, in 1830, where he served as prefect of studies. On his return to Rome the Jesuits did not accept him for ordination as a priest, so on the direction of the Bishop of Cork, Dr. Murphy, he was ordained in Lucca in Italy. As a curate in what is now St. Patrick's parish in Cork he gave devoted service among the poor during the severe cholera epidemic in 1832. Shortly afterwards he settled in London where he led a somewhat bohemian life centred around a brilliant literary set most of whom wrote for Fraser's Magazine, the forerunner of "Punch." Wit and wine, social and literary comment added spice to a boisterous lifestyle. Mahony was to find many of his fellow-Corkmen in the set, Dr. William Maginn, Thomas Crofton Croker and Daniel Maclise, while other luminaries included the young Charles Dickens, Tom Moore, Thomas Carlyle and William Makepeace Thackeray. Occasional additions to the set were the Cork playwright, Sheridan Knowles and the writer, William Hazlitt. Though Mahony occasionally said Mass and preached at the church of the Spanish Embassy, and said his Office throughout his life, he seems not to have engaged in any regular priestly functions. In 1834 he began contributing to Fraser's Magazine under the pen-name of "Father Prout," the articles full of elegant wit and classical learning and based on imaginary happenings in the life of a former parish priest of Watergrasshill, Father Andrew Prout who had just died. The articles appeared for two years and were later published as the "Reliques of Father Prout" with illustrations by Maclise. It was in one of them that the song, "The Bells of Shandon" appeared, modelled on old Irish melodies with a wealth of vowel rhymes. The author said that he wished it to be sung with the resonance of a dozen pianofortes "to rouse the heart and elevate the souls of the hearers, giving the glorious pealings of the bells altogether." In 1837 Mahony took off on a wandering tour of Germany, Italy, Hungary, Asia Minor, Greece and Egypt; in 1845 he took up residence in Rome, becoming a friend of the poets Robert and Elizabeth Browning. In 1858 he moved to Paris where he was often seen in company with Thackeray, and where he befriended anyone from Ireland who was down and out. Suffering from diabetes, his health began to decline and he became something of a recluse among his books. On May, 18th 1866, he died in Paris attended by a confessor and his sister. His body was brought back to Cork and the bishop, Dr. Delaney, presided in St. Patrick's Church at the solemn requiem and then the cortege moved through crowded streets as "Father Prout" was taken to be laid to rest in the Mahony vault at Shandon, beneath those bells "whose sounds so wild would, in the days of childhood, fling round my cradle their magic spells."

Shandon churchyard also contains the tomb of a forebear of Dr. Douglas Hyde, founder of the Gaelic League and first President of Ireland. Nearby is the finely-restored Skiddy's Almshouse, the oldest charity in the city while the new nurses' home of the North Infirmary marks the site of another charity, the Greencoat Hospital School. Generations of youngsters have hopped, skipped and jumped in the old laneway running alongside, while budding hurlers and footballers have learned to lift and loft a ball in its narrow confines. Familiar to all of them, as to the men who did business at the Butter Market and those who came to the church for services or burials, were the two figures of the charity-school boy and girl which stood over the former gateway, commonly known as "Bob and Joan." The school has considerable interest in the history of eighteenth century Irish education and its story was widely known in this country and in Britain through an account published by its founder, the Rev. Henry Maule, Rector of Shandon, and published in 1721 under the title "Pietas Corcagiensis, or a View of the Green Coat Hospital and other Charitable Foundations in the Parish of St. Mary, Shandon, Cork." The charity school movement was one of the pioneers of the modern concept of universal elementary education, being founded in London in 1699 by the Rev. Dr. Bray to bring Christian doctrine and simple reading, writing and arithmetic to the children of the poor in the hovels of the metropolis. A systematic routine for teachers and pupils led to the formation of the Society for the Promotion of Christian Knowledge; this set basic standards and its rapid success awakened public interest in the schooling of the illiterate masses. The Rev. Mr. Maule of Shandon was an early correspondent with the S.P.C.K. in London and in his "Pietas" he describes how his school became affiliated to the parent body and was formally opened on Sunday, 12th August, 1716, when the Mayor and Corporation came to service at Shandon, "dressed in their formalities and the sum of £48 1s. was collected for the use of the Charity." The name Greencoat comes from the fact that the charity boys and girls were dressed in green serge clothes made by themselves in the school. Maule describes the origin of "Bob and Joan" as follows: "and because many strangers or other well-disposed persons might be willing to bestow their alms as not to let even their left-hand know what their right-hand doth, therefore the Trustees ordered two charity-boxes to be fixed up in the school at the foot of the figures of two Charity Children dressed in their proper Habits." The two figures which were erected before 1721 may still be seen within the belfry. A fuller account of the Greencoat School was published by this writer in the Journal of the Cork Historical and Archaeological Society in its issue of December, 1972. In the church vestry may still be seen some of Henry Maule's books, including a bible in Irish. He was later to become a bishop of the Church of Ireland.

The whole Shandon area is rich with evidence of the Catholic revival of the first half of the last century and best exemplified in the red sandstone tower of St. Mary's Cathedral which shares the skyline with Shandon Steeple. There is mention of a chapel on the present site as early as 1730, while work on the cathedral began in 1799 under Bishop Francis Moylan. Following a fire in 1820 his successor, Dr. Murphy, engaged the Pain brothers to reconstruct the interior in what was described as "florid Gothic." The tower was designed by Sir John Benson whose other works in Cork included the old Opera House and St. Patrick's Bridge. Construction was in progress in 1862 under the episcopacy of Dr. Delany. Near the cathedral, still popularly called the North Chapel, is the well-known North Monastery School where the grave of Gerald Griffin, poet, playwright and religious brother, may be visited. Nano Nagle's nuns came up the hillside from Douglas Street to teach and cloth and feed the children of the poor, while Mary Aikenhead, whose home may be seen in Rutland Street off the South Terrace, had the happiness of seeing her Sisters of Charity established at St. Vincent's Convent. The name Shandon comes from the original Irish words, sean dun, an old fort, and the site dates back into the mists of history. On the site of Shandon Steeple there is mention of the Church of St. Mary in 1306 while in the seventeenth century Oliver Cromwell sheated his sword and read his bible while staying at Shandon Castle which stood nearby. Having savoured something of the spirit of this historic area it is best to return to the city centre by Dominick Street, even if only to see the old lanes that look down "on the pleasant waters of the river Lee;" they have the dignity of age and the memories of a long yesterday. Francis Street and O'Mahony's Place give way to Long's Lane, Widderling's Lane, Quarry Lane, Ferry Hill Lane, Rowland's Lane, Lloyd's Lane, Moynihan's Lane and Roman Walk. Should the bells ring out they will add their peal to the song of Father Prout:

With deep affection
And recollection
I often think
Of those Shandon Bells,
Whose sounds so wild would
In the days of childhood,
Fling round my cradle
Their magic spells.
On this I ponder
Where'er I wander,
And thus grow fonder
Sweet Cork, of thee;
With thy bells of Shandon,
That sound so grand on
The pleasant waters
Of the river Lee.

BIBLIOGRAPHY

Original Sources:
Minute Book of the Royal Cork Institution.
Minute Books of the Cork Butter Market.
Archival Material, University College, Cork.
Private Papers of Sir Robert Peel, British Museum, London.
Archives of the Society for the Promotion of Christian
    Knowledge, London.
Manuscript Autobiography of Daniel Maclise, Royal
    Academy, London.
The Day Papers, Cork County Archives Library.
Selected Parliamentary Reports of the Nineteenth Century.

Secondary Sources:
State of the County and City of Cork. C. Smith. 1815.
History of Cork. J. Windele, 1839.
History of Cork. C. Gibson. 1861.
History of Cork. M. F. Cusack, 1875.
Economic History of Cork City to 1800. W. O'Sullivan, 1937.
History of Cork. J. G. McCarthy. Pamphlet Reprint by Miros
    Press, 1974.
Daniel Maclise. W. O'Driscoll, 1871.
Daniel Maclise. Catalogue, the Arts Council of Great Britain,
    1972.
Guide Book to the Great Southern and Western Railway.
    G. Measom. 1866.
Dublin, Cork and South of Ireland. Stratten and Stratten,
    1892.
Cork, its Trade and Commerce: Handbook of the Incorpora-
    ted Chamber of Commerce and Shipping. 1919.
Souvenir Handbook of the Convention of Master Painters,
    Cork. 1910.
Paris and Irish Sketches. W. M. Thackeray. 1875.
A History of the Cork Medical School. R. O'Rahilly. 1949.
Wit and Wine. D and M. Coakley, 1975.
The Council Book of the Corporation of the City of Cork.
    Edited by R. Caulfield, 1876.
Annals of St. Finbarr's Cathedral. R. Caulfield, 1871.
The Industrial Movement in Ireland. J. F. Maguire, 1853.
Father Mathew. J. F. Maguire. 1875.
Tour of Ireland. A. Young. 1780.
Tour of Ireland. J. Windham. 1780.
A Philosophical Survey of the South of Ireland. T. Campbell.
    1778.

Life in Ireland. L. M. Cullen. 1968.

Problems of a Growing City, Belfast. Public Record Office of Northern Ireland. 1973.

Munster and the City of Cork. R. Hayward. 1964.

A History of the Middle Ages. S. Painter. 1968.

The Social Condition and Education of the People. J. Kay. 1850.

Reminiscences of Oxford. W. Tuckwell. 1907.

Studies in the History of Education. B. Simon. 1960.

Illustrated English Social History. G. M. Trevelyan. Pelican. 1964.

Victorian England. G. M. Young. Reprint, 1964.

The Age of the Railway. H. Perkins. 1970.

Victorian Cities. A. Briggs. 1963.

Victorian People. A. Briggs. 1954.

The City in History. L. Mumford. Pelican. 1975.

Selected Issues of the Journal of the Cork Historical and Archaeological Society.